SURGEON OR JACK OF ALL TRADES?

Surgeon or Jack of All Trades
A Mission Doctor in Tanganyika 1949-1990

by

Marion Bartlett
MB, FRCS (England)

Copyright Marion Bartlett © 2013
Produced in association with

www.wordsbydesign.co.uk

All rights reserved. No part of this publication may be reproduced, stored in a retrieval system, or transmitted in any form or by any means, electric, mechanical, photocopying, recording or otherwise, without the prior permission of the copyright holder or a licence permitting restricted copying. In the UK such licences are issued by the Copyright Licencing Agency, 90 Tottenham Court Road, London W1P 9HE.

ISBN: 978-1-909075-13-9 (colour)
ISBN: 978-1-909075-14-6 (monochrome)

For further copies, contact
Revd Timothy Fox, 40 Lakeber Avenue,
Bentham, Lancaster, LA2 7JN
Email: editimfox@btinternet.com

Just married

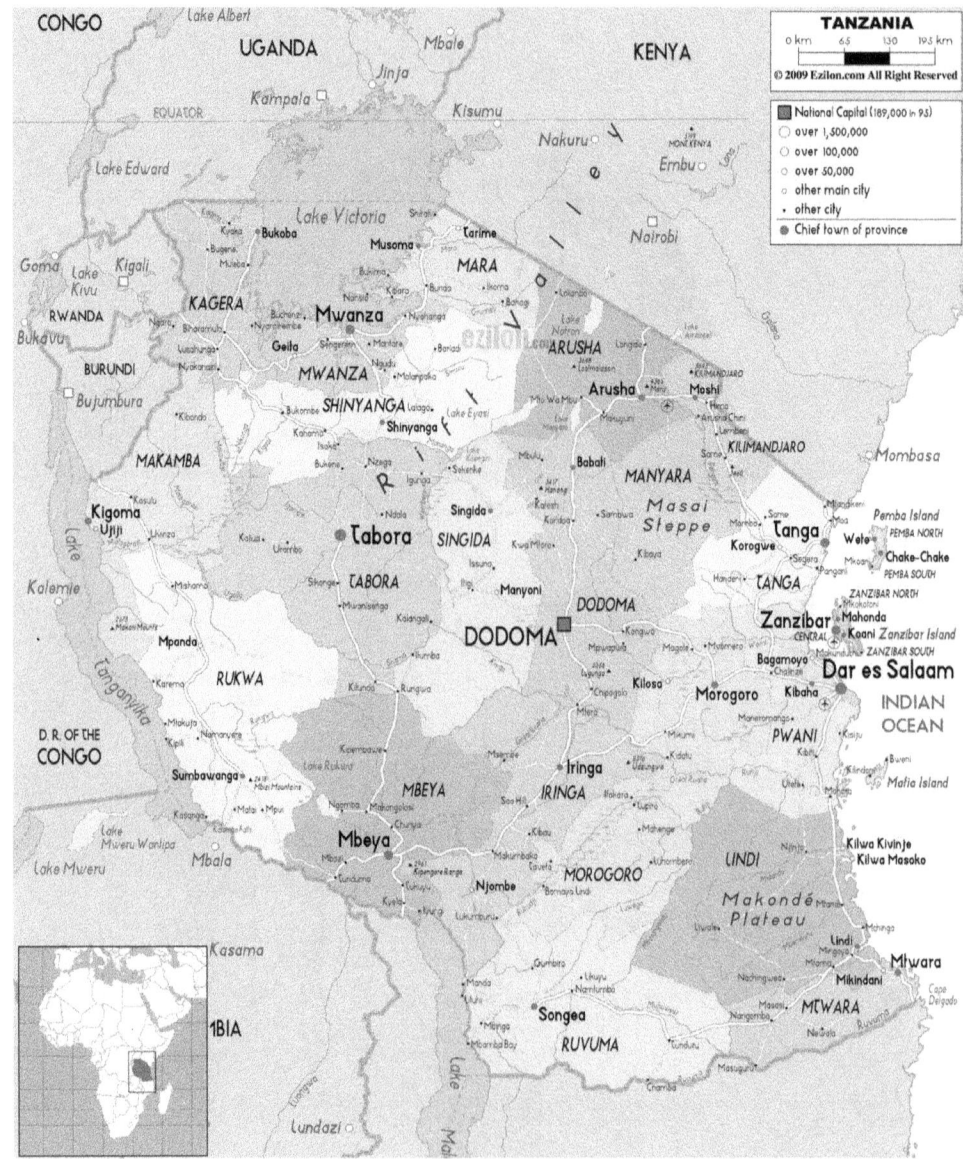

Acknowledgements

Jennifer Fox was the originator of this book. I met her when staying with long-term friends, Edith and Timothy Fox. She told me that I must write my memoirs. I replied, "I've tried and I can't, and I'm too old now anyway." After some discussion with Jennifer, Timothy and Edith, Jennifer said that if I would give her the facts she would like to write the story. We worked hard together for over a year but sadly, her health failed and in December 2012 she died. Without Jennifer's help this book would never have been written.

With so much work already done, Jennifer's brother-in-law, Timothy Fox and I decided that if I wrote it – and I had learnt a lot from Jennifer – he would see the book to production. Roger, Jennifer's husband, agreed and gave what help he could.

I had wonderful secretarial help from Angela Budgen while she was Secretary at the College of St Barnabas, and then from Tony Parker and his wife, Sylvia. From fellow residents of the College I received encouragement and practical help, including Fr Robin Osborne, Fr Michael Shields and the Warden, Canon Howard Such.

Timothy called in family members, his wife Edith who was one of the nursing sisters mentioned in early chapters, his sister Liesel Fox and Edith's sister Nancy Bibby for proof-reading, and also Canon David Bruno for help with this important task. Others, especially Dave Lewis, have helped with photographs and maps, and many friends have encouraged me when my own health presented problems.

I was delighted when Archbishop John Ramadhani, Archbishop of Tanzania 1984-1997, agreed to write a foreword to this book.

Marion Bartlett.

Contents

	Acknowledgements	ix
	Foreword	xiii
1	From Country Childhood to Hospital in Africa	1
2	Introduction to Life at Minaki	17
3	The Wider Vision – Working Together	45
4	Changes at Minaki but Hospital Routines Continue	67
5	Goodbye Minaki: New Challenge Ahead	87
6	Masasi, Lulindi, Newala and Rondo	105
7	Lulindi with a Difference	133
8	A Taste of Town Life	161
9	Magila and Muheza	187
10	A Dream Come True?	233
11	Zigualand – Handeni District	269
12	Zanzibar and Retirement	317
	Useful Contacts	353

Foreword
Archbishop John Ramadhani

It is with much pleasure I have received the request to write this foreword. I believe the composition of this lovely book was partly the result of my pleading with Dr Bartlett not to allow her rich experience, working in several places in Tanzania under the auspices of the Universities Mission to Central Africa, to be lost in oblivion. It is a matter of great joy to see this book written at all.

I first came to know Dr Bartlett when I went to St Andrew's College, Minaki, Dar es Salaam as a Form 1 student in January 1950. She had then just arrived in 1949 as a young doctor to work at the teaching church hospital, where medical assistants and other types of medical personnel were being trained.

Dr Mary Gibbons, the superintendent of the hospital and her husband, Canon RM Gibbons, the principal of the college were about to retire. Dr Phillips as she was known then took over the work of Dr Gibbons. Canon Gibbons who had moved with the college from Zanzibar in 1925 handed over his work to Canon Nash, a missionary in the Zanzibar Diocese since 1936. Canon Nash came to Minaki with his elder sister, Miss Gladys Nash, an experienced teacher of Religious Knowledge.

When I completed 4th Form in 1953 I was trained as a teacher at Minaki. There were no 5th and 6th Forms in Tanganyika or East Africa then. I did well in Miss Nash's classes in Religious Knowledge, to the extent of being recruited to take her classes when she went on leave 1958/9.

I did not welcome the idea of returning to Minaki to teach where I had recently left as a student myself. However, when I returned I met David Bartlett, a new chaplain to the college. We became great friends from our first meeting. I met the Bartletts at Korogwe in changed roles: Dr Bartlett as superintendent of Muheza designated district hospital and Canon Bartlett, the Vicar General of the Diocese of Zanzibar and Tanga as well as parish priest of Muheza parish, and I was the newly appointed Bishop of the diocese.

I have always enjoyed reading life stories of people. The thing which fascinates me is to see how they grapple with life and make sense of their world. Dr Bartlett's book portrays life in the mission field in her days. That story touches part of my past. It is an important peg to see how much we have travelled. Her book is like a picture which captures a moment for eternity. Thanks to her for writing it.

CHAPTER 1
From Country Childhood to Hospital in Africa

Parents: Happy Home: The Farm

Life for me began in a country Vicarage in Norfolk. I was four years old and don't remember much before then. Dad, the Reverend Alfred Arthur Phillips had been a CMS (Church Missionary Society) missionary in Szechuan Province, West China from 1892 until 1922, and was ordained priest whilst there. Mother, Josephine Amy Clouting who was an art student at the Slade Art School at the turn of the century, felt that she was called to missionary service and trained as a nurse midwife at the London Hospital. In 1912 she joined other CMS Missionaries to take the Trans-Siberian railway to China. After a brief stop in Beijing (Peking in those days), they went on to Szechuan Province (spelt 'Sichuan' now) in South West China and bordering on Tibet. They went on to Mienchow, the 'village' where Mother would be working. This in 2008 was the 'city' in the world news as the epicentre of the earthquake, which caused such devastation in the province.

It was beautiful mountainous country, far up the Yangtze River, and mother put her artistic skills to good use while there with colourful sketches of people, pagodas and other buildings, flowers and scenery, and also some watercolours which have been a pleasure to the family ever since.

Dad's first wife, Caroline, a lovely-looking lady in photographs, was from the Isle of Man, and sadly died during the Great War, leaving Alfred Phillips devastated. Gertrude, my half sister, was born in 1900 but their two other children died. In 1919 when war ended, my mother was overdue for leave but instead she accepted Alfred

Phillips' proposal and stayed on. She was now in her forties and Alfred well into his fifties. My brother Alan was born in 1920 and Mother brought him to England in 1921 when she was pregnant again, starting down the Yangtze by boat as she had come up nine years before. This time they were shot at by brigands as they passed through the towering gorges and had to shelter behind mattresses on the deck. Three months on the ocean liner can't have been much better, with Mother seasick and with an extremely active toddler to cope with! Our grandmother's home in Sevenoaks must have been a wonderful haven of rest until her second baby arrived on October 2nd. I was baptised Marion Josephine in St Nicholas Church in Sevenoaks.

Dad had heart trouble – we all did in our time – and he came to England on retirement from mission service in 1922. After three years as a curate in a Norwich parish, he was made Vicar of Great Plumstead, a small village five miles out of Norwich.

For me it was ideal country vicarage life with a large garden, fruit, vegetables, flowers, hens and even a pair of doves for a time; a croquet lawn (vicarage type), tennis court/bowling green, where the village came to play on summer evenings. Alan and I used to watch from an upstairs window as the swallows and swifts soared and called over the garden. Nearby was a farm with a delightful lady farmer, Emelene, who welcomed us at any time. I just loved all the animals and especially riding the great big cart horses as they brought crops in from the fields and we took them along to the pond for a drink. But with our quiet country upbringing we were shy children, and shyness sticks. Meeting people was always difficult, and speaking in public a lot worse!

It was there at Great Plumstead that I learnt about Jesus and the Bible stories, about prayer and worship and the Heavenly Father and his love. Sin and judgement also came in but not harshly, and the Cross and Resurrection with their message of cleansing and forgiveness, hope, joy and confidence about the future. It was the evangelical Christian message from parents who lived by it themselves. As a result I knew instinctively that the fairy which I definitely saw at the bottom of the garden was not really real in the same way that Angels were. One day as I stood watching a glorious sunset over the fields I called, "Mummy, I'm watching God painting the sky". It was not an old man with a big paintbrush, but to me quite obviously it was God, because he was the one who did everything in earth, sea and sky and heaven too.

Another thing that was quite clear to me right from those early days was that I would have to be a missionary nurse like Mother, not recognising it as a call from God, but just as a fact of life. What was certainly not clear to me then was how my name would change over the years. It was Molly (or Mé-mé, Chinese for 'little sister') until I went to school, when I insisted on my baptismal name, Marion;

'Miss Phillips' or just 'Phillips' as a student; changing dramatically after 4½ years to 'Dr. Phillips'; 5 years later, according to our strange English custom for surgeons, back to 'Miss'; in Tanzania 'Mama Daktari' or just 'Doctor'. Later came the biggest surprise of all when it changed to 'Mrs. David Bartlett'.

I had heard missionary stories about forests, hills and valleys, African villages with thatched huts, snakes and lions, bugs and fevers, and missionaries holding services and giving out medicines under trees. The first two visitors I remember from overseas were bishops. Bishop Song from Szechuan in West China must have been one of the first Chinese people to come to an English country village as early as the 1920's. He used to get up and pray at 4 am every day. Then came Archbishop Mowll from Sydney, Australia, who seemed huge to me. He was too tall to get into Dad's Austin Seven with his hat on so he went off wearing my green Scottish tam-o'-shanter! I don't think I learnt much about the life of a missionary from them, but stories about it in China came from Mother. Dad was rather quiet and studious, and very sadly his heart caught up with him and he died in 1933. It was a devastating loss for Alan and myself as well as for Mother. Dad could have told us so much in later years about his 30 years as a missionary in China.

School: Plans for the Future

At the age of 13 I went to boarding school at St. Michael's Limpsfield in Surrey, which was then a school for children of CMS missionaries. It took me a term to get over the horror of leaving home, complicated by a long and severe attack of tonsillitis, with no antibiotics in those days and the sulphonamide drugs just appearing on the scene. Serum injections were an innovation. But soon nature study, games, art, girl guiding, and music as well as routine schoolwork took over and I made lasting friends.

After a good school certificate the excitement came when Mother asked, "If you had £1,000, what would you do?" – knowing that a dying aunt had left me that sum in her Will. "I'd be a doctor of course" was the spontaneous reply! What a hope! Brother Alan was a scientist and mathematician from the day he left his cot, but little sister –"No, no!" Moreover this school didn't teach science, only botany, and I needed Higher Certificate or first MB (more or less equivalent) in science subjects. However the school came up trumps and I had five terms of coaching in physics, chemistry and biology and things went ahead. I was offered a place at the London Royal Free Hospital School of Medicine (LSM), which was 'for Women' then. A grant of £1,000 was promised by the SPCK (Society for Promotion of Christian Knowledge) and in those days £2,000 would see you through 5 years medical training if you were careful.

Medical Student During Second World War

In September 1939, just after war broke out, I entered the LSM, but instead of the college building in Hunter Street, I got on a train at Kings Cross Station with staff, students and equipment, to be evacuee-lodgers at Aberdeen University for two terms. Lovely digs in the town with excellent food (much straight up from the fish market), a freezing cold winter with skating, a welcoming Scottish church as well as the university, and of course, the fascinating studies we were starting, made it a really good start to our medical training.

All seemed quiet in London, so we returned for the summer term, but stayed on during August to fit in an extra term's work. We were there for the great docks fire and the start of the London bombing. We studied and slept in an underground lecture theatre at the college, and one night we were fire-bombed out. A few weeks later we reassembled in Exeter, courtesy of the university, and battled our way to exams in December.

This opened our way to 3 years of clinical studies, which should have been at the Royal Free Hospital (RFH), then in Gray's Inn Road, London. The hospital had been evacuated as much as possible to a wartime hospital at Arlesey in Bedfordshire and we spent our first 3 months there. After that the routine depended on suitcase, bicycle and trains, with 3 month periods in different hospitals around London, sometimes staying as long as 6 months at the RFH. We lived in a variety of 'digs', hostels, bed-sitters, and in one such period four of us slept on mattresses on the floor of the RFH out-patient hall, and were on call for emergencies. For this we received meal tickets for the hospital canteen, where the food was dreadful, but at least it was there on the spot and saved cash! All surgery was done in basement operating theatres to be safe from the bombing.

Despite all the problems we got a good basic medical training for which I was extremely grateful over the next half century, but it was sadly lacking in the other aspects of university life. Although exhausted after the ups and downs of those training years, I was soon looking for a job, always aware of the future I was preparing for.

Hospital Jobs and Mission Training

I applied for house surgeon (HS) at my home hospital, the Norfolk and Norwich, which had a good reputation and is now a university teaching hospital. This was 1944 and they clearly didn't want a woman and had not had one on the resident staff before, but men were scarce as many went straight into the Forces, so I became their first woman Resident ('Junior Doctor' now) and was soon hard at work. Experience there was excellent and after 6 months as HS, I moved to the medical side, so completing my year of hospital experience. It was not difficult to settle in and people, even the mostly Guy's Hospital-trained male Residents, soon became used to having a woman around.

After some weeks, my sister Gertrude, who had been on rather prolonged sick leave, came back to her position as records officer, and incidents sometimes occurred, relished (and perhaps caused) by the porters, who in those far off days felt that they ran the hospital from their den in the out-patients department, when calls got through to the wrong Miss Phillips! (Yes, we did have a phone system round the hospital, but not pagers or other clever more recent inventions).

Leaving Norwich was quite a wrench. In fact I have always been sad to leave jobs despite the interest and excitement of moving on to new interests and new challenges. I went back once or twice to do locums there and one of the ward sisters became a lifelong friend. When I left, the hospital secretary, a powerful man in those days, was kind enough to say that they would never have another lady doctor on the staff in case she was a disappointment, which I think and hope was an idle compliment!

I was a CMS candidate for mission service from the time of leaving school, so next came two terms at the CMS Missionary Training College, at that time using part of Ridley Hall Cambridge, as their property had been taken over for war service. By then I had met and been much influenced by Catholic theology and the Anglo-Catholic side of our Church. A weekend with Max Warren, General Secretary of CMS, and his wife Mary, convinced us all that I was not right for CMS, and in any case needed a bit more time. I had realised that surgery is a 'must' for missionary doctors because of distances and the scarcity of doctors. The wonder of the human body had come home to me in learning its anatomy. Surgery and its possibilities, which have made such amazing progress since my student days, took that wonder several stages further. So I must go ahead and learn more about it.

In those days, a surgical fellowship (FRCS) needed, for the first exam, a detailed knowledge of the anatomy and workings of the human body; for the final exam, a wide knowledge of general surgery and plenty of experience as a house surgeon (junior doctor in modern terms). The exams were rigorous, but there were no specifications about details of experience and no alternatives in specialist subjects, the one exception being ENT (ear, nose & throat). So it was pretty basic compared with the present version!

To tackle the primary fellowship, I had a part-time job in London teaching anatomy at the LSM (London School of Medicine), while attending lectures at the Royal College of Surgeons. A kind Anglo-Catholic Priest and his wife gave me lodging at their Walworth Rectory. This gave me the chance to absorb the wonders of the Catholic faith, which I found grew quite naturally from my childhood's simple teaching and beliefs. Of course, I have had times of storm and argument since then, and also of forgetting all about having any beliefs, but this six month period was a time of real deepening of understanding and of faith and renewal. Next I had a year at the Royal Sussex County Hospital Brighton, and then, as I was finishing a job at the King Edward the Seventh Hospital Windsor, came success in the final Fellowship examination. The only celebration which I remember was meeting a fellow resident when I got back to Windsor and was on the way to a bath. He was so excited when he heard the news that he squirted a whole lot of foam into the bath, giving me my first very bubbly bubble bath!

The Decision

Leaving Windsor in January 1949 I was being encouraged to apply for a job in Oxford to train in plastic surgery, but I had to consider very seriously the question of missionary vocation. Few women were taking up surgery then. I had seen only one other woman among the hundred or so taking the final FRCS when I did, and she was taking the ENT version. My reason was that I had been convinced for so long that God wanted me for medical mission work, and that I would need a basic knowledge of surgery for that.

Now, five years qualified and with FRCS (Eng) in my pocket, decisions must be made – it was the time for action. It had been a tough battle to get so far but a fascinating one, and as the Lord had brought me so far presumably I was needed somewhere in the overseas mission of the Church.

At the time I was staying in a flat in London with Ruth, a close friend from student days, and her mother and sister. Ruth had been 'converted' at school, but sadly was gradually losing her faith. Her mother and family were atheist and communist in their beliefs. They were friendly, kind and hospitable, and I always felt welcome there, and in spite of our different outlooks on life they clearly understood what was on my mind.

I approached the Society for the Propagation of the Gospel (SPG) at their headquarters in Westminster, Tufton Street, with its work in almost every country in the world. Their reply, in spite of my period of missionary training with CMS, was that I should go for a year to the Selly Oak College of the Ascension, Birmingham. Qualified five years and 'rarin' to go' I wasn't keen on that! My reaction was to go to Central Africa House, home of that wonderful old Anglo-Catholic missionary society, UMCA, the Universities Mission to Central Africa, which later joined with S.P.G. to form the USPG (the 'U' now standing for United). The origin of the UMCA was an appeal by David Livingstone in the Cambridge Senate House in 1857 for young men from the Universities to take the Gospel to Central Africa – what an exciting challenge! Its work was centred in Zanzibar and Tanganyika (now Tanzania) and extended west as far as Nyasaland and Northern Rhodesia (now Malawi and Zambia). The reply to me was, "Sorry, we haven't got the right sort of job for a doctor with your qualifications". What a shock! I had spent ten years training to be fit to work under what I had reason to believe would be 'missionary conditions', and now this. Had I got it all wrong?

Clearly I must do some hard thinking. Was I mistaken about a vocation to medical missionary work? Was it simply a hangover from childhood fantasies? Could I be happy and find fulfilment in plastic surgery if I could get into reconstructive surgery like the amazing work done by people like Sir Archibald McIndoe and his team in East Grinstead? The urgently needed rehabilitation of members of the armed forces with terrible burns and other injuries had inspired these surgeons to do something to give new life, hope and confidence to such people. Plastic surgeons had played a major part in this. The techniques and skills, which were developed during and after the 2nd World War, would still be needed for civilians in peacetime and for other victims of warfare.

Then came a telegram from the Bishop of Zanzibar to the General Secretary of UMCA – "ACCEPT PHILLIPS SURGEON ZANZIBAR". Illogically and against all previous ideas, a violent storm set in – "No, too late now, other plans in hand. No, No, No!" I tried to pray but the storm raged. But of course the Lord won, and I realised that if you have really and sincerely committed your life to him, he is not likely to let you go without an almighty struggle!

Destination Tanganyika

I went back to Central Africa House to get my marching orders, and was booked to sail on the Llangibby Castle early in May 1949. It was now February and I was to sail in May. I found I was to go to the hospital at Minaki, not on the Island of Zanzibar but in mainland Tanganyika 18 miles inland from Dar-es-Salaam (Haven of Peace), which was then the capital of Tanganyika. It was 15 years later, after Independence and the Zanzibar Revolution that the two countries, Zanzibar and Tanganyika, joined to form the United Republic of Tanzania.

Zanzibar Diocese in 1949 included the Islands of Zanzibar and Pemba as it does now, and also a broad strip of Tanganyika's east coast down as far as the Rufiji River south of Dar-es-Salaam. The first UMCA missionaries had tried to start their mission in 'Livingstone Country' up the Shire River, a tributary of the Zambezi. Malaria, which caused many deaths of people from overseas in those early days, was the main reason for leaving that area and making a new start on the island of Zanzibar in 1863. When the work was established there, a delegation of missionaries and local converts was sent across to Tanganyika just south of the beautiful Usambara Mountains, north of which lies Kenya. It is fertile farming country, with corn, fruit and vegetables in the valleys, orchards of oranges, lemons and limes, grapefruit and other tropical fruit, cardamom growing up in the foothills and other crops creeping up the slopes as far as possible. Large areas in the valleys were taken over for sisal, which was a very lucrative crop in those days. At a pleasant spot among those hills a mission station with church, school and dispensary, later to become a hospital with nursing school, was started, at Magila, where I was to work at a much later date.

By 1949 the Southern Region, south of the Rufiji, had become Masasi Diocese, and the Southern Highlands were included in the Diocese of Nyasaland. Dar-es-Salaam and Minaki were still under Zanzibar and it was much later that Dar-es-Salaam got its own bishop and cathedral. All I knew about Minaki was its situation in the coastal hills, and that it had a hospital with no surgical facilities and St. Andrew's College for boys. 'The College' included secondary school, teacher training college and students doing a medical training in the hospital. It was up to me to bring the necessary equipment, instruments etc. to set up a surgical department!! Again, as right at the beginning, "What a hope!" Theatre sisters know about that, not doctors even if they have just got their FRCS! It was an early lesson in, "If you don't know ask someone who does" – a rule of life which stood me in good stead on that and many other occasions. I presumed that there would be wards, and there were, but with mud walls and floors and thatched roofs.

Other jobs to tackle were to learn the language, which was Kiswahili, a language known by most in the country as well as their tribal languages; and to equip myself with tropical clothes (still in the era of clothing coupons) and personal supplies for 3 years. These had to include a topee (sun helmet), a double turai hat and mosquito boots up to the knee. Thankfully spine pads and cholera belts had recently been crossed off the list! Double turais were two wide-brimmed felt hats, one inside the other, and were a good idea for keeping the sun off, but I hardly used mine or my topee, as I didn't have to do long walking safaris. Spine pads were used to protect the back of the neck and upper spine from the hot sun, as this was thought to be the cause of sunstroke. Cholera belts were used to protect from 'chill on the stomach', which was thought to be the cause of cholera, until it was found to be a waterborne infection.

After doing all I could in London and the South about hospital, and especially operating theatre supplies, and my personal needs, I joined mother and Alan both now in Edinburgh. Language was a problem. I got a few Swahili text books, and found in Edinburgh a student who had been in Kenya and knew some Luo, a similar language: a kind offer, but not very useful! I did better later during our four-week sea voyage.

Now there was Mother to consider, elderly and far from well in 1949. At the end of the war in 1945 she was still living in Luscombe, a tiny hamlet in Devon, 2 or 3 miles from Harbertonford village. A girl in the post office there still pushed and pulled plugs in and out of the wall, to put telephone calls through and also carefully typed out incoming telegrams and gave them to a boy with a bicycle to deliver to the door. One morning Mother received a telegram from Alan saying, "SEND BONES". What stories must have gone round the village! Surely the girl at the PO couldn't have kept that news to herself? But at once it told Mother that Alan had been given a place at Edinburgh University to read medicine.

Alan had spent the war years struggling to complete his physics degree at St Catharine's College, Cambridge, while drafted into radar research instead of being called up into the forces. Realising that this was taking him towards nuclear research which he did not want, he decided that after the war he wanted to put his scientific knowledge into healing instead of possible destruction. This took him into a career of radiology and oncology including research. After retirement he spent over 20 years giving scientific and medical advice to antinuclear activists.

In those days medical students when studying human anatomy had to have a half set of bones. In 1939 I had spent £5 on mine, a vast sum of money then, so I was delighted that they would help Alan on his way as well.

Mother joined Alan in Edinburgh in 1946 and was at first housekeeping for a family of students. Sadly she was frail and ill when I reached Edinburgh and was in the Royal Infirmary when I left for my journey to Tanganyika. But she was full of enthusiasm for my plans and would love to have known that when she died ten years later, her legacy would provide for building the church at Muheza near Magila, where my husband and I were working later. A comment that she made was that she was not nearly so nervous for me about lions and snakes as about meningitis and typhoid fever – for which, of course, there were no specific treatments then. It turned out to be malaria which gave the trouble, as drug resistance started giving serious problems at that time, with each antimalarial drug in turn becoming ineffective.

How simple it had all seemed at the age of four when I wanted to be 'a missionary nurse like Mother'! Does God 'call' four year olds as he did the prophet Samuel before that age? Mother thought so. It was then, when I was all lined up ready to go to Tanganyika, that she told me that I was her 'Little Samuel'; she had 'presented me to the Lord' as Hannah had presented Samuel. How wise of her not to tell me before, when I still had decisions to make. It was sad to leave her in hospital but Alan would take care of her.

Arriving in London early in May, all packed up and ready to board the Llangibby Castle, I found that a dock strike had started which was very frustrating. The Walworth rector and his wife very kindly welcomed me back and we waited day by day for news of the strike. The rector's wife suggested that a former curate, who was in London and apparently not over-worked, should show me some of the sights of London. Wartime had not been good for sightseeing so I enjoyed the outings. However, the sequel was a sudden entirely unexpected offer of marriage, which was certainly not in my scheme of things just then! I found no difficulty in making that decision. In any case UMCA asked its members to commit themselves not to get engaged or married during a 3 year tour of duty.

Four Weeks on the Ocean

At last early in August the Llangibby Castle was ready to go. I travelled with other UMCA missionaries including Audrey Fisher, a middle-aged teacher returning to Minaki, and also Sister Mary Bernadine CSP (Community of the Sacred Passion) who heard, when we reached Mombasa, that she had been chosen as the new Reverend Mother of her community. She gave me very welcome lessons in Kiswahili on the ship, and I was soon to get to know her community well as I worked with them at four different hospitals at different times. The community was founded in 1911 for work in Africa, with the help of Frank Weston, a famous early Bishop of Zanzibar. Their mother house in Tanganyika was at Magila, 'Msalabani' in Swahili, which means 'Place of the Cross'. In England at East Hanningfield in Essex, they ran the last leprosy settlement in England, moving to Effingham in Surrey when the residents had no further need of them. In Africa many were teachers and nursing sisters, some very highly skilled in midwifery. Outreach to maternity and child welfare work in the villages was one of their specialities. The teachers played an important part in girls' education over the years.

The journey was a great experience for me, that is, after I had recovered from the effects of storms in the Bay of Biscay! Gibraltar with its rocks and apes; the Mediterranean bright and beautiful, and going ashore at places like Genoa; Port Said, hot and crowded, a first taste of the Middle East; the Suez Canal with camels, sand and the blazing sun, and then Port Sudan and glass bottomed boats to see fantastic fish – things one missed later on when we travelled by air. And remember we hadn't yet started to see these exotic things on television, though Geographic Magazines did their best.

Mombasa was our first East African port, fascinating at first, but with five days there, sleeping in our hot stuffy cabins while cargo was unloaded and loaded, rather took the edge off the enjoyment. It was my undoing: I went down with a high fever and spent the last days of the journey in the ship's sick bay with a diagnosis of malaria. So I had to swallow my first course of quinine pills. We all took our paludrine tablets regularly, but at once came to terms with the fact that malaria prophylaxis is a tricky subject because of resistance developing to each new medication which is invented or discovered. Malaria is such a scourge in the tropics, despite efforts with mosquito control, insecticides, bed nets and other measures, so that our hope now has to be in the production of a vaccine. But every few years we are told, "It's on the way" – and –"Ten years till we get it"', but apparently it is a really complicated problem!

Arrived!

When we sailed through the narrow channel into Dar-es-Salaam's picturesque harbour on 8th September 1949, the Lutheran church near the wharf caught the eye, with the town rising behind it. Our eyes were soon on Dr Mary and Canon Robin Gibbons on the quay waving a welcome. Canon Gibbons was the principal of St Andrew's College, Minaki. Dr Mary had built the hospital and was in charge of it and of the medical training. We were soon rowed ashore (no deep water docks for the ocean liners then) with our cabin luggage quickly cleared by customs. Miss Fisher and I were welcomed by the Gibbons' and taken to their car, with only 18 miles of bumpy track to Minaki. Bumps didn't matter as the ride was lovely, winding up through palm trees, low scrub and a few small settlements, and then up onto a ridge with a glorious view, now under bright moonlight, of wooded hills and clearings for crops stretching into the distance. After a sudden steep uphill turning we reached Minaki, turning off again just before the hospital towards the college and stopping among a small group of houses, where my home would be for the next 12 years. Staff and some of the boys came out with lanterns to meet and greet us. Dr and Canon Gibbons went off to their house on the left and Miss Fisher and I were taken to the ladies' quarters on the right, for talk, refreshment and then bed and the sounds of the African night. I had arrived.

Chapter 2
Introduction to Life at Minaki

Home, College and Village

Minaki was a well-known name in Tanganyika by 1949, well-known for St Andrew's College and for Minaki Hospital. Canon Robin Gibbons was the principal of the college, which was a combined boys' secondary school and teacher training college. It also included the medical assistant students, who were being trained in the hospital by Dr Mary Gibbons and her staff. Mary welcomed me as a much needed second doctor, who she hoped would set up a surgical department.

The hurricane lamp carriers who took Miss Fisher and myself on arrival to a small group of dwellings nearby, were two or three teachers and three nursing sisters, all missionaries. Three of these had roomy but sparsely furnished bedrooms in an old two storey German house. It had an open space between them, right across from front to back and closed only by crisscross burglar wire at the ends. Upstairs the space was our sitting room, cool and breezy, but rather wet during heavy rain! Downstairs there were large burglar wire gates to secure the house. The German building was a reminder that, until the end of the 1914-1918 war, Tanganyika had been a German colony, and it then became a British Mandated Territory under the United Nations. I was taken to the fourth room in this building – and much later on, one of them became my office. Several little single storey buildings nearby were houses for the other ladies, and one was being built for me. These had cement floors and corrugated iron roofs; there were plenty of small windows with burglar bars and wooden shutters – no glass – and a six-foot partition to divide off a small bedroom. Beds had wooden frames, with poles for mosquito nets, grass webbing for springs, and grass mats for mattresses. I found these cool and comfortable, though some found them rather hard! In the bedroom there was a smallish tin bath, and I found that I could lie down in it (not all at once of course) and really enjoy it after a long tiring day!

Our dining room and kitchen were separate buildings nearby, and cooking was done on a Dover stove, the standard type of kitchen range. Thirty years later, when I was doing the cooking for my husband and myself, I used a small round charcoal stove, and made our bread in a brick oven built in the back yard. In these early days, we had a cook and 'house boys' between us – a considerably reduced form of the colonial custom of cook, houseboys, dhobi (washermen), garden boys, etc.

St Andrew's College had been at Kiungani, on the island of Zanzibar, until 1925, when Canon Robin Gibbons, the principal, brought it over to Minaki. This was a settlement in German days, 18 miles inland from Dar-es-Salaam, on a rough road past the future airport; it was 600 feet up in the Pugu Hills. By the time I visited Kiungani, on the coast, just outside Zanzibar town, it was overgrown with trees and bushes, but the site has since been restored as the Diocesan Centre. Mary Westall, a UMCA teacher at Korogwe on the mainland, decided in 1924, at the end of her first 3-year period in Tanganyika, that doctors were needed even more than teachers, and she herself should train to be one of them. After full training at the Royal Free Hospital in London, she returned in 1931, now married to Robin Gibbons.

She built Minaki hospital, drew up a syllabus to train medical assistants (MAs) and started to train them. The students (male) became members of St Andrew's College. They were trained to assist doctors in hospitals or to run dispensaries in the surrounding villages. It was a three year training which included much experience in the hospital wards and out-patient departments, laboratory and dispensary (pharmacy) as well as in classes. Government hospitals soon started to train MAs and much later, girls as well as boys could be trained.

In 1949 there were only three boys' secondary schools in the country: a Government one at Tabora, 200 miles inland from Dar-es-Salaam; a Roman Catholic one, St. Francis College, Pugu, 3 miles from Minaki; and St Andrew's College, Minaki. Thankfully that information was out of date in a few years time!

Next morning, as the sun rose soon after 6 am (being only 4° south of the equator, it always rose between 6 and 6.30 am), I could begin to look around. I could see the low hospital buildings near the road we had come in on, and the college on the other side; the Gibbons' house was over to the left, and further off on the right, our chapel. Beyond that was the little village of Kalole, with family houses for the African teachers and hospital staff, with some space to grow vegetables. Our beautiful chapel was central to the life of Minaki, with room for all the boys on mats on the floor, and seats at the back for all staff. All services were in Swahili, so church Swahili as well as hospital Swahili must be understood by newcomers as soon as possible. Our day started early, as it was customary for us to be in chapel well before the daily 6.30 am Eucharist. All chapel singing, as well as that in village churches, was unaccompanied, and all in plainsong; we had a very good hymnbook, mainly adapted from English hymns, with local style ones gradually being added to the repertoire.

A lovely occasion for using both styles was at the centenary celebrations in 1980 of our cathedral, which was on the island of Zanzibar. (See chapter 12) The choir from St Alban's Church, Dar-es-Salaam came over and sang in London–school-of-church-music style, and Zanzibar Choir responded in local style and rhythm. Zanzibar Cathedral has an organ, and it is amazing how it manages to stand up to the heat and humidity.

The Hospital and its Staff

Our day in the hospital started with brief prayers together at 8 am, and then my first job on the first day was to find my way round and meet the staff in their different places of work. All buildings were single storey. Some, like the laboratory, outpatients rooms, dispensary and those to be used for operating theatre, had cement floors, tin roofs (corrugated iron or aluminium, known locally as 'bati'), and walls of cement blocks or burnt brick. The wards, apart from maternity, were just lodging places really, having thatched roofs, mud floors, and walls of mud brick dried in the sun, or 'mud and wattle' like walls of English cottages long ago.

As I went round, I found the MAs hard at work – Daudi Mfuko in the laboratory, assisted by Clement Mdoe; Alfred Magombeka and Dennis Mhina doing ward rounds, or already seeing outpatients; Anthony Msei, who had just passed his pharmacy exams, in the dispensary, supplying the ward and outpatient staff with all the medications they needed, and ready to do the same for out-patients when they had been seen. It was called 'dispensary' because in those days most medications were made on the spot. Liquid medicines were mixed, pills rolled, and ointments mixed on a marble slab with a spatula. Paul Mhina, the senior MA, would be somewhere around, and in future would be my very able assistant in theatre, when we had one! The question was soon in my mind: "Which is more urgent, to improve the wards or to start some surgery?"

The three nursing sisters, Ruby Marshall, Penny Webb and Joyce Wortley, had a small office and store, and the maternity and labour ward was in their hands, helped by whatever nurses and midwives we could get hold of at the time. That was a problem for us, as the nurses' training school for our diocese was 200 miles away at Magila. Girls had not yet got used to leaving their home area on their own, so for qualified nurse midwives we had to rely on wives of the MAs. Local girls could help and be taught gradually.

Christmas in Kenya and Future Changes at Minaki

It was September when I arrived at Minaki, but after malaria on the ship I didn't really regain my health. In December Dr Gibbons sent me to Nairobi, to be treated by a doctor friend of hers, and I stayed at the CMS guest house. The treatment went well, and at the guest house I found Margaret Howard, whom I had met before at a CMS summer school at Malvern; she and a cousin were teachers at a

CMS school in the foot-hills of Mount Kenya. They took me off to their home for Christmas, amid hills and farms and woods, and with a dramatic view of the mountain, changing every day in mist and sun and storm. Mt. Kenya is not as high as Kilimanjaro, but is rugged and spiky and impressive, while the drama of Kilimanjaro is the way its summits suddenly appear through the clouds, as though floating in mid-air. 'Kilima' in Kiswahili means 'hill' or 'mountain', so 'Mount' is better omitted. My first Christmas in Africa was with these kind cousins, and then I returned to Minaki refreshed and ready to get down to the job in hand.

The prospects for surgery changed abruptly when I got back. Robin and Mary Gibbons were due for overseas leave in January, and they would have to retire. I should be on my own. Robin's eyes were being damaged by the anti-malarial drugs then available. Quinine is a fierce drug, though a very useful one; mepacrine, the yellow one, is slow acting and has plenty of problems, and paludrine, which we took weekly, will prevent but not cure malaria. Soon chloroquine was available, but long use is also dangerous for the eyes. The Gibbons went on leave in January 1950 and returned briefly later in the year to finalise their affairs at Minaki, pack up, say their farewells after their long and valuable services to health and education in the country, and then return to England.

The hospital and training unit were in our hands – the nursing sisters, the medical assistants, and the fairly new doctor who still had much to learn! As well as all the clinical work, there was the administration, the teaching programme, and an urgent building programme to finance and put into action. Eating and sleeping had to be fitted in, as well as a bit of praying, and perhaps even some recreation! I also found that I was needed to help in co-ordinating Church medical work with that of other Missions, and our work with Government, because I lived near Dar-es-Salaam. More of that later. It was then that I first realised that I was there to be 'Jack-of-all-trades' and not just surgeon or even just doctor. This became increasingly evident as time went on. We were too few on the ground to have 'specialists' or to say, "But that's not my job", even when it came to drains and architecture or planning the health service!

It may seem strange to regard surgery almost as an optional extra, but this was because of the locality. The Sewa Haji Hospital in Dar-es-Salaam, only 18 miles away, was at that time the best hospital in the country. It was soon to be replaced by a larger and more modern one which became the teaching hospital when we had a university with a medical faculty. So local people had better access to hospital facilities than many others in the country. When, later on, in 1962 I went down to Masasi Diocese in the Southern Region to work at Lulindi Hospital we were much more isolated. We were also training nurses who had to have surgical experience. Surgery was essential there, and good facilities were already well established.

Admissions and Diet

At Minaki I quickly realised that one had to develop a new concept of how a hospital functioned. Admitting a patient started with, "Je! Umekuja kukaa?" ("Have you come to stay?") A bit of persuasion either way might make a difference, but was not the deciding factor. Patients, especially men, were surprisingly keen to have operations; hernias were common, and they wanted to get rid of them. But any procedure, especially for the women, often needed consent from a specific relative, usually the senior maternal uncle, who might live miles away – very troublesome in emergency situations! A helper nearly always stayed with the patients, and that was necessary in some of our hospitals where food was not provided. At Minaki we provided the staple diet of ugali and beans twice a day (ugali is an almost solid maize meal porridge), with some vegetables. When we could afford it we gave some uji (porridge) or bread and tea with sugar for breakfast. We were amused some years later, when my future mother-in-law, visiting near Christmas time, asked, "Do the patients enjoy their Christmas dinner?" I am sure they did, but not the turkey and plum pudding that Mother was thinking of! David Bartlett was acting chaplain to the college at the time, and it was at Minaki that we first met.

Celebration of a Life Saved

One year our students had a real Christmas feast. A family living 6 miles away showed their gratitude for our services by inviting them all, over 40 of them, to a feast at midday on Christmas Day. Not long before they had brought one of the family to us, completely collapsed from severe internal haemorrhage, which resulted from a ruptured ectopic pregnancy (a pregnancy developing outside the womb). An operation and our first blood transfusion had saved her life. The first bottle of blood came from a teacher from England who knew he was 'Group O IV'; the second was from the patient's brother. We could only do direct cross-matching at that time. We were already good at saving and returning the patient's own blood, but it was not enough in this case. After the festal sung Eucharist on Christmas morning, the students who were on duty got on quickly with their hospital work. Then the staff took over for them and they all hurried off with high hopes, which were certainly not disappointed. Their return must have been a cross-country run, as they were back before dark, safe from lions and other wild life, and in time to join us for the joyful sung Evensong at 6 pm.

Languages and Training

In a country with many tribes each with its own language, we were blessed with a universal language, which most people knew, Kiswahili, usually referred to as 'Swahili'. English was also widely known, particularly by young people who hoped for further education after primary school. The teaching of all medical and nursing students was in English, and this was for two main reasons; it gave them access to far more text books than Swahili; it also gave them access to more advanced courses in future after some work experience. This was important, as for many, their schooling had been difficult, so it had not shown their real potential. Medical assistants, if they did well in their work and continued their studies, could apply for entry to an Assistant Medical Officer course, and if successful, be employed as doctors, and take on far more responsibility and also get a higher salary. Other medical categories, as well as nurses, had similar opportunities.

Language was a problem with some patients. There are so many different tribes in Tanganyika, each with their own language, and for some, such as the Maasai, this is quite unrelated to Kiswahili. Inevitably there are some, mainly elderly ladies, who never bother with Swahili, but among staff and students, someone could often be found who could help.

Teaching our students was usually a delight, with eager boys wanting to catch every word, though occasionally completely misunderstanding it! Miss Fisher, teaching English grammar, says that one day when she said, "Any questions?", a particularly bright boy (whom I met later when he was ambassador to China),replied, "Miss Fisher, I haven't understood a word you have said". Rather disconcerting for a very experienced teacher!

The MA course was for three years; it was like a simplified doctor's course with little in it of the background subjects. Anatomy was like a really good first aid anatomy course, and no chemistry or physics were included. In the laboratory, use of the microscope was important for diagnosis of malaria, intestinal worms and other parasites. As well as the signs, symptoms and treatment of diseases, especially the ones common in the country, they needed to know how they spread and how to teach people to prevent them. Health education would be part of their work as well as handing out pills and medicines. Many MAs would find they needed to know some nursing principles, as trained nurses were in short supply at that time. Our classroom teaching was important, but even more so was 'hands on' teaching – looking down the microscope in the laboratory, and getting to know the different medications in the dispensary. In wards and outpatient clinics they saw how we made a diagnosis and decided on treatment. Under supervision they could then do some of the treatments themselves. So there were teaching jobs for us all, Daudi and Clement in the laboratory, Anthony in his dispensary, Sisters and MAs in wards, and the team in theatre.

We struggled with cleanliness in wards and sterility in theatre, having open windows for light and air, with nothing to keep out dust and flies, even in the theatre. Amusing though was an incident in theatre, when a pretty sensible student appeared to be just wandering round waving his arms in the air. "What are you doing Benedict?" said a slightly ruffled doctor. He replied politely, "Catching flies, Doctor!" He was catching them by making a grab with one hand, shaking the hand and listening for the buzz to be sure it was there – I don't know what happened after that!

Doctors, Herbal Doctors and Witch-Doctors

There are several terms in Swahili used to mean 'doctor'; but with shades of meaning they are difficult to define. In setting up her training for medical assistants, Dr Gibbons decided to use the word 'Tabibu' for them, so they were known as Tabibu Clement, Tabibu Paul, etc. Anthony with his similar grade of training, was also called 'Tabibu'. 'Mganga' would be the obvious one to use for Dr Gibbons and myself, but it usually referred to herbal and witch-doctors, often the same person, so I was called 'Mama Daktari' or just Doctor. Witch-doctors could intend good or evil for their 'patients', and herbal doctors, while normally working for good, could easily do harm, because they had little control over dosage. With our treatments the problem was sometimes: "If I take a little it is good, so if I take more it will be better" – or even worse – "If it is good for me it will be good for my baby".

Tabibu Clement's time at Minaki was short and was my first experience of the deeply rooted fear of witchcraft. I always found this fear quite understandable in people exposed to constant dangers. An infant may die tomorrow from malaria; vital crops may be washed away over night or just wither away if the rain doesn't come, and then there is nothing to feed the family on. Witchcraft or evil spirits – is it so different from touching wood or crossing fingers? "Oh no, I am not superstitious, it's just fun" – or is it "just in case"? Clement, already a respected and efficient member of staff, who had been fortunate enough to have a year in England studying laboratory work in Bristol, came to my house one day looking sad. "Doctor" he said, "I know you will find this difficult to understand, but please try. I shall have to give in my notice". It was a shock – I really didn't want to lose him, as a good worker and a good influence on staff and students. "I am being repeatedly threatened with witchcraft by another member of staff. We Africans have a fear of witchcraft deeply buried in us, passed on by generations of ancestors. We, as Christians, know in our heads about the power of God in Jesus Christ, but in our hearts is still the fear and unrest, and we don't know how to handle it. I shall have to go." It was not hard to find out who the other member of staff was. His work was valuable, but I had other problems with him. Having got rid of Clement he also resigned, leaving no-one in the laboratory.

Clement had a useful career in government service, and when he retired about 20 years later and returned to his home village at Lewa, near Korogwe, in the foothills of the Usambara Mountains, David and I were at Magila, in much the same area. We heard that he wanted to discuss the possibility of becoming a priest. I also had my eye on him for a job on the administration side of the hospital, as he would still be young, only about fifty. We shall meet him again later, when David and I set off on our motorcycle to find him!

Tabibu Dennis Mhina who had laboratory experience, nobly took over the laboratory after this staffing crisis, and also the teaching of laboratory work and anatomy. Maria, his wife, was a nurse midwife trained at Magila. During her first pregnancy she very nearly died of eclampsia, but in fact lived to raise a family, and she outlived her husband into the 21st century. Dennis was one of the later-ordained priests, and he and Maria were a kind, gentle couple, who must have done much good to many people during their lives. Similar things could be said about many of the staff in their different ways.

Tabibu Anthony Msei had been taught his pharmacy and dispensing by Dr. Gibbons, who was essentially a pharmacist herself. After about 14 years running our dispensary, he did valuable work in Government service. He stayed on at Minaki until the situation changed there, and then left and was put in charge of hostels for medical assistant students and others, first in Dar-es-Salaam, and later in his home town of Tanga, 200 miles further north on the coast. Anthony had various ups and downs in his life, but was eventually able to fulfil his great wish to be ordained to the priesthood. Anthony's youngest son, Augustine, came to England in 1998 to study in London, and during his time there he gradually went into severe kidney failure. Our heartfelt gratitude goes to the National Health Service, as the Royal Free Hospital managed to find him a suitable kidney and performed a transplant. Immense gratitude also to the unknown donor and family!

David Bartlett and Other Missionaries and their Work

During my 12 years at Minaki, David Bartlett popped in and out of my life as did many other members of the Mission – we became rather like an extended family, exchanging news when we met, helping each other when we could, enjoying the company of most, and doing our best with the others! David and a friend of his, James Potts, who came rather later, came well within the first category; they both came to Zanzibar Diocese with a special interest in theological education. James has remained a very good friend ever since. I don't think it occurred to either David or me that in 7 or 8 years time he (David) would be suggesting something more!

David's first two years in Tanganyika were spent in parish work in Zanzibar Diocese, which gave him time to become proficient in the language, and to experience parish life, local customs and worship, while working with an experienced Tanzanian priest. This was Yohana Jumaa, who later became the first Tanzanian bishop of the diocese, and would then be asking us to rejoin his staff. After a short home-leave David moved further south to Masasi Diocese, to St Cyprians College at Namasakata, near Tunduru, which is about 220 miles inland from Lindi on the coast. St Cyprians was 'right in the bush', with local style buildings of poles and mud walls and thatched roofs, paraffin lamps, water carried in, and with 6 or 8 miles of treacherous track between them and Tunduru. They had no telephone or other modern assets of course. How they got their supplies I am not quite sure – I saw no sign of any vehicle except David's motor-cycle when I stayed there while on a tour of Masasi Diocese in 1957 with Marion Robinson. She was the doctor at Lulindi Hospital where I worked later. At the time it was thought best to train priests for our group of dioceses in the circumstances in which they expected to work, but before long there would be changes. Meanwhile a new venture had started at Kalole, the staff village at Minaki. Here a very small number of men with sufficient background education, would be trained in English for ordination, thus giving them access to a wide variety of reading matter, and fitting them for a wider variety of ministry. The Kalole course continued for a few years and then closed, as English started to be used much more at St Cyprian's.

David's first spell at Minaki was as acting warden at Kalole, two successive wardens having been called away to become bishops! Mark Way was to be Bishop of Masasi, and then John Poole-Hughes went to Njombe in the Southern Highlands, the Diocese of South West Tanganyika. After retirement Bishop Poole-Hughes returned to his native Wales and in 1975 was made Bishop of Llandaff. Later on David came to Minaki for a few months as acting college chaplain. By then, staff changes meant that the two nursing sisters and I, now Joyce Townsend and Edith Horton, got to know him much better. We valued his easy friendliness, and his dry sense of humour, making fun of some of the difficult things of life! Then one day he got involved in a dogfight (he loved dogs and usually had one of his own), and as a result we reckoned him to be our first 'private in-patient' in one of the big rooms in the old German house.

During the early period when David was at Kalole, he turned up at my house one afternoon, asking if I could possibly go to Pugu, only 3-4 miles away, to see an Asian lady, whose family were begging for me to go to see her. I didn't normally go out to see patients, and in any case had no transport, as it would be unheard of to ask for the

College lorry to take me. The only other transport was David's motorcycle, but it was back in the days when lady missionaries were expected to be rather 'proper' and in any case I had no trousers! Nervous of the views of the more straight-laced of my colleagues, but because this was in some way 'special', I donned a back-pack of essential items and committed myself to the back of David's small motorcycle ('piki-piki' in Swahili). I clung on, not being used to that sort of transport on that sort of road, and the only thing to cling onto seemed to be David's waist. We arrived safely, and I did what was necessary for the patient. Next came the inevitable effusive thanks and the present – bananas – not just a huge bunch, but 'mkungu' (Swahili for a branch of bunches)!

In spite of my protests David insisted that they be fixed to his pack, so it is not difficult to imagine the angle at which I was clinging on, to say nothing of the effect on the stability of our small vehicle. The steep stony hill was our downfall; at one of the bends we landed in a heap in the middle of the road. Mercifully there were no injuries and no traffic, and the bike still functioned, so we arrived home safely and I was able to creep in unnoticed; the problem was going to be accounting for the glut of bananas! Little did I know how often in later years I would travel on the back of David's motor-cycle, or on my own beside him!

Some Surgery at Last

It was a joy in those early days when our surgical facilities were up and running. A prime mover and really super theatre sister was Ruby Marshall, who later became Sister Ruby CSP, when she joined the Community of the Sacred Passion (CSP). At Minaki she was hospital matron and theatre sister, housekeeper for us ladies, and also did her share of teaching. The other two sisters coped with all the wards and the maternity work, as well as stores, and shared night-calls with the MAs, calling me when they needed me at night, or of course during the day.

Hernias topped operation statistics at Minaki, of which many were planned operations; a few of these were small and routine, while others had adhesions, and some were huge. It was difficult to know how best to repair the huge ones using nylon supplied by a fishing tackle shop, which worked well on the small ones. An example of this came unexpectedly. My local holiday usually included visiting other centres of medical work, and in 1954 this took me to Lake Nyasa (now Malawi) on a visit to a friend with a dispensary on the lakeside. She also had a new baby. Then, hitching a lift on a fisheries research boat down the lake, I arrived at night to visit the UMCA-supported hospital at Liuli. We shone a search-light onto the land; I was rowed ashore, and the whole village came out to see what was going on! The doctor there, Ursula Hay, was quick to ask if I would do a hernia for her, which was booked for the next morning. I saw why when I saw the hernia! I had a similar request at Lulindi when visiting Masasi in 1957. That time it was for a hysterectomy, needed for out-sized fibroids, which were a not uncommon problem.

It was quite a challenge to switch from holiday maker/information gatherer, to surgeon (I was not qualified as a gynaecologist), and in a strange operating theatre – probably strange in more ways than one! I did enjoy these opportunities, as they were a challenge and a change from my 'Jack-of-all-trade' work on most days.

At Minaki and elsewhere I was usually the only doctor, and had no trained anaesthetist. If there had to be a general anaesthetic, I had to be instructing a nurse, as well as doing the operation. Spinal or local anaesthetics were used where possible, but could add to the problems for serious surgical emergencies. Delay in getting emergencies to the hospital meant that instead of simple release and repair, a hernia needed resection of the bowel or some other major procedure. It is hard to believe now that in those days we used home-made intravenous fluids, with re-sterilised giving sets, and re-sharpened needles; instruments were boiled, needles and 'sharps' were kept in trays of spirit; gowns and drapes were sterilised in what looked like pressure cookers on primus stoves. Surgical gloves too were re-sterilised after being patched (like bicycle tyres) when pricks or holes were found. Gloves were not always available for deliveries or even for removal of retained placentas if our maternity services had become very popular. (I was quite relieved to get an HIV test while on leave, after we heard about the HIV/AIDS problem.)

Injuries were also high on the list: animal injuries and falls from trees; cuts, burns needing skin grafts; and gunshot injuries, usually accidental, but not quite always. Acute appendicitis was a rarity, its place on the emergency list taken by ruptured ectopic pregnancy. We were popular for women with women's complaints, as they would naturally prefer a lady doctor to an unknown one, probably a man, in Dar-es-Salaam. So we soon had to take on their pelvic problems, including huge fibroid tumours, often complicated by previous infection. I was very glad of my basic general surgical training, on which one could build experience in gynaecology, and in other of the more specialised situations when they turned up. Opportunity came when leprosy experts asked me to relieve pressure on nerves in the arm causing weakness and curling up of the fingers, and I could soon see how to do it. Also poliomyelitis is often followed by severe deformities of the legs, for which fairly simple surgery followed by physiotherapy often enables a child to become upright and mobile again.

Fractures were a problem without x-rays, and we had no electricity until 1959. Some I could safely treat, and that included hip fractures. During my time working in England, 'pinning' of hip fractures was just coming in, and this of course needed good x-ray facilities. Hip replacements were hardly more than a pipe dream. I was familiar with the old method of 'balanced traction' in which the whole leg is slung up from a beam over the bed with sufficient traction to make it comfortable and stable. Results were usually good, but for adults it meant 8-10 weeks flat on the back in bed. The time was shorter for small children, who had a gallows frame over the bed, the child flat on the back with the legs straight up in the air, which amazingly they soon got used to. We even had reason to treat newborn babies in that way on more than one occasion, when there had been difficulty with delivering the baby. We were really nervous when the first 2 or 3 day old baby, Violet, was brought in with one thigh all wobbly and clearly broken. We slung her legs up from the frame and I am sure some of the nurses thought I was making a big mistake. Happily both Violet and the later ones did well, but Mother had to get into a very queer position to suckle her child!

Our Surroundings

Wild animals and other hazards meant that few cases were brought in at night, for which we were thankful, especially because of lighting problems. Diagnosis would be by hurricane lamp, and in theatre by Tilley pressure lamps which gave out a lot more heat than light when we were struggling with something tricky during a hot night. But tropical nights were special. The clear star-light or moon-light was absolutely silent for a time. Then suddenly it came alive with sounds of night birds or howling hyenas and an occasional lion's roar, wild pigs grunting, frogs at times in the year really yelling from any watery place, and then the 'komba' or bush baby. He is a sort of outsized squirrel, who has a loud shriek and I think must wear outsized army boots by the noise he makes clattering over tin roofs! He is also liable to climb the palm trees and get drunk on the palm wine. Our cook collected this to make our bread (instead of yeast, while others of course use it for more sociable purposes!) We would find 'komba' in the morning, a small round bundle of coarse fur, snoring under a nearby bush, so we knew why our bread had gone flat!

Another distant haunting sound at night was drumming, eerie and suggestive of witchcraft and the fear of evil spirits. This is often connected with tribal rites of passage or illness, celebrations or misfortunes. I suppose we all have our different ways of expressing and dealing with these things and the emotions which go with them. For a new missionary the eerie drumming is another thing to get used to. I very much appreciated the respect for the ancestors, and awareness of them, the 'living dead', whom I think of as the 'dear departed.'

Minaki was a settlement surrounded by African bush, miles of low trees and shrubs with clearings for villages and fields of corn (maize), cassava, vegetables, and other crops, and even hill rice. It was ideal for a varied wild life. Goats and chickens were kept, but cattle only if they could be immunised against sleeping sickness (trypanosomiasis). The animal form was endemic along the coast, but fortunately for us, the human form remained confined to certain areas inland. Lions had caused trouble in the past among the students, killing one who was out too late. On another occasion one caused panic, by chasing a wild pig into a dormitory – no casualties that time. Snakes were fairly common, but many of them not dangerous; a python was seen on one or two occasions, and at a later time and place, puff adders would spray their venom into the eyes of our dog, making her very cross, but doing no long term damage. Leopards were specially feared, as they attacked without provocation, aiming for the face and eyes. A man I saw had lost one eye, and also parts of one hand which I had to patch up as best as I could.

Gunshot wounds in the different places where I worked were nearly always accidental and often from faulty guns, used for shooting for food or protection from dangerous animals, or to protect crops from predators, mostly wild pigs. A man out shooting wild pig had his gun explode in his hand, leaving little that could be salvaged. My mother had faced a similar situation in China when a 'brigand from the hills' was brought to her with a shattered hand, which she, as a nurse, had to amputate. She was rather anxious when, much later, he wanted to see her, but it was only to tell her that he was all right because "he could eat his rice".

Two miles up the hill from Minaki is the Boma (literally fort) which is the headquarters of the Kisarawe district commissioner (DC) and his staff, all British in our time there. The local tribe are the Wazaramu, and their chief officer, the Wakili Mkuu, with other local authority (LA) officials, also had their offices at Kisarawe. The LA had certain areas of responsibility in the district, making them a valuable link between the DC and local people.

We were glad to accept occasional invitations to Kisarawe for lunch on Saturday, always an almighty curry, with all manner of accessories, including banana, various fruits, egg, cheese, nuts, and always grated coconut. I disliked curry, but as it was about our only chance of a meal out, I decided that I must get on and like it. I soon succeeded. Another welcome invitation was for tennis, which once included Dicky Gower, who was DC there but sadly for only a short time. He was a brilliant player who really livened things up, and later provided English cricket with his well known son David Gower. The forestry officer's wife, Mrs Howe, was a character. She delighted in telling us, as she bounced her first baby mercilessly up and down (which he seemed to love), "The Queen was at my wedding", her husband having at the time had the Windsor Estate trees under his care.

New Wards at Last

The new hospital wards were an urgent need. Canon Neville Nash, a seasoned missionary and headmaster, replaced Canon Gibbons in 1951, and was soon joined by his sister Gladys, a retired teacher, with a name for country dancing which she soon started teaching the boys. Father Nash helped me plan and get built our three new wards. We decided on the old Nightingale type, 24 bed wards, cheaper to build and easier to run than others. The wards had concrete floors and pillars, sun dried brick walls, and bati (tin) roofs; there were rows of beds, small lockers, and not much else. Money trickled in, and the men, women and children got their more manageable and much more hygienic wards. Ward rounds with teaching became possible! The MA on the ward gave a fairly formal report on new patients and on the progress and problems of others. We had a laugh on my 40th birthday, when Tabibu Alfred started at the first bed with a new patient: "This old lady is aged forty". I had to tell them what the sister and I were laughing about, but admittedly I did sometimes feel a bit elderly! Alfred's English was correct. 'Mzee', meaning 'old person' in Swahili, is a term of honour and politeness for a person older or senior to oneself, or just to show respect. 'Old lady' sounds different in English!

Looking for funds for the building project increased our feeling of being rather peripheral to the diocese. We were 200 miles from its headquarters which was at Hegongo then, very near Magila. We had the feeling that 'the powers that be' might have felt more involved if it had been Magila or Korogwe hospital which was in such urgent need. The Gibbons were a pretty strong pair, able I'm sure to pull in all the support they needed, so we must learn the technique ourselves. Running expenses of the hospital were financed in a variety of ways. We received a quarterly subvention from UMCA via the diocesan treasurer; patients' fees were of necessity small, but helped a little; Government grants helped cover salaries of trained staff. We will hear more of 'grants' later. Gifts from friends and supporters overseas were vital, especially for projects like the new wards, theatre equipment, and making an existing building suitable to use for surgery.

It was fun choosing names for the new wards. The women's ward was given St. Veronica, who according to tradition showed kindness to Our Lord on his way to Calvary. The children had St Monica for the girls' side and her son St Augustine for the boys. We chose St Benedict for the surgical patients, as by then I was in touch with the Benedictine Abbey at Nashdom in England and the Benedictine way of life.

The old wards were still useful for ulcers, and these could be serious, some due to yaws, which was happily being completely wiped out when penicillin became easily available. Yaws was a condition common in the tropics causing horrible ulcers, mainly on the legs, which went deep and refused to heal. The soles of the feet became hard and horny, with multiple deep and painful corns. Severe joint pains were thought also to be caused by yaws in the later stages. It was a condition which responded to the same drugs as syphilis, and was caused by a similar organism, though not transmitted sexually. Injections containing bismuth and arsenicals were used, as for syphilis, but we all forgot about them as quickly as we could when the 'all-powerful penicillin' came along! Infected wounds and burns were admitted to these old wards. This was not ideal, but it prevented infecting others; this applied to infectious diseases too.

Cases of chickenpox, not usually being dangerous, had to go into a corner of a main ward, and one day the tall, thin, gentle MA Alfred came to my house really worried. "Doctor", he said, "I'm very much afraid that the case of chickenpox in St. Augustine's ward has turned into smallpox" – a polite way of saying that we had made a bad mistake in diagnosis. This of course was some years before the exciting day when WHO could announce that smallpox had been entirely wiped out all over the world.

My first case of anthrax was quite exciting. It is a dangerous skin infection, caught from the hides and skins of domestic animals, and it quickly develops severe toxic effects, and often leads to death if not treated. A man came one morning when I was teaching students in out-patients, and he was the perfect teaching case, with all the textbook signs and symptoms which I had never seen before. He was perfect for treatment too, as by then we had penicillin, which in big doses produces dramatic cure of this dangerous infection, and it did just that for our patient.

Changes to the Training

Soon after Dr Gibbons left Minaki, I realised that our training of medical assistants was coming under threat. The health ministry was starting to raise the standard of MA training, as part of the drive to make real improvements in the medical services of the country. This training would require better staffing and facilities than we could provide. Students would be from Standard 10 instead of Standard 8. Realising the importance of better services in rural areas, the policy was to set up rural health centres run by medical assistants. Nurse midwives would handle maternity and child health services, and all staff should be committed to health education for all – fathers as well as mothers, men as well as women. Each district would have a few health centres, and around them a ring of dispensaries run by rural medical aids (RMAs) and village midwives (VMs), both with similar but less advanced training than for MAs or for fully qualified midwives, but following the same sort of programmes. After discussions at medical headquarters, and with our bishop, William Scott-Baker, and others concerned, we decided to change to RMA training. Our trainees would be available to staff both mission and government dispensaries.

RMA training was a two-year course, and was on the same lines as the MA one. It must be simple and straightforward, and practical for the situation in which they expected to work. They must know about the common diseases and their treatment, and the laboratory tests which they could do themselves with a microscope and little else. Most important was for them to know which cases they could treat (and how to do it); and of those who needed to go to the health centre or hospital, which were urgent and which, like an uncomplicated hernia, could go home and think about it.

RMAs would be first in line to help village people to improve their health, and babies and small children were a high priority. Diet, cleanliness and protection from mosquitoes and malaria, and quick treatment when needed could help a lot. If milk was scarce, there were vegetable proteins like beans which could be used if properly prepared. Fathers and village elders must be drawn in to feel a responsibility for helping to tackle the sad statistics of infant mortality and that of young children. Our trainees would be at the front line for this, as an important part of the national maternity & child health service (MCH). Worms, especially hookworm, were another preventable, and also treatable, cause of sickness, and of death from anaemia. The district authorities worked hard at encouraging people in hygiene, and especially in digging pit latrines, which helped a lot in prevention of worms, and also of the dysenteries, and of cholera when that became a big problem later on. There were vast areas where there was no hope of water-borne sanitation. The old style country general practitioner would have been a good role-model for our RMAs, with his care for all those in the village or town area for which he was responsible. First aid would be an important subject for RMAs, especially resuscitation and control of bleeding, splinting fractures, and deciding what to do next for the patient.

All students in the college were given Red Cross first aid training and took the official exams. One afternoon the Governor, Sir Edward Twining, came with his wife to watch a display and to give out Red Cross certificates. At the end, Lady Twining, who was a doctor, suddenly said to me, "Are you coming to the leprosy lecture in Dar this evening? Come and spend the night with us at Government House (!) and I'll send you back in the morning". A great opportunity but alarming, yet how could I refuse? A hasty visit to the hospital, and then to find a respectable dress, and I was off in their Mercedes. What would my colleagues think of this escapade? At Government House drinks with the high and mighty were followed by dinner, where in some surprising way, I found myself given the seat on His Excellency's right as 'Senior Lady'; strange and a bit scary for one still a fairly 'new missionary'! It was quite a relief when Lady Twining excused us to go to the lecture, adding to HE, "And to save time dear, may we use your cloakroom?" Breakfast was brought to my room, where the veranda looked out onto immaculate lawns and borders, and the vast expanse of the Indian Ocean. Headed note-paper was provided, so I scribbled a note to Mother, and then the Mercedes arrived and I was swept back to real life at Minaki.

The Lorry: Who Can Drive?

The only transport at Minaki after the Gibbons left was the 3-ton lorry. It was used for supplies for the college and hospital, and for students' transport for outings, for sending them off for their holidays, and for very occasional emergencies. It seemed a bit risky to me that no-one on the station, except our very devoted driver, Daudi Sala (literally 'David Prayer') could drive any vehicle, let alone a lorry, unless David Bartlett, who was used to tanks and armoured cars during the war, happened to be with us. It seemed a good enough reason for me to ask Daudi to give me instruction. I had driven a car a few times in England with a provisional wartime licence, and Daudi was an excellent teacher. Driving the lorry reminded me of carefree childhood days, high on the back of the huge farm cart-horses, bringing in tumbrels of wheat or barley, or mangel-wurzels for animal feed. My orders then were, "The horse must walk in the outer wheel marks at gateways, or the wheels of the cart will bring down my gateposts"! My small brain said "Why?" But I did what I was told and it worked, and gradually I understood why. I was careful to follow Daudi's orders when he had me backing round a winding track through a glade of palm trees before taking a test. Perhaps his name helped.

Liz Leeson, the maths and science teacher, also later learnt to drive the lorry, and much enjoyed it – she was much more of a tough guy than I was! When she left Minaki, she spent the rest of her life, first doing marine biology in a sail-boat down the east side of the Americas, going ashore from time to time to teach and earn some money. Next she made three attempts to cross the Atlantic Ocean solo in a very inadequate sailing boat, ending up without going further from Britain than Madeira, where she spent the rest of her life in marine biology and other interesting pursuits. She wrote a fascinating autobiography, 'Alone on a Crooked Mile'.

For business or pleasure, places could be booked on the Saturday lorry trip to Dar-es-Salaam, which went to collect supplies. We often returned perched up on top of the loads, pretty precarious and bumpy, but it gave a good view of the scenery! Shopping for us was minimal, because income was minimal; our food and lodging were supplied by UMCA, via the diocese, plus Sh.11/- per week (55p) as pocket money. I often had things to do at Medical Headquarters, or needed to see Father Walsh of the White Fathers, who co-ordinated the medical work of the Roman Catholic missions. Lunch for me was often with friends, or with the two CSP Sisters who worked in Dar. I had an occasional afternoon crewing for Dr Barratt from Medical Headquarters in his rather heavy and clumsy yacht. We had a lovely harbour area to sail on, and islands just off the coast, where one could go ashore. Dr Barratt would kindly drive me home, as I was too late for the lorry's return. Dar has attractive palm beaches which many enjoy, but with little shelter I found the sun just too much. Newcomers are warned of the danger of using the shade of a palm tree, because of what may fall down from the top!

St. Francis' Secondary School, Pugu

We got to know the Irish Holy Ghost Fathers who ran the boys secondary school at Pugu, 3 or 4 miles from Minaki, through sports competitions and occasional 'shows' which they put on. I remember a spectacular Gilbert and Sullivan, and also an amazingly good production of Macbeth, with considerable amusement caused by the all-male, all African cast, in Shakespearian English with an Irish/Swahili accent! Our college 'shows' were presented in a much simpler local style at that time and went on for ages, but later a very gifted headmaster's wife (Elizabeth Pentney) produced some excellent plays at Minaki, bringing out plenty of hidden talent.

Our other contact with the Pugu students was in the hospital, and especially during an outbreak of typhoid fever, for which at that time we had no specific treatment. Giving TAB injections for prevention to some 600 students and staff of the two colleges, and as many as we could collect in of the local population, was quite a big and definitely unpopular job. Sadly one of our students did die of typhoid in spite of our efforts, and another was unconscious for days, but then recovered.

Lent to Easter

The cycle of the Church's year was the background of our life at Minaki, and also of that of village and town parishes. Lent was always during the time of oppressive sticky heat, when we were all longing for rain. We knew it would come, and then we expected to be swamped by violent storms with rain day and night. In our area the term 'the rains failed' meant much less rain and for too short a period to bring the vital crops to maturity. But whatever the weather, as the Lent season progressed, I became conscious of the special atmosphere, both in and out of chapel. Services, led by

Father Nash or the college chaplain, were beautifully and reverently sung. The solemnity and awe of Holy Week were followed by the joy and excitement of the Resurrection when Easter dawned. This all emphasised our life together at Minaki as a Christian community. For the students these formative years must have made a big difference when they went out into the 'great big world'. For me as a newcomer, it was certainly a joy. Another enormous help was the knowledge of the prayers of faithful friends and congregations overseas at times of stress, as well as in the happy times.

In my newsletter of June 1950 to friends and supporters I said:-

> It was a wonderful experience having Holy Week and Easter here, after so many spent in the rush of English hospital life. All the week one could feel the atmosphere of quiet expectancy among the staff and boys. It started with the long Palm Sunday Services, including a procession round the church carrying palms, green ones straight off the trees. After that each service brought us nearer in thought to Good Friday, and then led us on to the triumphal theme of the Easter Mass. It was wonderful to me that the boys held onto the atmosphere all the week – - – and how it changed from the quiet awe of Holy Week, to the absolute triumph of Easter; it was there all the time, while working in hospital and classroom. The singing too was beautiful, and helped us, especially when our lack of knowledge of the language might have made us miss the English services. We certainly have a lot to be thankful for here.

Medical work in Tanzania could be exhausting, and was always stressful because so much needed to be done, and there was so little to do it with. The parable which Jesus told of 'Building on the Rock' was very relevant, the Rock being Christ himself and his Church. These were our reliable support, while trying to serve him in wards, operating theatre, classroom or literally 'stuck in the mud' and trying to get home!

Home Leave

We all looked forward to home leave which was expected at roughly 3-year intervals. By February 1953 Dr Lesley Sitwell from Kideleko was able to come to Minaki, and was well able to keep things running while I was away, as she had been in the diocese since 1945. After the usual last minute scramble I was ready on time to board the 'Kenya Castle'. It was an interesting and restful journey, and I was met at the London docks by my Uncle Charlie, who put me onto the train to Cambridge. I had instructions from my brother Alan about the local bus to take for Bourn, a few miles out of Cambridge, where he and his wife Joy had an attractive thatched cottage, and Mother lived with them. Alan was working in a radiotherapy research unit at Addenbrooke's Hospital in Cambridge. It seemed quite unreal to step off a bus in an unknown English village, and I felt a bit nervous surrounded by white faces, and everything and every person moving so fast!! I must have looked lost, but Alan soon appeared, and I knew I had arrived home. It was only a few steps past very English fields, and homes with their much loved Spring gardens, to find Mother waiting at the cottage window, and Joy in the kitchen, preparing an excellent supper for us.

Overseas leave was a wonderful experience, meeting family and friends, travelling round to different places, enjoying familiar foods, and the familiar scenery of town and country. For me it was a relief not to be always 'on call' day and night. I could sympathise with mothers who long for the baby to learn that nights are for sleeping – all through! At Minaki we always looked forward to the arrival of the mail bag; in England I looked for Tanganyika stamps when the postman called.

Our leave normally gave us 4 months in England. The first and last months were for seeing families and friends, and for re-equipping ourselves with clothes and other necessities for the next three years. It usually also included replenishing some hospital supplies, or getting new items. The middle two months were for going round the country, telling people about our life and what we were doing;

this could be in small groups in people's houses, or in meeting halls and churches. I had become used to standing up in front of students in classrooms, but all my earlier fears came back when it came to big meetings and congregations!. But I really wanted people to know about our work, and its ups and downs, failures and successes, and about the people we worked with. I wanted them to see what their money and prayers were supporting, and to realise that they were actually doing the work, as well as those of us on the spot. A good supply of colour transparencies were life-saving when I could show them, as they fired me up, so that I could talk enthusiastically as though to a group of friends, about hospital, students, patients, scenery; about village life and the roads with their sand or mud, stones and rocks, potholes and floods; of staff and their problems, and of our life together at Minaki. For some listeners this might be an introduction to the needs of 'those far-off places', as they were at that time (1953), when few people travelled far, and news travelled slowly; others had been faithfully working and praying for years, and their devotion and enthusiasm did as much for me as my talk could possibly have done for them!

As well as all these activities during our home-leave, we needed refreshment and renewal of our inner lives and the chance to think over our calling to serve the Church in this particular way, in my case, as a mission doctor. Sometimes there would be a mission conference to attend, with a chance to share thoughts and experiences with others involved in mission work. A retreat or other quiet period could be planned to review the past and prepare for the future. Also visits were paid to Mission Headquarters, at Central Africa House in Great Peter Street (London) in UMCA days. There were news, ideas and plans to discuss, and problems to sort out. A medical check-up was fitted in, hoping that they wouldn't find some exotic tropical parasite lurking somewhere and about to cause trouble. The time passed quickly, and it was soon time to start packing.

Leave could be tiring, with so many people to meet and talk to in so many different places, and in spite of difficult farewells, I found that I was impatient to get back when the departure date got near. This would be my last four-week sea journey. I for one was glad that future journeys were by air; I enjoyed the experience of going by sea and calling in at interesting places, but also liked the sudden change that air travel gave between the two different but closely linked parts of my life.

Chapter 3
The Wider Vision – Working Together

Early Days of UMCA

When David Livingstone appealed in 1857 for young men to go and take the Gospel to Central Africa, a group of them from Oxford and Cambridge responded, and soon others from Durham and Dublin, and also some young ladies joined them. Under the title Universities Mission to Central Africa (UMCA) they made their way in 1860 to the east coast of Africa, to what was then Portuguese East Africa, now Mozambique, and sailed up the Zambezi River into its tributary, the Shire. When they went ashore and set up camp, they were taking on an entirely new thing in an area almost unknown in the West. It was tribal country, under tribal chiefs and elders, with no national boundaries, and no central organisation. Tribes were often at war with each other, and the East African slave trade was still active. Education would have been by word of mouth, from generation to generation. Illness, including spirit possession, was treated by 'Waganga', witch doctors, using herbal medicines as well as charms and exorcisms, with drumming and dancing, and various tribal ceremonies. Spirit worship played a major part in tribal life, connected of course with the practice of witchcraft and the respect and veneration of the ancestors. They were people who must have had a deep sense of the spiritual world around them. Ninety years later, when I went to Africa as a UMCA missionary, most things had changed, but this deep spiritual sense remained. In 1860 I suppose all inland tribes had a form of Animist belief; by 1949, Islam, Christianity, and Animism were said to be the faiths of almost equal numbers, with Islam strongest on the coast, and some mainly Christian areas where Missionaries had been working longest.

The Tanganyika I went to had a central government which was responsible for a health service with hospitals in towns, and dispensaries in some villages.

There was also an education programme with primary schools in each district, and just a few secondary. Many results of 'civilisation' were in evidence. There were roads, railways, bus services; towns with schools, shops and stores and a few factories, lorries, cars and motor-cycles, churches and mosques. The towns even had piped water and electricity, but not yet for all residents.

Large areas were still isolated by miles of uninhabited 'bush', broken up by small groups of simple dwellings. Most people were subsistence farmers with their fields around them. The lucky ones had a stream or well nearby, others having to walk miles each day to get water. Even the few main roads could be impassable during the rain, with bridges broken down or the dreaded 'black cotton soil', which when turned to mud can defeat even brilliant drivers of 4 wheel drive vehicles with any number of gears. When living 200 miles from Dar-es-Salaam 20 years later, our local bus proudly displayed the sign 'spanna mkononi' meaning 'spanner in hand'! The driver often needed more than spanner and string, and spares were still hard to get.

Until December 1961, government was in the hands of the United Kingdom under United Nations Mandate. Tanganyika had been a German colony until the 1st World War, and the older buildings in major towns and at District Headquarters showed this, as did our two storey building at Minaki. Roads were rough and pot-holed, and trains ran at an average of 15 miles an hour; services were primitive and limited, but a good start had been made. Officials were at that time almost entirely 'wazungu', expatriates, but as well as development and improvement of services, the policy of the Government in its different departments, and of the Missions, was to prepare local people to take leading positions as soon as they could. However no-one expected things to move so fast that 'Uhuru', Independence, would come at the end of 1961!

Christian Medical Missions: Relations with Government

Coming to Tanganyika and finding myself in charge of a hospital and medical assistant (MA) students in training, my time and energy were at first entirely used up getting used to the language, new surroundings and the job in hand. There was also the wider picture to look at: the medical services of the country, the place of Minaki and of other Mission medical work within those services. Roman Catholic, Lutheran and Anglican medical missions were active all over the country, as well as Mennonites, Moravians, Seventh Day Adventists and others in more localised areas. Our mission, UMCA, supported work along the east coast, and in the south right down to the Mozambique border, while the Church Missionary Society (CMS), mostly Australian, were active in the central and western areas right up to the border with Uganda and Kenya. Government's medical work was based on district hospitals at the district Headquarters all over the country, with larger hospitals in the few major towns. These later became well staffed specialist hospitals. Missions, on the whole, were working in rural areas, though later developing some really good specialist hospitals. The importance of outreach, and getting to the people 'off the map', influenced the planning of our work. Missions also saw the importance of training good nurses and midwives, and others like our MAs were needed all over the country. For the Christian boys and girls, a few years in training in a Christian setting was a good preparation for life in the great big world with all its stresses and strains.

The over-all picture showed that about half the total medical work in the country was in the hands of Christian missions. As time went on this would become the work of the local Church, supported by the wealthier Church overseas. Mary Gibbons and other doctors were determined that there should be full co-operation between the different providers of medical services, between the missions amongst themselves, as well as with Government, and it was clear that with so much of the work in our hands, we could expect to have some input into central planning and policy. A Mission Medical Committee (MMC) was set up soon after Mary Gibbons came on the scene. All doctors working with the Missions were members, and this included the Roman Catholic missions, which at that time kept themselves apart in many ways.

As Minaki was the nearest mission hospital to Dar-es-Salaam, and so to Government medical headquarters, I was soon asked to take over from Dr Gibbons as secretary to the MMC, and so to form the main link between ourselves and Medical HQ, not a job I would have chosen, but it turned out to be a very interesting one. Getting to know some of the officials whom I met there was helped very much by Paddy Shiel. She was the administrative assistant who was responsible for everything to do with missions and the grants which Government paid towards our work, and for the different committees that I might be involved in. She and her mother lived in Dar es Salaam, and I was soon being invited to lunch and even an occasional weekend if I could get away for one. The committees would be those concerned with medical and nursing trainings, their syllabuses, exams and standards. They were also responsible for the distribution of medical resources around the country and of the grants allotted to each mission, and for the Medical Registration Board which had recently been set up. This was in the process of deciding what medical qualifications would be acceptable for registration, which was very important for some missions, wanting to bring in doctors from various different countries. It was to prove the most difficult of my duties over the next 10 or 12 years. How could we possibly know the standards in Nebraska and New York, let alone Moscow, and in all Australia?

The series of chief medical officers and their deputies in my time I found a bit fierce, and to be handled with caution! An exception was Dr Barratt, second in command for a time, who was rather bland and very friendly; it was he who had a small but rather unwieldy boat at the Yacht Club, and who occasionally invited me to crew for him on a Saturday afternoon. It was very enjoyable and relaxing to be idling (mostly) on our beautiful harbour, or out to the islands off shore. The Dar-es- Salaam sailing fraternity spoke of the 'six o'clock calm'; the breeze dropped at sundown, and if the tide was running out they would be home very late for supper!

Dr CW Davies (Bill) was concerned mainly with training; he could be fierce at meetings when Mission training and the syllabuses were being discussed, especially when I was arguing for more financial help for our training schools. However it was soon evident that he was both knowledgeable and sincere in his planning. I got to know him and his wife Joan, and stayed with them once in Entebbe, when he became Chief Medical Officer of Uganda. David and I kept up with them after our retirement in England. I took the opportunity on a journey to England to visit Entebbe, going on to Mulago Hospital and Makerere University in Kampala. My main interests there were work going on to bring out useful textbooks for our type of medical training, covering the subjects which they really needed and in English terms which they would be likely to understand. It was a chance also to meet Dr Denis Burkitt, who was enlisting the help of mission hospitals with his research into a tumour of the jaw, which occurred only in children in the tropics. It later became known as 'Burkitt's tumour'.

Training and Upgrading

Relationships of Missions with Government on medical matters were good, both before and after Independence, though sometimes 'tricky', as money was scarce, and we were always asking for more! I think that sometimes, especially in our training schools, they felt our religious principles and practices were too prominent and having too much influence on our planning and decisions. However we all wanted good medical services and good training, and they needed us to help to provide it. We were all aware that many students who entered the training programme had come from places where it was a struggle to get schooling, even up to Standard VIII, (or VII when VIII was abolished). This was the entrance level for Grade B nursing and RMA training and for MAs while we were training them, and it was also a struggle. There were bright boys and girls among them who could go much further. This led to the idea of progressive training after a few years of work experience. RMAs could, with further training, become MAs, and Grade B nurses could attend a specialist course in subjects like theatre work, children's nursing, midwifery or psychiatric nursing, and so be registered as Grade A. As well as giving them fulfilment in their work, more responsibility and a higher salary, it was a good use of resources, and at that time the higher grades were nearly all expatriates. MAs also could be up-graded to assistant medical officer (titles changed later) and so be called 'doctor'. The country badly needed more Tanzanian doctors, as well as nurses in the 'Nursing Officer' Class. This was becoming more important in many positions of responsibility nation-wide as Independence was approaching.

When we were in Zanzibar in 1995 I met a good example of this principle. Quite an important looking middle aged gentleman came up and greeted me effusively as his former teacher. Puzzled, I asked a few questions and found that he was a retired judge! His name sounded familiar. He had been a former Minaki RMA student, and not a particularly good one! He passed his final examination, worked in a district dispensary, while studying until he could get into Dar-es-Salaam University, where he studied law. Rising further up the ladder took him to a career, though it cannot have been very long continued, from a reluctant RMA to a judge.

Exploring the Country

Paddy Shiel, with her responsibility at Medical H.Q. for liaison between 'them and us, took trouble to see as much as possible of Mission medical work, and it was also important for me to know more about the work in our diocese. Early in my time at Minaki, Paddy and I arranged a joint tour of the hospitals and dispensaries in our diocese, and we included a Lutheran hospital in the same area. We had no medical work on Zanzibar or Pemba Islands, although we were at that time still part of 'Zanzibar Diocese'. Apart from Minaki the medical work was all in Tanga Region, and this was the area which later became 'Tanga Diocese'. Tanga Region is north of Dar-es-Salaam, going up to include the Usambara Mountains and westward to the Pare Range.

I had already visited Masasi Diocese in the Southern Region, going right over westward to the shore of Lake Nyasa (now Lake Malawi), to Liuli Hospital and Manda Mission and Dispensary. I also visited two great RC Benedictine settlements, with their abbeys, farms, schools and medical work, at Ndanda and Peramiho. Ndanda, not far from Masasi, had a separate hospital and settlement for people with leprosy which was a common problem in the south of Tanzania. Down near Lake Nyasa I was ferried across the river in a canoe by a man with clear signs of the infectious form of leprosy – not a danger for the casual traveller but I did wonder about those who used the ferry every day. Frequent close contact is what spreads the infection.

I was quite excited about the trip with Paddy. What would the roads be like after the heavy rains? How would Paddy and I get on together, at close quarters for two weeks, and perhaps with differing views about 'our' work, and I perhaps somewhat protective of it? Happily it turned out very well and we enjoyed being able to discuss freely, on the spot, how the work we saw fitted into the policy and practicalities, as well as priorities, in situations where the needs were much greater than the combined resources which Mission and Government could supply completely.

A Memorable Tour Round Our Diocese, 1951

Magila was the centre of our diocesan medical work and it was where the mainland work of UMCA had started about 80 years before. The diocesan centre was just near at Hegongo at that time, later moving to Korogwe, 35 miles further inland. Magila is a beautiful place in the foot-hills of the Usambara Mountains, with church, convent and hospital, surrounded by farms and fruit trees, forests and streams, and in the valleys extensive sisal estates, a very lucrative crop in the past. Corn (maize) and other crops were planted as far as possible up the hill-sides, and cardamoms higher up than that, and there were African violets too if you knew where to look for them. Avocado pear trees bore fruit prolifically, mostly where we 'wazungu' (foreigners) had planted them near our houses. When in 1971 David and I started to work there, we planted an avocado pear stone in a 4 gallon paraffin tin, where it moved about with us to different dwellings until we had built a parish priest's house at Muheza, and it was able to settle into good solid ground, fruiting really well in 1981. But of course we then moved on, and only enjoyed one more fruiting season after that! By then it was a stately tree which our cat loved to climb, sometimes just to annoy the dog (our two cats and the dog had wonderful games among the grapefruit trees which surrounded our house and church at Muheza); I too climbed that tree to collect the fruit in season! It was a useful supplement to our diet at a time when even basic foods were in short supply.

Magila

In May 1951 Paddy and I flew up to the coastal town of Tanga, and then were driven 25 miles westwards (inland) up a potholed tarmac road to Muheza, a pleasant little market town and District HQ. After that it was all dirt roads until we got back to Dar. Three miles up a sandy, rock-strewn track took us into the Usambara foot-hills to Magila village, and then St Augustine's hospital, with its out-patient department, wards, operating theatre and office. Looking on up the road is the tall solid stone-built church with a back-drop of the mountains, and then the CSP convent, the community's mother house, which is a two storey building with cloisters around a bright, well kept garden. Beyond that was the nurses training school (NTS), and then the midwifery hospital, St Elizabeth's, with a small orphanage. Of the buildings, the NTS was the least impressive, but we had evidence in the hospital wards and operating theatre that the nurses were well taught and efficient. As one of the first two training schools in the country, it was also an early one to train young student-midwives. Midwifery training was tricky 25 years before, when CSP started it at Magila, because the African tradition was that it had always been only married women with families who could be birth attendants. It was 30 years after our visit that we were able to build a much more modern and very attractive nursing school with a new 'modern' hospital. The CSP nursing sisters were responsible for all the hospital work we saw at Magila, with the help of Dr Dulcie Adkins, a UMCA doctor of over 20 years standing. The Tanzanian nurses in both parts of the hospital were those trained at Magila, and the MAs who did the out-patient clinics were from Minaki.

Back on the main road going west, inland, we reached Korogwe, and visited St Raphael's hospital. It is near the church, which later became the Cathedral, and situated just above the old town. About a mile away the new town was being set up, with a government district hospital, but a smaller hospital near the old part of the town was still needed, especially for work with mothers and children, for which St. Raphael's ran an extremely active MCH Department. The Sisters at Magila had fewer attending their MCH clinic at the hospital, but needed much more out-reach to the surrounding villages. It was quite an obsession with some of the older Sisters, but an extremely useful one!

Kideleko in Zigualand

At Kideleko, some 60 miles south of Korogwe, was another 'bedded dispensary', run by two nursing sisters, missionaries, with oversight from the doctor at Korogwe – later on they were able to have a doctor stationed there for a while. This area is Zigualand, the land of the Zigua tribe, 'Uzigua', and Kideleko is not far from the district headquarters at Handeni. It is cattle country, very different from the arable and fruit farming area around Magila. Thirty years later David and I lived at Kwa Mkono, also in Uzigua, so we got used to miles of low scrub, interspersed with fields of maize, beans and cassava, which is a life-saving crop. Cassava is able to survive drought as well as floods, so has the reputation of a crop which has saved many lives, the other crops depending so much on the right rain at the right time. Guavas, small mangoes (sometimes having the reputation of tasting of turpentine), citrus fruits and bananas are the fruits which I connect with Uzigua. We got used to goats and calves strolling in at one's open front door; one year they frolicked into the church before Christmas, and enjoyed a meal from the straw of the Christmas crib! Outside the village were herds of huge gentle Maasai cattle, with their long curved, dangerous-looking horns, as well as the smaller local breed, and goats and chickens everywhere.

Zigua houses were round and beautifully built, with intricate systems of poles to carry the heavy thatched roof; walls were of thinner poles tied on horizontally with creeper, and lots of mud slapped on, which dried in the sun. The central area for the family had a cooking fire near the centre, with a hole in the roof for the smoke. Around this was a corridor for the cattle and goats, and chickens who of course wandered everywhere. At Kideleko the church was built in a similar way, but was rectangular in shape, and wide enough to hold 600 people with ease. It was 25 years old and in good condition, which did credit to the quality of the poles and to the standard of construction. The thatch would need regular inspection and repair, and the walls could be strengthened with some more mud from time to time. As well as the three hospitals, our 1951 trip took us to dispensaries, most with dressers in charge at present, but clearly needing the RMAs with their fuller training. Some were run by CSP Sisters, and these had thriving MCH clinics and some beds for maternity cases, as well as providing the sort of GP service that all were giving. Both Government and Missions, which Paddy and I represented, gave high priority to getting better services available in more dispensaries, in terms of both care for the sick and maternity and child health, including health education, and awareness of what could be done in the villages to reduce and prevent many diseases. From Uzigua we returned to Korogwe, to plan our next two visits; these were to remote spots in the Usambara Mountains, north of Korogwe. It would be a treat for us, as well as being good examples of the many isolated places which our combined health care system was trying to provide for.

Both days started with beautiful and in places spectacular drives up into the mountains. On the map neither destination looked far away, but with all the twists and turns and hairpin bends, each added up to 50 miles or more. First we went to Bumbuli, to a Lutheran mission, with a hospital at which they were just starting to train medical assistants. They wanted advice from Paddy about requirements and regulations for the training, and to discuss with me the actual practicalities of doing it.

The Lutheran Centre in the Usambaras

The drive to Bumbuli started on the main road from Korogwe running north to a small place called Mombo and then on north and west to Moshi. At Mombo we turned off to the right towards Lushoto, where since German days there had been a European settlement up in the hills. The road was a masterpiece of engineering – ten or twelve miles of hairpin bends, carved out of the hillside, and such strong re-enforcement of the road itself and of the mountain-side rising sheer on one side and dropping down on the other to the valley with its stream and cultivation, that it was firm and solid from German days, until it could be converted to a good paved road in the 1980s. At intervals we crossed tough little stone bridges built over the many mountain streams. Near the top the precipice side was re-enforced with tall eucalyptus trees planted near the edge. At times I was glad not to be the driver. At sharp bends, with mountain on one side and precipice on the other, heavy-laden lorries might suddenly appear, rushing to get their produce down to the market! For passengers all attention could be given to the scenery, down to the valley on one side, and with brief gaps looking through to the plain, and everywhere trees clinging on where they could. The long distance views were of course seen much better on the return journey.

Soni was an attractive little market town, where we turned off along a winding road through the hills, still climbing through the tall forest trees, and past a turning to a Roman Catholic mission. It was a bumpy road, narrow in places, and had survived the rains quite well that year; I found it in a very different state 10 years later, due, it seemed, to serious re-construction in a year when the rain never stopped between October and the following May! The result then was mud, mud, mud, and then more mud!

Reaching Bumbuli, we came first to the village and Lutheran church, and then the Mission area and hospital, with mountains rising behind. We were given an American welcome by Dr Jensen, the doctor in charge, and soon joined Mrs Jensen and some of the staff for refreshments. We were to spend the night at Bumbuli, so were shown to our room. Next came quite a detailed tour of the hospital, meeting other staff on the way, and getting a good idea of all that was going on. The buildings were mainly old German ones, well equipped, well staffed, and busy. The staff were from several European countries, as well as Tanzanians and Americans. There were three doctors, and a number of trained nurses from overseas as well as locally trained nurses, and those still in training. It made our Minaki staff look very small! The training school buildings looked very adequate.

Dr Jensen was glad to show us the problem areas of their work, as well as the good features. A feature which we were shown on a walk round the site, and which Minaki would have valued enormously, was a gorgeous torrent cascading down the mountainside, which supplied hospital, training school and staff housing with both water and electricity. There was a lot to talk about.

Dr Jensen had clear ideas about the training, and plenty of questions to ask. He was happy about Paddy's side of things, rules and regulations, including staff. They were already receiving money from Government for the hospital under the Grant-in-Aid system; he would also welcome the grant allowance for the training, though clearly money was not such a problem as it was for us! Having so recently taken over the running of our training, I could hand on some hints, including some of the inevitable problems, and was very glad to discuss it with someone so keen and interested.

'Grant-in-Aid was the system whereby Government gave financial support to medical work specifically approved to form part of the medical services of the country. As well as approval of the work itself in relation to other facilities in the area, staff, beds, students, standards, etc; there were naturally some stipulations which we must agree to if we wanted this help. The service must be open to all, of whatever creed or colour, and with no 'preaching to captive audiences' or other unfair pressure towards conversion. It was up to us to show Christian love, compassion and service in our work, with information and help available for those who wanted it, but not to use our work as an unfair way of proselytizing. In the hospitals where I worked, we did go as far as going round the wards on Christmas morning with a Christmas tableau of Mary, Joseph and the Baby (a newborn Christian baby if possible!), telling the story of the birth of Jesus, and singing a carol. We found that all alike enjoyed this little scene and wanted to rejoice with us at the arrival of the new baby who was so important to us. All matters of grant distribution went through the 'Grant-in-Aid Advisory Committee' held two or three times a year, and the MMC had representatives on it to present our applications and express our views. Decisions were then made depending on the funds available. The grant system covered approved training of nurses, MAs and RMAs; it continued after Independence, with further variations and developments. Bumbuli hospital was clearly doing a good job in a place otherwise short of medical services. Facilities for training MAs in the country were in short supply; approval of grants should not cause any problem in their case.

We went on to discuss the wider picture of medical services in the country, their distribution between town and country, and the balance between hospitals and outreach in the use of funds. Paddy and I both saw that Dr Jensen could become a very useful member of some of the government committees, as well as of the Mission Medical Committee.

By evening we felt free to find out more about other work being done by the Lutheran Mission in this area, and to join them in their evening worship. We also heard about a major development which was being planned jointly by Lutheran and other missions, at Moshi, a fast developing town about 200 miles up north on the road we had started out on from Korogwe. This was the Kilimanjaro Christian Medical Centre (KCMC), which over the years developed into a specialist medical centre, with a variety of more advanced medical and nursing trainings. Both David and I had reason to value their services some years later. After a really good night, Paddy and I returned down the mountains by the same route, getting plenty of lovely views out onto the plain and over to the Pare Mountains.

Kizara and a Mountain Walk

The other venture into the mountains started with a 50 mile drive from Korogwe, and then nearly two hours on foot, climbing through forest on a mountain track, to Kizara; this had been an early centre of mission work by UMCA. It was thrilling to follow the path up through tall trees with hanging creepers, over rocks and past waterfalls, trees which seemed to hang over us on one side, and a sheer drop on the other. Sudden views appeared on the precipice side, of the valley below, or of the plain stretching out to more hills. We met people coming down, and sometimes wondered how we would pass each other, especially if they were carrying loads, but soon we were exchanging African style greetings and news, which continued as we passed, getting fainter as we continued on our journey. It was astonishing to see some turn off down what I suppose was a path, but appeared to be going vertically down a precipice! Rather out of breath, and with some aching limbs which we tried to ignore, we came out into a flattish cleared area, Kizara village, with its easily recognised church, a primary school and a dispensary. Nearby were the homes of two missionaries, one the parish priest, who would soon be replaced by a Tanzanian priest, and the other Beatrice Hart, a schools supervisor. Her work took her to all the schools dotted about in the villages on the hills eastwards towards the coast.

We were soon in the dispensary, meeting the dresser and village midwife who worked there. Between them they were able to treat many of the sick, and both were encouraged to work hard at showing the local community what could be done to improve their health and prevent disease; also to co-operate on the maternity and child health side. Village midwives (VM) were older ladies, previously the 'birth attendant' in the village, who had the advantage of experience, followed by quite a short period of training in the local hospital. This would be about cleanliness and how to avoid infection during delivery, what to look for which should lead to urgent transfer to hospital, and more about prenatal care, and the care, nutrition, and immunisations of babies and small children. We spent some time with the dresser and VM, looking at their records and supplies of medications, equipment and facilities, and discussing their problems. This gave us an insight into the planning of services and of the teaching programme for RMAs, who we hoped would be gradually replacing these dressers, whose training had been very limited. It also showed the numbers being seen, and gave an idea of how many of these needed to get to hospital, either urgently or to arrange for 'cold surgery' such as uncomplicated hernias,, or for long term treatment as for TB, or the still fairly rare cases of diabetes, or heart disease. After this Miss Hart took us off to her house for lunch, which gave us the chance to talk with her about her work, and to hear about the parish and the people, weather, crops, and life in general in their isolated circumstances. The parish priest was away for a few days, visiting the villages around. Kizara parish consisted of small settlements scattered round in the hills, with few sizable villages. Eastwards, towards the coast, it adjoined the similar parish of Kigongoi, where a CSP sister ran a bedded dispensary. There were a few beds for general patients and for maternity, and the dispensary cared for the sick as well as for maternity work and infant and child care (MCH). In the 1970s, when David and I were at Muheza, we drove down to Tanga on the coast and to Maramba in the foot hills, and then climbed on foot for an hour to reach Kigongoi. Years later the Sister reminded me that I had 'mended her leg' when she broke it up there. Of course it was the Lord who healed it, using the resources which humans and animals have developed. I just made sure it was straight and put it in plaster!

The villages between these two centres had small Christian communities, who met in schools or houses, or small mud and stick churches, but at church festivals they would trek in to Kizara or Kigongoi. They often came for Evening Prayer the day before, spent the night with friends or in the church, and very happily joined in the festival service next day. This was often followed by a village feast, before they set off for home, refreshed by the Eucharist and the fellowship with other Christians. All this helped to give us a clear idea of what would be possible in the development of medical work in these fairly remote areas of the country

Darkness would fall soon after 6 pm, so we set off early down our forest track. It was the same path as we had come up by, but seemed very different. The steep safe side, with all its mighty trees looked much the same; the precipice side gave superb views into the distance, but now looked even more dangerous and almost threatening! How did these tall trees manage to hang on above and below us? Was the ground going to slip away under our feet at the narrow corners? Were we going to slip off a rock or some stones and find ourselves facing the abyss? But then our total attention was taken up by a troop of the rare Colobus monkeys which inhabit those woods. Beautiful with their jet black and white bodies and black tails with white frills on the end, they were leaping past in the trees, showing their amazing accuracy and skills. Then one mother paused on a branch, took a good look at us, and then held up her tiny black and white baby for us to admire. Then she leapt off to join the troop, and we continued on our way back to Korogwe.

Our long, tiring, and extremely interesting day impressed on us how vital such dispensaries, with their maternity care and concern for the new-born and toddlers, are for places like Kizara and Kigongoi. For a long time yet, much work would be involved in keeping them supplied with staff, equipment and supplies; vaccines would be a special problem, needing reliable refrigeration, whether kept on the spot or supplied regularly. We were thankful for a good night's rest arranged for us by the lady missionaries at Korogwe: a nurse, a teacher and a Mothers Union worker, and Lesley Sitwell, the doctor who looked after Kwa Mkono and Kideleko dispensaries, as well as Korogwe Hospital.

Kwa Mkono: Bedded Dispensary

Next morning we set off south towards Handeni and Kideleko in Uzigua; our two week tour was coming to an end. After about 30 miles we turned off to the left at a village called Sindeni, down a rough track to Kwa Mkono. This was a sizeable village, with two primary schools (a secondary school much later on), a bedded dispensary, as well as the church of St Francis. A group of CSP sisters lived there: Sr Magdalene and another sister were in charge of the dispensary with the help of two medical assistants (MAs), some Magila-trained nurse-midwives, and visits from Dr Lesley Sitwell.

The Sisters, backed by Dr Sitwell, were already doing what they could for the health and well-being of mothers and babies and others in the surrounding villages. Sister Magdalene was becoming aware of the number of children unable to walk at all with paralysed and often deformed limbs (usually legs) which prevented them from getting any schooling. This led some years later to setting up the Kwa Mkono Polio Hostel, which became well-known by the time I next visited Kwa Mkono in 1980. The deaths and deformities caused by poliomyelitis were one of the reasons that whenever possible our hospitals and dispensaries make a priority of getting vaccines to babies and others. Smallpox vaccine was essential also for years after this. I saw my last case of smallpox in 1968, when there was a small epidemic in the southern part of Tanzania.

Our visit to Kwa Mono was on a Friday. This I remember because at Korogwe we were generously given two boiled eggs each (the tiny local ones) for breakfast; for lunch the Sisters had made an excellent egg curry, two (or was it three) eggs each this time; and for supper at Kideleko, as a change, the eggs were scrambled! Meat on Friday was frowned upon, fish was not seen away from the coast, cheese was a very rare luxury, and red beans (maharagwe) were ordinary and everyday, and we all tried our best for visitors!

From Kwa Mkono we returned along the track to the main road, and 30 miles on reached Handeni, the district headquarters, where we called in briefly at the district hospital, and then went on a few miles to Kideleko. The small hospital there was under the care of Dr Sitwell at Korogwe, and run by two UMCA nurse midwives, supported by MAs and nursing staff. St Paul's Kideleko was one of the flourishing boys' middle schools in the diocese, with a Welsh lady teacher, Eira Lloyd, an English priest headmaster, Geoffrey Wilkinson, and African teaching staff. Not many years later it would be in the hands of Minaki trained teachers, sometimes aided by VSO or other volunteers from Britain, Canada or America. We were glad of the opportunity to worship with the local congregation in their lovely church on the Sunday. Next morning a bus took most of the day to take us 120 miles or so to Morogoro, to catch the night train to Dar-es-Salaam. It had been a most enjoyable and informative safari, really useful to both of us. Our various committees and discussions needed to be realistic about practicalities and priorities, as well as aiming at on-going improvements in the services which Missions and Government between them could provide, and I should be able to speak with far more confidence after seeing some of the work and the problems at first hand,

Back to Base and a Little Research

Years of experience taught me that, on return from time away, there was always something 'going on' – an outbreak of something, or a plea from an anxious sister-in-charge: "We've tried everything, please come and see him soon", or "We can have theatre ready in 10 minutes, she really does need a caesarean, I'm worried about the baby's heart-beat", followed on good days with "And there are coffee and sandwiches in your room"! This time nothing urgent, though there were a few cases of typhoid around, which turned out to be the start of a small epidemic. The really interesting news was, "They have come to make a film called 'Simon's People' (for UMCA), and they want you for a scene in the ward". The ward used was the first new one, with no roof yet, so nice and light for filming, as we had no lighting except what the technicians brought with them. 'Simon's People' was a medical version of 'Man of Two Worlds'. MA Clement Mdoe was the leading character, a lad from a village way out in the bush, who had walked many miles to get some schooling and then a lot more miles to get to Minaki to train as a medical assistant. He wanted to help to provide medical services to more of his compatriots. It emphasised the contrast between his home village and the relative sophistication of life at Minaki, and the stresses and strains for him and his family, who had worked so hard over the years to encourage and support the bright boy of the family. Now he seemed a very different person, and both he and his family had to find a way to handle the changed situation.

The typhoid cases gave us a lot of work. First came the arrangements for isolating and treating them, as they needed a lot of nursing care; chloramphenicol and the other clever drugs were not available yet. We must try to find out where the infection was coming from, and get hold of lots of TAB vaccine calling in everyone possible for the injections. With St Andrew's College, Minaki staff and students, as well as those of St Francis Pugu, and as many local people as we could persuade to come, and giving two injections to each, it made plenty for us to get on with! The principal, Fr. Nash, had his injections with everyone else and he was a person who was never ill. Next morning he told us that he was woken in the night by terrible pain in his arm and felt so ill he was sure he was going to die. The next he knew was waking as usual in the morning, wondering what it was all about! Some of us were not so lucky!!

Research was not my line. My attention was all on the patient in front of me, the diagnosis and treatment; yes, and why has he got it? Who else might have the same problem? How to prevent it? and similar questions. But I was very thankful to know that others were equally absorbed in the necessary research. However we did get involved in simple ways in two interesting research projects.

Rats were an abiding problem, coming in from the bush, stealing food and the grain for planting, and crops in the fields. They chewed blankets, bed matting, anything they could get, including the covering of electric wiring in the Land Rover. The ultimate problem came when they chewed people's toes in the night! The subject had to be in a very deep sleep of course, but the real danger was for sufferers from leprosy who had lost sensation in their toes, and it was a serious hazard for them.

We were asked to try out a new rat poison, and were supplied with plenty of it, doubtless very expensive at the time. We readily agreed to anything which would get rid of our rats, despite the gory details. We were told to mix plenty of the poison in ugali, the stiff, almost solid food that people ate every day, and to lay baits of this all around. The rats, we were told, died a sudden painless death from severe internal bleeding, because of the very large dose in the bait. We had to collect the dead rats and hand them in at a centre in Dar-es-Salaam for post-mortem examination. I'm glad we didn't have to do the post-mortems! The resultant medication is of course supplied in exceedingly well regulated dosage, under the names, 'warfarin', 'coumarol', etc and has saved many lives from the perils of thrombosis.

The other research concerned the very distressing tumours which we saw in young children, starting in the jaw and disfiguring the face and finally destroying the side of the mouth and cheek; death was from bleeding, or spread to other parts of the body, or from starvation, as they couldn't take any food. Dr Denis Burkitt, stationed in Kampala, Uganda, was researching this deadly tumour, which appeared to be confined to some areas of tropical Africa. Every month we received a form from him on which to report the details of any cases seen and then of their progress. We were sent a small supply of the drug, methotrexate, which was quite new at the time, and which he found had some effect on the tumour. We were told what dosage to use, depending on the child's weight. Replacement supplies were sent regularly from Kampala. Later there were added questions about other tumours which he and others there were studying. The jaw tumour soon received the official name 'Burkitt's Tumour', and gradually alternative and improved treatments and regimes were developed.

When David and I were working in Dar-es-Salaam in 1968 – 70, we were able to meet Denis Burkitt, when he came on a visit. By then his research included tumours of the gut as well as Burkitt's Tumour. He was studying the relationship of tumours to diet, and the effect of changing from traditional foods to a western type of diet. Many of us were beginning to think that this must be influencing the changing incidence of problems such a heart disease and diabetes too. Denis and a colleague came to supper with us, bringing a Dundee cake in a tin – a rare treat! The research had progressed a long way since I had met Denis in Uganda 12 or 14 years before, and it was good to see him again and hear about his recent work. A cousin of his later took charge of the MA training at Bumbuli.

CHAPTER 4
Changes at Minaki but Hospital Routines Continue

The Future Brightens for the Rural Medical Aids

Changes in our medical training at Minaki, from medical assistants to rural medical aids, took their time to settle. From staff and hospital point of view the training didn't change much, but students latched onto the idea that they had been 'downgraded'. It was difficult for them to see that it was the MA course which had been 'upgraded' to provide better staff for hospitals. MAs would now come from Standard 10 or 12, RMAs still from Standard 8. The course would be very similar to the old one, but directed more to village work, and it was the RMAs who would provide the higher standard aimed for in the villages, when they replaced dressers who had only a very basic training. It took a while for the students to get over their persistent awkwardness resulting from the supposed insult, before they could see the important place they would have in giving village people a better service! We had to weather a period when students took offence easily, losing the cheerfulness and enthusiasm which we were used to. Newly qualified RMAs, doing their hospital year before leaving us, thought they knew everything, and expected the same responsibility as the senior MAs!

By 1956 I was able to say in my newsletter, "Morale among our students has improved". They had come to see that their new qualification had its place in the scheme of things, and to take a pride in their work, and to start enjoying it again. They would have several villages to look after, not just wearing a stethoscope and handing out pills, but helping the people to improve their lives and that of their children, as well as being able to treat the sick. The joy of teaching students eager to learn, and to work with newly qualified staff, had returned. Once more, "Tumshukuru Mungu" (Thanks be to God).

Home Leave: Travel

Dr Lesley Sitwell was able to come to Minaki again in 1956, so by autumn I was back in England. It was my first experience of air travel, and exciting, because the cheap flight which we used 'hedge-hopped' up Africa, giving good views, although it was rather bumpy over the Sahara! The small plane with about 25 passengers came down for the night at Nairobi, Khartoum (or Waddi-Halfa) and Malta, and landed also briefly at Entebbe Airport in Uganda. Cairo was another possibility and on one occasion it was Benina in the desert near the North African coast: a cafe with a nice cup of tea and biscuit and two or three flowers in a tin can on the table. What a contrast with the next stop at Lyons in the restaurant and other facilities! Once we had 24 hours in Malta, because the radio on the plane from England wouldn't work; on another occasion a ship I was on broke its cable in Malta harbour. Sad to say my chief memory of Malta is dull skies, steady rain and chaotic driving, which I'm sure doesn't do credit to the beautiful and celebrated island! We gradually progressed to shorter journey times and occasionally had direct flights between Heathrow and Dar-es-Salaam.

'Home Leave' was a thing we all looked forward to. In those early days we were really cut off from England and from our family and friends. But of course we were not nearly so cut off as my parents had been in China, where tours were normally seven years, and longer during the 1914-18 war, and their mail was extremely slow and unreliable. Visits to us in Africa from Europe were very rare, and 'youth' had not yet started hitch-hiking round the world. That came later and then one had mixed feelings on seeing a group of back-packers approaching, especially if the cupboard was almost bare!

The Pleasures and Duties of Home Leave

The joys of England for me began with the English countryside. Then, after family and friends, came English flowers, autumn ones this time, apples, proper baths and undisturbed nights. The round of visits to parishes and other supporters was still a duty because of my dislike of standing up in front of an audience, but where I had got to know people it became much easier. Smaller groups were much easier and a new set of transparencies to show made a big difference. Seeing the scenes and the people on the screen brought back my enthusiasm, I forgot my nervousness and I could pass on the joys and sorrows, the excitements and disappointments of our life in a mission hospital. Sometimes there was a mission conference to attend with people with news of the Church from all over the world, some doing similar work to ours but in a different culture. We could discuss facilities and problems and get renewed enthusiasm and some new ideas. Some contacts soon became lifelong friends.

Shopping lists, both personal and for the hospital, occupied time on each leave. Air travel for this and future leaves was a welcome change in most ways, but brought the problems of weight allowance and freight costs for hospital supplies. One leave later on with David, we bought two motorcycles for the diocese and had them flown out (costing no more overall than sea transport). We picked them up in Dar-es-Salaam when we arrived, and rode them 170 miles to Kwa Mkono where we were living then. One was for David and the other for another priest, as they were being used increasingly for parish and deanery work.

Family Matters

Leave was very enjoyable, but rather exhausting with so much travel, talk, meetings, and also the reverse culture shock. It was all so very different from what we had got used to, and naturally not the same England as I had said good-bye to three years before. My leaves in 1953 and 1956/7 were based at Bourn, near Cambridge, where Mother was still living with my brother, Alan and his wife,

Joy. In 1958 Alan accepted a job in clinical and research oncology in Edmonton, Alberta, so, now with two small boys, they emigrated to Canada, moving again after two years to the United States, to a similar post in Flint, Michigan. Alan's physics degree at Cambridge and radar research during the war, followed by a medical degree from Edinburgh, gave him an ideal start to a career in radiotherapy, at a time of so many exciting developments in diagnosis and treatment of cancer.

Mother had held her own so far, and moved to my half-sister, Gertrude's home in Norwich, and so she was well cared for when the family moved away. Attacks of angina had started some years ago, and after about a year her heart gave up the struggle. Strangely it was David who brought me the news – it had come to him as 'Head of the Station' as he was acting chaplain at Minaki at the time. He came to tell me with his much-loved dog Fupi, who was a cross between Rhodesian Ridgeback (head and body) and Dachshund (Chippendale legs). Fupi seemed to understand the situation, and did his best to give me a comforting hug, which is difficult to do when you are short ('fupi' in Kiswahili) and barrel shaped! In those days we didn't go off to England for illnesses or deaths unless we were really needed.

When returning to Africa in 1957, I was very aware of Mother's frailty. Her angina had started even before she moved to Edinburgh ten years previously, and by that time it was becoming troublesome, confining her to the house and garden unless taken out by car. My doctor cousin, Frank Clouting, a GP in Lincolnshire, had kindly lent me an old car, a small Ford, during the 1956/57 leave, which was most useful for trips around the country. English traffic wasn't too bad then, though on later leaves I found the speed and amount of traffic, as well as motorways, all a bit much after our very different road conditions in rural Africa! I had to go up to Whitby, to talk to the Sisters of the Holy Paraclete about medical work in Tanganyika, and especially what we were doing at Minaki, so I took my Mother with me for a change of air and holiday.

The medical profession hadn't got much help to offer to angina patients in the 1950s – just the little pill under the tongue during an attack – but she was all right in the car, and we had a great time. However the country around Whitby is not like East Anglia which the old Ford was used to, and on an afternoon drive we got to the bottom of a very steep hill, only to find that we couldn't get up the other side. We both kept calm, both being used to crises, Mother from her years in China, but I did wish that my passenger was a strong youngster, who was able to get out and push, rather than an elderly lady liable to have an angina attack at any moment! Then I remembered having heard that reverse gear is lower than 1st forward, so with some difficulty in a narrow lane, we turned round and then were able to creep up the hill, or was it a mountain? We arrived triumphant at the convent, and Mother, quite undaunted, was looking forward to our next outing!

Back to My Second Home and the Daily Routine

When it came to the days for packing up, farewells and going off to Heathrow, I realised that, like Tabibu Clement in the film, 'Simon's People', I had become a 'Man of Two Worlds'. That is lovely in one way, as I felt at home in two very different settings and cultures, but it was not all easy going. Sometimes I felt that I didn't quite belong to either!

The flight soon took my thoughts on to Tanganyika, and Dar-es-Salaam, and then the welcome when I reached Minaki made it a real home-coming. Soon I was back in the daily routine, similar in the six different Mission hospitals where I worked during over 40 years in the country. These would soon become known as Church or Diocesan hospitals. The 'Missions', first UMCA, and then USPG, continued to give us marvellous support with both staff and money, as well as prayer, but the local Church obviously had to take much more responsibility for all aspects of our medical work, hospitals, training schools, and out-reach to the surrounding areas.

For me one of the joys of working in our Church hospitals was that we were always near to a church, and unless the priest was away, there would be a daily Eucharist, usually at 6.30 am. With the Eucharist and then hospital prayers (brief, and before regular work began) we started our day with some thought about what we were there for. Also the parish priest was nearby to help and encourage patients, relatives and staff, especially at times of severe illness and stress, and of death and bereavement. Moreover, when we were celebrating happy occasions, and giving thanks for new births and recovery from severe illness or accident his presence was always welcome. This included places like Minaki, and Kwa Mkono, where I worked later, where a majority of patients were Muslim. Without discussing it I felt sure that many Muslim patients and their relatives were aware, as I was in those times of anxiety and sadness, and also in celebrations, that we were both praying to the one God.

The day's routine at Minaki centred round the teaching as well as the patients. After seeing any patients who had caused worries overnight, I started with a teaching round on one of the main wards. The MA in charge of the ward, or sometimes a senior student, gave a report on progress of the patients, and a more detailed one on new patients. After the round, I went to the out-patients department, where MAs were already hard at it, and I saw the patients for whom they needed advice, as well as those I had booked for follow-up. Students were with me, and were helpful for language problems, while getting teaching and first-hand experience of diagnosis and treatment of patients. At some point in the morning I tried to find time to call in on the other wards to see new patients and any problems. The last hour of the morning was for classroom teaching, and there was always plenty to catch up with if others were doing that. In other hospitals with nursing training I was less involved in classes, and mine were often in the afternoon. When the Minaki operating theatre was up and running we had an operating list on two mornings a week, and that applied in the other hospitals where I worked. At any time routines were broken up by emergencies, medical, surgical or obstetric, so changes to the timetable were common, and we were often catching up!

Lunch at 1pm and the regulation afternoon rest were usually punctual at Minaki, but often very far from it elsewhere! The afternoons were less predictable; after a cup of tea, it might be more teaching, cases to see in hospital, preparing work or time-table for the boys, drug orders and correspondence, and sometimes a walk with an off-duty sister. Compline was sung in chapel at 6.30 with the students all filing in, looking as though butter would not melt in their mouths. I'm sure they enjoyed the singing, and the feeling of community and security it gave them, even if followed by bursts of laughter as soon as they got out of the door. Our supper followed soon after.

Our cook, Saidi, who was so clever with the wood-burning dover stove, lived quite near, and was with us early to start the fire in the morning, and late to see to the supper. One day he had been locked up over night for some error in behaviour, minor I'm sure. He turned up as usual to get our breakfast next morning. When the authorities came looking for him, pretty angry that he had broken out of his cell, he said quite confidently, "Well, of course I did: I had to get here in time to give the ladies their breakfast". It seemed quite obvious to him, and it seemed they understood, as they were quite lenient with him!

I had an Aladdin lamp in my house, so with a good light I could get on after supper with teaching notes, reading up about any tricky patients that were bothering me, correspondence, and the other jobs waiting to be done. Aladdin lamps use paraffin (kerosene) and have a delicate mantle which gives out a strong but mellow light so are pleasant to use. They are quite tricky creatures though, and the slightest draught sends them up in smoke, blackening the glass and ruining the mantle, and blackening the whole room too if not dealt with soon. That was the trouble with paraffin refrigerators, which in a sudden draught would flare up and blacken everything in sight before going out. If they wouldn't behave properly, the traditional advice was to empty everything out, (including the paraffin of course!) and turn the fridge upside down! By the time we were living at Kwa Mkono in 1983, we were thankful to get one that didn't have those bad habits!

Changes in St Andrew's College

When I got back from leave early in 1957, changes were on the way at Minaki. By July we had all gone into action. That pre-independence period was a time of change, sparked off I think by the many changes going on in surrounding countries; if we wanted progress there was bound to be change. St. Andrew's College would become a boys' secondary school under a board of governors, with Government representatives as well as bishops and other church people on it. Large grants would come from, or at least via, Government from development agencies. The college would be almost entirely rebuilt, including staff housing. The Teacher Training College would move to Korogwe; the medical training would have to separate off. We, the medical team, must find a site near the hospital, and somehow or other find some money to build 'St Luke's Medical Training School'. We should need dormitories, one or more classrooms, office, dining room/meeting hall, and at least two staff houses, but we would still share the college chapel.

St Luke's Medical Training School Planned and Built

All this had been going round in the back of my mind since returning from England a few months before, so I was glad when Archdeacon Sydenham, our Diocesan Treasurer, turned up in July to discuss site, buildings, funding, etc. The comment in my newsletter about the site chosen by 'Syd', as we irreverently called the Archdeacon, was "small, cramped, and sloping, and thoroughly unsuitable!" ... "but a much better one was soon found" ... "and Syd was quite ready to agree that it was the one that he had approved"!

Margaret Makins was an architect doing town planning in Dar-es-Salaam. She had been an assistant to my Uncle Charlie when he was architect to the Office of Works in Edinburgh. In spite of problems with her ancient car, which boiled on hills, and our appalling road, wrecked by torrential rain, she, an ardent

Presbyterian, took an interest in our project, and nobly came to Minaki to give us her extremely valuable advice. The layout needed careful planning because of sun and prevailing wind direction, as well as the sloping ground. The semi-permanent building materials which she recommended gave us strong and good looking buildings with very little more expense than the materials we had used for the new wards. In all this planning and in getting the buildings up and running, we were helped enormously by Canon Nash, the college principal since Canon Gibbons retired.

It was at this time that we decided to buy the 'Penguin'. She was a small black Peugeot van with a white roof to keep the sun off, and was used for carrying loads or students or both, as part of our independence from the college. She was extremely useful, but not quite as roadworthy, or shall we say as good at bad roads, as we might have hoped. This showed itself when she had to battle with thick, slimy mud on exciting mountain roads! She wasn't too keen on those when she took us to Bumbuli in the mountains a few years later.

The Blessing and Opening of St Luke's Medical Training School

Our new buildings were put up to the glory of God, and to enable us to press on with the work, which we, and our supporters overseas, were trying to do for him. So it was natural that we should want to ask God's blessing on them, and on all who would use them, and it was customary to have all our buildings blessed whether hospital, school, dwelling house or whatever. Local people had their strong beliefs that spirits lived all around us, in buildings, trees, mountains and other natural objects and wanted to get rid of their evil influence. We from overseas had varying and often less well defined beliefs, but all wanted God's Holy Spirit to be the strongest influence around us. All of us wanted to offer these buildings to God for his purposes, which of course included the safety and welfare and freedom from any sort of evil, for all those using the building.

A visit from Bishop William Scott-Baker, in February 1958 gave us a good opportunity to ask him to bless the training school and staff houses. College staff and students joined us, and we all sang hymns while the bishop, in cope and mitre, accompanied by the hospital students and the chaplain, went all round outside and then inside, dedicating the buildings to God's service and asking his blessing on them. Ten days later our 38 students moved in, and the two members of staff to their new houses.

On 4th March the official opening of St Luke's Medical Training School took place, performed by the Hon JP Attenborough CBE, Minister for Social Services, accompanied by Mrs Attenborough, and other official guests from Government and District and Local Authority. Appropriately Archdeacon Sydenham came to represent the bishop, which gave him the chance to appreciate the very suitable site chosen for the buildings! We had the usual delays and crises that morning: the new St Luke's badges for the boys' shirts, which needed sewing on of course, arrived that morning. In putting up the important plaque, the masons sprayed cement around on the whitewashed wall. Then at midday a boy with a cut tendon in a finger turned up, and I had to settle down to the ticklish business (for one not doing it every day) of getting it well repaired.

However by 4 pm we were all sorted out, and ready to serve tea to the guests as they arrived. The college Scout troop were on patrol, and escorted the guests down to their seats outside the training school, where the whole school had assembled. Mr Attenborough, who knew the Gibbons well, spoke of the history of the medical training and of the valiant pioneering work done by Dr Mary Gibbons. He then flung open the doors of the hall, and unveiled the handsome plaque donated by my helpful architect friend, Margaret Makins. Light relief came when two very small girls, daughters of the medical staff, hand in hand, approached the platform hesitantly. The smaller one had a huge white bonnet on and a bouquet in her hand, but was distinctly doubtful about handing the bouquet to Mrs Attenborough! Her small companion made sure that our visitor got her flowers. When the guests had gone the boys had a feast, and then a dance, to which we 'wazungu' (Europeans/foreigners), the two sisters and I, were invited. Of course we joined them briefly, to celebrate together in our new buildings, but we soon left them to have their own fun.

Staff Changes: Teachers, Sisters and Medical Assistants

By 1959 the 'mission ladies' had decreased in number. It was a shock to us all when in 1957 Miss Fisher, the teacher I had come out with on the Llangibby Castle in 1949, had a serious stroke and died in the government hospital a few weeks later; Liz Leeson had gone into government service; Gladys Rhodes and Juliette Mullins, nurse-midwives, had been replaced by Edith Horton (Fox) and Joyce Townsend; Edith Perrett moved with the teacher training college to new buildings in Korogwe.

The medical assistant staff had changed too; Joachim Macha, a Lutheran, and our first MA from Bumbuli, had joined us. His wife, Ephrosia, was a nurse-midwife, and both were really useful additions to our staff. MA Joseph Angwazi was a St. Andrews College student, who also trained as MA at Bumbuli, and joined us at about that time too, but because of later developments, he was not with us for long. However, I met him again in Zanzibar, where after an interesting career in various jobs, in retirement he was able to come as Warden of the Visitors' Hostel in Zanzibar for a few years. He was still involved in various activities including 'women's rights'. Of course I too wanted women to have their rights, but my feeling was that we didn't need to go on shouting about it in England. Joseph made me very aware of how much there was still to be done in many other countries, and that in order to be heard one might need to shout!

Julius Nyerere

In June 1959 the new laboratories in the college were completed, and were officially opened by Julius Nyerere. He had been a teacher at the Roman Catholic secondary school at Pugu, and had been at Edinburgh University a few years before, together with John Keto, one of our teachers. John had got to know Mother and Alan, but they didn't meet Nyerere. In 1959 he was leader of TANU, the Tanganyika African National Union, later becoming Prime Minister, and then our first and much loved and admired President. My first meeting with him was when, as the anxious father, he brought his wife Maria along from Pugu with their newborn first baby. The baby was flourishing, but it was Maria's first and was a precipitate delivery; she was in urgent need of help from me!

I met 'Mwalimu' (teacher), 'Father of the Nation' as people called him, on various later occasions, but all rather different, as by then he was the VIP. In 1968 Bishop Trevor Huddleston of South African anti-apartheid fame, stayed with us in Dar-es-Salaam when he was leaving Masasi Diocese and on his way to the UK. He and Mwalimu were very good friends, and shared many ideas about development and progress in the country. We were invited to his farewell sundowner at the University, and amongst others found ourselves listening to an amusing exchange. It was between Mwalimu (Nyerere), who was a faithful though somewhat unorthodox Roman Catholic, his English secretary, and Bishop Trevor, Anglican of course. The subject was indoctrination as practised by Communists, but also, the secretary suggested, by the Roman Catholic Church. Nyerere was always keen to point out that his aim was to learn all he could from very different ideas in very different countries. He could choose what he considered best and most suitable out of each, and so create an African socialism, which would be acceptable and would work well for Tanzania. Time would show how successful this would be, but meanwhile he had gained the respect, honour and co-operation, and also the love of the nation.

Electric Light at Minaki

The next big event at Minaki was the coming of electricity later in 1959. This was all part of the big development of the college, but for the hospital it was a serious problem to raise the funds which we should need. However it was a real joy when the time came to be able to 'switch on'. We should also need money for a proper overhead theatre light, but meanwhile we could use the spotlight on the mains, without any problem about getting it recharged.

An Eventful Leave in 1960

My next 'long leave' was due in spring 1960, and my sister Gertrude welcomed me to her home in Norwich. Before leaving Tanganyika I had deep discussions with our bishop and others about the extent of building and development, which we should need if Minaki was to continue as a successful hospital and medical training school. I was told to do all I could to raise lots of money, and, as local doctors and nursing sisters were still in very short supply, to scout round for likely ones in the UK. "What a hope" – came to my mind again as in earlier years, and this time I couldn't think of an answer to – "If you don't know ask someone who does?" But I'd been told to do it, so something must be done!

Day one in England was nearly a disaster – my mind had clearly been rather over-occupied. Gertrude was determined to meet my plane on arrival, but at Heathrow airport there was no sign of her. There were no mobile phones then, and there was no point trying her home phone; enquiries all round the airport gave no result; finally I decided I must set out on my own. Having settled into a coach which would take me to the Victoria Coach Station in London, I glanced out of the window, and there was Gertrude. How she got there I never knew. She joined me in the coach just as it was starting off. Apparently I had told her that I should be arriving at Gatwick! Just a slip of the pen when I meant Heathrow!!

It was lovely to be back in England. Gertrude, now 60 (more than 20 years older than me) had just retired, and we both had many friends in Norwich. I was booked to go to the Oberammergau Passion Play with a doctor friend in May, and then on for some more holiday in Austria; later on, to Edmonton, Alberta, to see Alan and Joy and their two little boys in their new home, and they took me for a week touring in the Canadian Rockies with them. In between these two adventures I met a friend in London who paid for my one and only visit to the Chelsea Flower Show.

On the work side, a pretty full programme of visits and meetings had been arranged with UMCA. One day, not long after arrival, I was at home with Gertrude, chatting and ironing a petticoat ready to go out to give the first talk at a boys' school just down the road. I was planning to tell them about the wonderful hospital and school where I worked in Tanganyika, and how much was planned when I got back. The postman arrived, and I opened an air letter from our Bishop: Minaki hospital and the training school were to be closed at the end of 1961! I turned to Gertrude and said, "No, we haven't received this letter, put it away until I come back". Looking back at my petticoat I saw that I had burnt a large hole in it! The bishop's decision I realised later was the right one, as by local standards Minaki hospital was very near to other medical services. The staff and money we should need to modernise it could be better used where people were in much more difficult circumstances. But the way it had come about was unfortunate to put it mildly, and it made the work side of my leave even more difficult, because the information was at present 'confidential'. I have no recollection of how I coped with talks in parishes and schools, except having the thought, which I suppose was a prayer, "Dear Lord, you have put me in this position, you will have to cope with it somehow".

Sad Losses

There were many good and interesting things about that leave, including Austria and Oberammergau, Edmonton and the Rockies with Alan and family, and time with my sister, Gertrude, which we had hardly ever had before. But there was one more problem: on my return from Canada, Gertrude had a very swollen leg. Rest with the leg up and limited exercise were the instructions from the surgeon whom we both knew well. He had been the registrar at the Norfolk and Norwich Hospital when I was working there 15 years before; I had assisted him at many operations, and even had my knuckles rapped in the early days! Gertrude was impatient. This I well understood, but I was nervous and disturbed about her, right until I had to leave her and return to work. In October, back at Minaki, I heard that she was having an operation. A week later we heard that very sad result: "The operation was successful but the patient died". It was her heart apparently. I heard on November 2nd, All Soul's Day, and I was shattered. I went out and sat on my doorstep that night, and read the long slow office of the Commemoration of All the Faithful Departed out of the Benedictine Monastic Diurnal, and I found it comforting. Gertrude was a very active and sincere Congregationalist, and she would not herself have prayed for people who have died. But I am sure in my own mind that the Lord uses our prayers as he wishes. I think of my prayer for someone as simply committing them in love to God's care, and of course we are already in that care all the time, and that is true too even for those others who don't know it.

Alan was at the time on holiday in the Canadian Rockies, and the 'Canadian Mounties' went out to find him to bring the news. Friends acted for us at the time, but when I could be spared in December I went briefly to England to get Gertrude's bungalow and other affairs sorted out.

Gertrude had always made me feel that I shared the bungalow with her. It was on the outskirts of Norwich and I got to know some of her neighbours, as did Mother during her short time living there. The three little girls next door called her 'Grannie Phillips' and ran in and out quite freely. I always hoped I would live there some day, but the next best thing was that, while she needed it, a member of some family friends, who were like family to us, used it for as long as she could. After about 10 years it was sold, and gave us a very good start to buying our retirement bungalow when we needed our own home in 1994. House prices had doubled in those 20 years, but Alan, always so kind and generous, enabled us to buy our own very pleasant little bungalow in North Walsham, near Norwich.

My one remaining aunt, Elsie Savage, lived in Riverhead, near Sevenoaks in Kent, and I had expected to have a base there when next in England, but sadly when it came to the time, in 1964, she became ill, and died the very day I arrived. It was one of the difficult and sometimes sad things about our life, as for others who worked far from home, that we were not there for parents, aunts and others when they became ill or old. However, I did realise, as time went by, that being cut off from our previous surroundings helped us to become totally committed to the place, the people, the work, and above all the local life of the Church in our area. Divided loyalties didn't have to be considered because to go was not a practical option. Questions like "Ought I to go?", "Will I be in time?", and "Who's going to look after my job here?" didn't have to tear one apart; life just went on. I found though that I was hit twice by the shock and sadness of deaths, as when I did return 'home' the person was no longer there!

St Luke's Hospital, Minaki

Ambulance – African style!

Dr Julius Nyerere opens new school laboratory

Marion Phillips at gathering to mark closure of St Luke's

St Luke's Pageant to celebrate 30 years of medical training

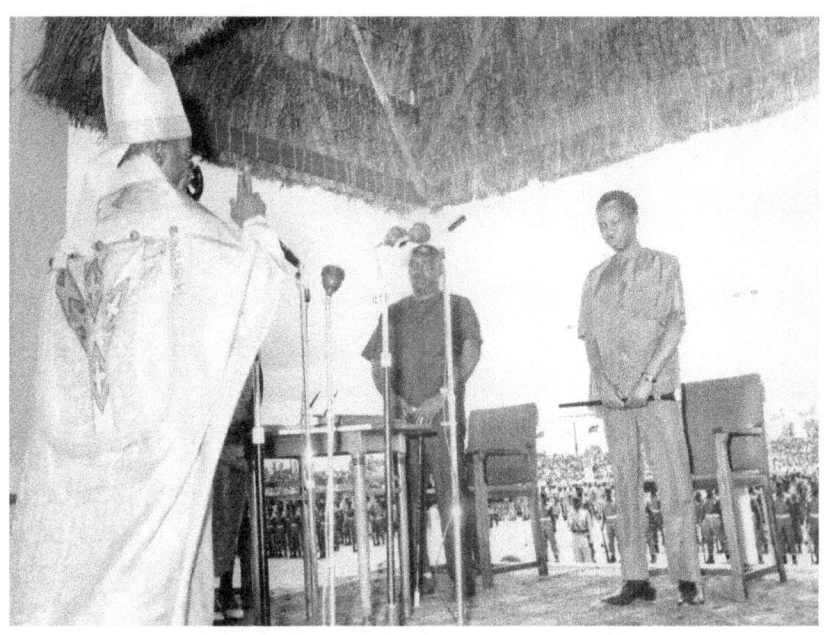
President Julius Nyerere at prayers during independence celebrations, Dec 1961

CHAPTER 5
Goodbye Minaki: New Challenge Ahead

Back To Base

Arriving back from leave at Dar-es-Salaam airport early in August 1960, I found that Bishop Scott-Baker was there, so my anxiety about a first meeting after his rather shattering letter was soon dealt with. It also gave an early opportunity to discuss arrangements about the closure of the hospital and training school, and the future of the staff, both local and expatriate. He assured me that for the actual packing up and closing he would arrange for UMCA to send someone to do the job. There was going to be a lot to do before the closing date at the end of 1961.

Staff Futures Discussed

The present RMA students could complete their two-year course, but a 3rd year of suitable practical experience had to be arranged for each one for next year. Future jobs for staff would need discussion, and some could move on soon as there would be less teaching and gradually fewer patients. The two nursing sisters, Joyce and Edith, would be needed in the diocese at Korogwe and Kideleko respectively. They could stay till the end, and we should need a couple of MAs with strong arms, for help with decisions, and also as good company to keep our spirits up! Packing up a hospital where, in spite of problems, we had all enjoyed working, and then sending everything off in lorries over appalling roads several hundred miles, would be quite a challenge. I for one never quite believed that someone would come and do it for us – and so it turned out! Yes, he did arrive, but took one look at the job, caught the next ship going south, and we heard no more!

Masasi Diocese and Some Personalities

My own future was quickly decided. Dr Frances Taylor was a veteran missionary doctor of 30 years standing in Masasi diocese, in the southern region of Tanganyika. She wrote at once to ask me if I would be willing to take over Lulindi hospital, 30 miles south of Masasi. Dr Taylor's base at Mkomaindo hospital was near the small town of Masasi, with Mtandi, the diocesan centre, also just near the town. Frances had created a network of dispensaries throughout the diocese, with Mkomaindo as her base. I had heard about Lulindi hospital from Dr Leader Stirling. He was another outstanding character, who had joined Frances at Masasi in 1935. Soon he went on to Lulindi and built the hospital there, and worked there and in the surrounding area until 1949. I also knew the three doctors who had followed each other at Lulindi since then.

Leader Stirling was a remarkable person, who had come to help Frances when she was battling along on her own in Masasi Diocese. Having built and developed Lulindi hospital and nurses training school, he became a Roman Catholic in 1949 and moved to Ndanda, the Roman Catholic Benedictine settlement between Masasi and the coastal town of Lindi. At Ndanda the Benedictines had a good general hospital and leprosarium. The Benedictines had another hospital north of Nachingwea, where I had landed on arrival, and later Leader moved on there and set up a RMA training school. I visited him at Mnero in 1957 when I was visiting Masasi Diocese; we sat up half the night drinking black coffee and talking! Leader had not had a specific surgical training, but had built up his skills over the years, and put them to good use, whether in a well-equipped hospital like Ndanda, or in a makeshift hut in the bush. This was eventually recognised when he was given an honorary fellowship of the Royal College of Surgeons (England): I had to pass some pretty tough exams for mine! Leader's paths and mine crossed many times during his long and interesting career. In January 1999 I was astonished to receive a letter from him, now living just outside Dar-es-Salaam with his Tanzanian wife and family. He wrote to congratulate me on 50 years since obtaining my

FRCS(Eng), a jubilee about which I had quite forgotten. I never knew how he had found the date; Leader must have been well over 90 by then!

Lulindi Hospital had 120 beds officially, though later I found that a few local wooden ones were often slipped in for emergencies. These were frequent and multiple, and after a time no-one noticed the extra beds! The nursing school had a long and excellent reputation. On the Makonde plateau, 18 miles away and 3,000 feet above sea-level, at Newala, the Sisters of the CSP ran a hospital for maternity and children. This would also be under my care for a while, until we could get another doctor.

Some Interesting Outside Events

Quite ready to agree to go to Lulindi when Minaki hospital closed, I became even more enthusiastic when I heard that Father Trevor Huddleston, of South African anti-apartheid fame, was shortly to be consecrated as the new Bishop of Masasi. Bishop Scott-Baker and the UMCA readily agreed to my move. Fr Huddleston's consecration was to be in England, but there were problems about the enthronement. The Masasi area was in the grip of a meningitis epidemic, and a large gathering at the cathedral for the enthronement would not be allowed, as that is just the way to spread meningitis. St Nicholas' Church Dar-es-Salaam, newly built and expected to be the cathedral when Dar-es-Salaam became a diocese, was chosen instead. We were delighted that our RMA students were asked to lead the choir for the event; Tabibu Anthony Msei would be the choir-master. This was on November 30th 1960, but before this there was another big event, this one at the other end of the town, at

St Alban's church. The Archbishop of Canterbury, Geoffrey Fisher, came to inaugurate the new Province of East Africa, thus giving us more independence from Canterbury, England. Ten years later Tanzania would become a separate Province, with our own Tanzanian archbishop, John Sepeku, by then Bishop of Dar-es-Salaam Diocese. We welcomed these changes, as they gave the local church responsibility for its own development; it also encouraged closer co-operation between the dioceses, with their very different traditions, related to their supporting missions, CMS and UMCA.

Archbishop Fisher made a brief call at Minaki before leaving the country. He showed much interest in the college and the hospital and in the type of medical training which we were doing. It was good for us to have these outside events to give us a break from our own plans and problems. It seemed so sad that, having only just settled into our newly built training school, and the fairly new wards and other developments in the hospital, our next job was to close it all down! But we had to learn to see it as a task completed to the best of our ability – many patients had been treated and helped in the hospital, lives saved, healthy babies born, distress relieved, and also our succession of students were now carrying out healing work all over the country. But the coming 12 months would have its problems and difficult decisions: we were going to have plenty to do and to think through during this final year.

Celebration

Then, part way through the year, into our somewhat fraught situation there came a brilliant idea: Edith Horton and Anthony Msei were the prime movers, and staff and students alike entered in with enthusiasm. On St Luke's Day, 18th October 1961, we would have a great celebration of 30 years of Minaki Hospital and medical training. It would be a triple event – a garden party, a pageant of 'The History of Medicine', and festal evensong of St Luke. The 'great and good' would be invited, the Bishop of course and other diocesan clergy; the acting Governor (the Governor had left because Independence was imminent) and other representatives of the administration including the Wakili Mkuu (head of our local authority) and the district commissioner; and of course our helpful friend and architect, Margaret Makins.

When the day arrived we were all in chapel early to start our celebrations, with the Bishop celebrating the sung eucharist. After necessary work, which was not much, as there were few patients by then, Joyce, Edith and I were busy getting the tea organised, when in comes the bishop with a long face, saying gloomily, "I feel it's going to rain; my asthma is coming on." Without hesitation, Edith came out with – "If you feel like that about it Father, please don't come here, we're busy preparing for the Garden Party." No-one would take offence at Edith's half joking rejoinders ("Cloth ears" or "Observation nil" were favourites when someone had missed out on something). So off went the Bishop, mumbling, "Oh these women! But what would we do without them?" And it did rain, but only light showers so far. The 'short rains' had started early, and in 1961/62 rain continued right through until May, which caused plenty more complications for us!

At 4 o'clock the guests began to arrive for the garden party, during which guests and servers retreated into our little dwellings when driven by a shower. The 'garden' had been created within the past few weeks; apart from a few bushes it was just one or two recently planted flower beds, but the zinneas and African marigolds did their best. By 5 o'clock the rain had stopped. This was just as well, as the stage was outside the back of the big German house, and the audience were right out in the open. The choir, the same boys as the caste of course, were upstairs in the open space between the bedrooms, normally our sitting-room; changing rooms were the downstairs bedrooms; stairs were in constant use, and entry to the stage was from the centre, or round one side of the house. The pageant had been thought out by Anthony and Edith, both musical and with an eye for drama. Each incident in 'the History of Medicine' was read out by Anthony in English, in the person of St Luke, with the Bible used where possible, while the players mimed it on stage, clad in costumes created by Edith. The choir upstairs then sang it in Swahili, set to the rhythm and plainsong of the psalms. Meanwhile some rushed up or downstairs to join the choir or get ready to go on stage.

The scene started with Moses and the Brazen Serpent, a length of gilded creeper held up on a pole by Moses, as the Israelites gazed up at it and were healed immediately. Naaman visited Elisha; after some argument, he washed in the Jordan, and was cured on the spot, shouting, "There is no God in all the earth but the God of Israel." The lame beggar at the Jerusalem Temple Gate was healed by Peter, and danced off into the audience and then up to join the choir! Hippocrates dictated his oath; and finally of course David Livingstone arrived at his camp near the Shire River, giving out pills to a very sickly looking crowd, to show the origin of our medical efforts in this part of Africa. The finale was a tableau representing present day medicine, as all sang a specially written hymn about St Luke and the drama.

The provincial commissioner showed after this that he had done his homework by giving a very appreciative short speech, praising the work of the hospital and training school. During the 30 years, 200 young men had qualified as MAs or RMAs. Of those, 130 had qualified during my 12 year period at Minaki. A number of dressers had also been trained. Of course he was suitably enthusiastic and complimentary. The Bishop's final words have stayed with me, and have come in very useful over the years. His message was, "Except a grain of wheat fall into the earth and die, it abideth alone; but if it die, it bringeth forth much fruit." Only one of my assignments in Tanzania could be called 'a success' by ordinary standards, and that one, Muheza Hospital, [see chapter 10] had seemed the nearest thing to failure on a number of occasions. It brought home to us that some enterprises do their job and then something different takes over, while others develop over a much longer period, and have what is seen as a 'successful future'.

After the speeches we took our perhaps somewhat weary guests up to Chapel for a burst of praise and thanksgiving for all God's blessings on the hospital and training school and their staff and students. Solemn evensong, with some really good hymns of joy and praise for God's goodness, was the right note to end on. Now we could see our time at Minaki as a task we had completed to the best of our ability; now we were handing it back to God, preparing for the next job he had for each of us.

Have You Ever Packed up a Hospital?

For Joyce and Edith, Anthony and Alfred, and myself, the very next job would be to see off the remaining students, make last arrangements for the very few remaining patients, and then start to close things down. From time to time the sisters and I had expressed some nervousness about the packing, but the attitude was: "Oh, you women stop fussing; UMCA will send someone to do it". They did, but he had come, and gone; so we set to work. There were a lot of wooden cupboards in wards and store places, so we turned them on their backs, packed all the 'stuff' inside them, and called a carpenter to nail the doors shut to form lids – sounds easy doesn't it?

Someone had remembered to order the lorries! One complication was that the loads were going to three hospitals at three very separate places. Kideleko and Magila were on the same route, 200 and 300 miles away respectively, and those would be all right if we got the lorries off quickly. But one large load had to go to Lulindi in the Southern Region, normally about 450 miles away, along the coast road from Dar-es-Salaam to Lindi, and then inland about 100 miles to Lulindi. But the road crossed the Rufiji River, quite near the coast, and it has a formidable delta, with dreadful tracks on either side, leading to the ferry; all of us who have worked in Masasi Diocese have horror stories to tell of that road! After years of planning and fruitless discussions, an all weather road was finally built a good deal further inland, with an all weather bridge. But our laden lorry would have to go right inland via the Southern Highlands, Njombe, Mbeya and Songea, a whole lot further and a whole lot more expensive.

We were tempted to the sin of pride about our packing as the only thing that was broken was the marble top of the dispensary table, which slid off the back of the lorry when it reached Magila! Edith was the packer of all the glassware, from dispensary, laboratory, wards and our own quarters, and it must still give her a glow of satisfaction that all arrived safely!

'UHURU' – INDEPENDENCE

By 1st December two tired MAs were ready to go off for some well earned rest before starting their new jobs. Three exhausted 'wazungu', Joyce, Edith and I, were pulling ourselves together, writing last reports, saying a lot of good-byes, some very emotional ones, and bracing ourselves to set off in the Penguin, our small black and white van. It was destined for Kideleko, but was to take us first for some holiday up to Lushoto, in the mountain area beyond Korogwe.

Before that came the great event for which everyone was preparing: 'UHURU' – INDEPENDENCE. What a privilege it was that we were taken to the stadium in Dar-es-Salaam, on the eve of December 8th 1961 for the thrilling ceremony, among enormous rejoicing crowds. As the new Tanganyika flag was raised at midnight, a huge prolonged cheer went up. We knew that the flag was also being raised on the summit of Mount Kilimanjaro, the highest mountain in Africa. It was a wonderful occasion, not marred by any rough behaviour, and we 'wazungu' were able to be there just as part of the crowd.

Of course things didn't all go smoothly afterwards, when people went back to daily life, and found all their problems were not solved over-night. Progress was slower than everyone hoped. It was easy for people to think, "Now everything will be all right, everything will be perfect". The word 'Uhuru' means 'Independence', but its basic meaning is 'freedom', so it sounded as if everything would be free; some were indignant when asked to pay a fare on buses! It is hard to realise that all the things which so badly need to be improved take time, money, and all sorts of expertise and hard work before they can come up to our hopes.

These problems and many others faced the new administration, but there was plenty of determination. The great leap had been made, Uhuru was here, the future had arrived! People had real confidence in Julius Nyerere, the first Prime Minister. Next year, when the Republic was formed on 9th December, he would become the first

President, spoken of as 'Mwalimu' (teacher) and 'Father of the Nation'. Two years later the United Republic of Tanzania was formed, when Zanzibar joined in union with Tanganyika.

Our Eventful Holiday

By mid-December jobs were done and I felt ready to take to the wheel, so we three, Joyce, Edith and I set off for our holiday in the Usambaras. It was quite a long way for one used to driving 18 miles to Dar-es-Salaam! The first lap was to Dar-es-Salaam, and then 100 miles due west inland to Morogoro. Next day our route turned northwards to Kideleko, where we spent a couple of nights, making sure about the equipment we had sent to them, and telling them when the Penguin and Edith expected to arrive. The plan was for me to drive them there after our holiday, dropping Joyce at Korogwe on the way and leaving Edith and the van at Kideleko. I should go on to Dar-es-Salaam by bus and train, en route for a plane to Nachingwea, and on to Masasi; the bus depended on the road remaining open, which it didn't!

From Kideleko we went on north to Korogwe. Continuing north, we followed the road that Paddy Shiel and I had taken on our eventful tour of the medical work of our diocese. We had included on that tour a visit to the Lutheran hospital at Bumbuli, which took us along an exciting road winding up into the Usambara mountains. It is the last section of the road from Dar-es-Salaam to Lushoto, but for Bumbuli we had turned off at the small market town of Soni. The rain continued, but the Lushoto road from Dar-es-Salaam has been considered to be an all-weather road since German days. It has to be, because those who can afford it have always had their holiday and retirement homes in and around Lushoto. It is beautiful mountainous country, cool and comfortable after the sticky heat of coastal and other low-lying parts of the country. His Excellency the Governor's Lodge was on the outskirts of Lushoto; Paddy Shiel and her mother, a friend of the governor's wife, Lady Twining, had once been included among the select party invited there for Christmas. It would be the President's Lodge when Julius

Nyerere became the first president of the United Republic of Tanzania at the end of next year. The drive up the winding, climbing road to Soni, and this time on through an open farming area to Lushoto is beautiful, even in the rain. It was my first experience of driving such a road, with its precipices on one side and steep forest covered mountain on the other, blind hairpin bends and narrow stone bridges, and lorries rushing down, so I was leaving the scenery to Edith and Joyce.

The parish priest at St George's Church Lushoto ministered to a mixed congregation, so services were in English as well as Swahili, which made a change for us. He had two guest rooms, and could welcome tired missionaries needing a break. There were Roman Catholic and Lutheran churches also in the town, and it was Christmas time. We had many invitations to lavish feasts, as well as to candle-lit carols at the Lutheran church, and we enjoyed the Christmas services at St George's. There were intervals in the rain and we had some good walks, enjoying the scenery and the surroundings, and people's gardens, with what to us was a wonderful display of English summer flowers. One lovely garden belonged to Sister Eileen, whom I got to know well later on as a skilled dentist. She grew up in a Dutch Roman Catholic orphanage in these same hills, later joining their community. The Sisters took her to Holland, where she had a period of apprenticeship in dentistry. She was a brilliant person, artist, musician, gardener, seemingly skilled at whatever she put her hand to. She was extremely kind to people like ourselves, as well as to all and sundry of the local people who came to her with dental problems. She gradually developed her dental skills, and by the time David and I sought her help, no less a person than President Nyerere was going to her for dental care, as well as various Roman Catholic dignitaries. Once while doing a filling for me, she was talking to someone behind me about some sacred music she had been writing, and I found that he was an archbishop! It didn't seem to alter the success of the filling. It was people in Sister Eileen's position who gave us such headaches when we met on the Medical Registration Board;

she was a very good dentist but with absolutely no registerable qualification!

Rescued: Bumbuli Lutheran Mission

After a wet but very enjoyable and restful time at Lushoto (restful between the parties!), we set off for Bumbuli, and the Lutheran Mission, with the hospital which Paddy and I had visited 10 years before. Returning by the road on which we had come to Lushoto, we turned left at Soni, the little market town 8 or 10 miles along. For me, now at the wheel, it was breath-taking, but perhaps worse for my passengers, who knew that I could safely do a caesarian section, but had little experience of my ability in this new role, and the rain was seriously heavy now. Our interest in the views and the scenery faded as conditions deteriorated; the road had been 're-made', and being just a dirt road, it was now mud, mud, mud, and then more mud.

Several miles and dozens of hairpin bends into the mountains, we found ourselves floundering about in a quagmire of red soil, which the rain had turned into slippery, sticky, horrible mud. Penguin wasn't at all happy, and the Driver even less so. Why had people told us, "Oh that road will be alright, it has just been remade"? My thought was: "Oh for a four-wheel drive vehicle with umpteen gears, and perhaps also someone with more experience at the wheel!" Soon we were hopelessly stuck, covered with mud and all distinctly overheated! Five miles or so to go… What on earth were we to do?… No mobile phones of course in January 1962.

As so often happens in these apparently hopeless situations 'someone turned up', in a sturdy vehicle, with all the right tackle to pull us out onto firm ground a few miles on, and thankfully we found that the Penguin could take us on to our destination. On arrival, the Bumbuli Lutherans quickly seized us and our vehicle; we three were washed, dried, cooled off – or was it warmed up by then? – and fed. Soon we were relaxed and able to exchange news, as well as giving thanks for our safe arrival.

We had several enjoyable and interesting days there, meeting doctors, nurses and other staff, joining in prayer and worship, and seeing how the hospital had developed, with its fairly new and very well set up training school. The two MAs who had come to Minaki, Joachim and Joseph, certainly did credit to their teachers. Dr Jensen was still in charge, and his supporting staff, some from Europe and some from America, as well as local staff, seemed strong.

The rain continued, and in fact went on until May, so our route back to Korogwe and so on to our new places of work, was on a track over the mountains which our hosts knew. Kind and helpful to the end, one of them led off in a Land Rover, and we followed carefully behind, up hill and down dale, until we came to the final hairpin bends, and out onto the main road. Rocks and precipices were the hazards on that part of our journey, and this driver had learnt a few useful things during the last few days about both, as well as about mud!

The road south was, unsurprisingly, closed beyond Kideleko, so buses were not running to Morogoro; we dropped Joyce at Korogwe where she would be working. Then poor Edith, having not driven any vehicle for several years, had to take the Penguin on 30 miles to Kideleko, where she would be working. That road was well used, and she would have someone with her.

I had to get somehow to the south, first to Dar-es-Salaam, and then on by air to Nachingwea, the air-strip near Masasi. Tanga, with its port, is 70 miles from Korogwe, and a bus would take me there. Fortunately the Durban Castle, doing a round trip from England to South Africa and on, was expected in Tanga, and I could get a ride as far as Dar-es-Salaam. On board I found Eileen Farrell, a friend of my sister Gertrude, so we enjoyed a couple of days together, including a brief landing in Zanzibar.

On to Masasi

Thankfully I could fly on to the south from Dar-es-Salaam, and a few hours in the air would save me following the hospital loads on their lorry journey of several days, and no doubt more appalling roads, to reach the same destination. David and his dog Fupi had gone down by coastal steamer a year before, and it seemed that I had reason to be thankful not to be using that route. Rough seas, overcrowding, and for David a distressed little dog, 'tied to the mast' (literally I think) amongst various other animal passengers, had made the trip far from pleasant.

Our small plane left Dar-es-Salaam at 7 am, and they kindly gave the passengers a cup of tea and a piece of plum cake soon after take-off. Nearing Nachingwea it was exciting watching the ground below as we circled over trees which appeared to cover the ground in every direction. I was telling myself that planes landed there every day, so it must be all right, but it was a relief to see a clearing appear. Leader Stirling told of an occasion when, after circling a number of times, the co-pilot walked down the plane telling passengers "Sorry, we're going on to Mtwara to land, as we can't find the air-strip." Leader had turned towards the window, pointed down, and calmly said, "There it is", and the plane landed the next time round! Of course our plane landed safely on a very adequate landing ground, and it was great to see Frances Taylor striding across the tarmac to welcome me to Masasi Diocese.

Nachingwea, where we landed, was 30 miles north of Masasi, but that road relied on a bridge over the Lumusuli river, which had been washed away! A detour of about 60 miles would be the route now. We should have to take a road east towards Lindi on the coast. Near Ndanda, the big Roman Catholic Centre, we should meet the main road and turn back west to Masasi. I soon got used to "road closed" or "bridge down", or more often no warning, but just arriving and finding nothing. In Swahili one could say, "I went to his house and met him. He's not there", so I suppose one could say it about a bridge as well. The drive, with Frances at the wheel, gave me a wonderful introduction to this great veteran doctor of Masasi Diocese. "Never stop for hens", she would exclaim, as she hurtled along the narrow roads with hens scattering in all directions. The hens were in luck that day, as not even Frances could drive at full speed in the pouring rain on a bumpy dirt road. By the time we reached Masasi a lot of wisdom had been imparted, about the diocese and its medical work, and what would be expected of me at Lulindi and in the surroundings, and at Newala. I felt sure that I should enjoy working with such a dynamic personality.

Medical Planning for Our Dioceses

In August 1961, shortly before I left Minaki, Dr Taylor and I were among those called to a great meeting of bishops, doctors, diocesan treasurers, CSP sisters and others, from the three dioceses in the country which were supported by UMCA. These three, Zanzibar, Masasi and South West Tanganyika Dioceses, were soon to be divided. But in 1961 they included the whole of the east coast, and the south of the country, from the coast to Lake Nyasa (now Malawi) and also the Southern Highlands. Many of us had realised that our medical work needed some re-planning and co-ordinating, as we tried to bring it more in line with present day expectations. The out-reach and village work were vital. Good base hospitals were necessary too, not only for their curative facilities, but also essential as centres for training nurses, midwives, and paramedics like our MAs and RMAs at Minaki.

The meeting was called to discuss the suggestion that these three dioceses should work together to develop one medical 'Centre of Excellence'. This would include specialist medical and surgical services, training facilities for nurses and midwives, paramedics of different sorts and technicians, and the many other services of a modern hospital. Frances Taylor recommended her hospital at Mkomaindo, Masasi, as a suitable hospital to develop in this way. A specialist hospital there would supply a much needed service in the Southern Region, an area which many felt to be a neglected or at least isolated part of the country.

To move the nursing school from Lulindi to Masasi would make it more accessible, and this was already being considered. If the hospital could be developed, including some specialist facilities, the nursing school could take on Grade A training. Until now our training centres were for Grade B only, and nurses had to find other places to get 'up-grading' courses in order to take nursing officer or other senior posts. Mkomaindo would need almost completely new buildings for hospital as well as nursing school. More staff would be essential, including some specialists. Building costs would be enormous by our standards, but with the bishops supporting the project, and especially Masasi's well known new bishop, Trevor Huddleston, this might be possible.

Capital costs were one thing, but so many third world projects fail because they have made little provision for the running costs. The ever present example is the roads: generous donors make good roads at great expense, but running repairs don't happen without money, and the roads soon become seriously dangerous as well as thoroughly annoying!

Mkomaindo hospital, Masasi, was the favoured place, though in retrospect I realise that it had many disadvantages. Situation and site were good to supply a service to the Southern Region, but access as well as space for development would cause problems for anything on a larger scale. In fact no inter-diocesan hospital was built, as each diocese felt it must do what it could for its own area, by developing an existing hospital. After a few years, developments did take place at Mkomaindo hospital. It became officially the district hospital for Masasi Diocese, with more nurses and doctors, and other improvements. The nursing school moved there from Lulindi, into good new buildings next to the hospital.

It was at Magila that ten years later I became involved in building a new hospital and nurses' and midwives' training school at Muheza, the small market town three miles from Magila. We built these to replace both hospital and training school at Magila and also the Government district hospital at Muheza. The Government hospital was built 40 years before, in 'temporary buildings'; these, like those at Magila, were quite unsuitable to be developed into anything approaching modern medical facilities.

By the time we did that, the Government had agreed to a new category of grant-in-aid, under which Church (mission) hospitals could become 'Designated District Hospitals' (DDH) or 'Hospitali Teule' in Swahili. These did the work of a district hospital, and received a grant which theoretically covered its total running costs; staff could also be seconded by Government when needed. At Muheza we also received a substantial contribution towards building costs. However, we were not at all surprised to find that much outside support was needed in order to run the enterprise at anything like the standard and work load required of it; also specialist staff were needed from outside the country.

Masasi Diocese: Rondo

For the present, January 1962, being new to Masasi Diocese, I must put this important planning to one side. My next job was to find out about life in the Southern Region and, in particular, about my new home and work in Lulindi and at Newala. I must also get to know more of the diocese and of its other medical work. Frances Taylor would soon be retiring and a new doctor David Gill, was expected before long. He would be based at Mkomaindo, and would also be made District Medical Officer for the extensive Masasi District. A group of three other doctors, with a Franciscan (SSF) connection, were to come soon after Frances left, to run the hospital and take charge of its developments. These would all be new to the country and to the diocese. No doubt more jobs would come my way.

Early in Trevor Huddleston's time as Bishop of Masasi Diocese, a very desirable site became available at a bargain price, on the Rondo Plateau, a high area inland from the coastal town of Lindi. Bishop Trevor took the opportunity to move St Cyprian's Theological College from its isolated spot at Namasakata, near Tunduru, to this site on the Rondo. David Bartlett, after his leave in England, moved with the College to its new quarters, and soon became Warden.

The Rondo became a favourite spot for short breaks for tired missionaries and Dr Taylor was a regular visitor to its dispensary. Sister Susanna, CSP ran the dispensary, which looked after the students and their families, and also families from the surrounding villages. High priority was given to maternity and child health

(MCH), as Sister Susanna, like other CSP nurse midwives was an MCH enthusiast. Paddy Shiel and I, when in 1951 we did our tour of my former diocese and met the Community at Magila hospital, realised how keen and knowledgeable they were on this subject. This included the whole period from the early days of pregnancy, until a healthy infant was safely delivered, nursed and weaned onto a good nutritious diet. Sister Susanna was never so happy as when delivering babies! When Dr Taylor retired, this dispensary would be under my supervision, being 'only' about 100 miles from Lulindi.

James Potts, whom David knew quite well already, came from Korogwe to join him as chaplain to St Cyprian's College. Before long an attractive new chapel was built to replace a rather unsuitable makeshift building which I think had been used as a gym before. Ample side windows gave views right over the hills, and later, beautiful stained glass was put in. Creation was the subject, on one side dazzling panels of sun, moon and stars, and on the other the development of plant and animal life on earth.

With James and David there, and Sister Susanna, one of the three CSP sisters there, my visits for work or rest or both were something to look forward to. They also had a rather rough and ready tennis court, which I remember using once, but when I went again a goat was grazing on it!

Lulindi, Newala, developments at Mkomaindo, and the Rondo, as well as other outlying dispensaries all came into the picture of my new life. I should have a Land Rover, and a driver to look after it and share the driving; it would be a much more mobile life, and I guessed would have plenty of surprises. Masasi Diocese in January 1962 was starting a new chapter in my life, and in many ways that I had certainly not expected when Frances Taylor invited me to come and work there.

CHAPTER 6
Masasi, Lulindi, Newala and Rondo

A Change of Scene

Lulindi, how shall I describe it? I was there for only six and a half years from 1962 but much was packed into that time. In many ways my work in Masasi diocese was a complete contrast to life at Minaki.

Masasi is in the southern region of Tanzania, 90 miles inland from the sea port of Lindi, which is 300 miles south of Dar-es-Salaam. Masasi diocese stretched from the Rufuji River in the north to the Ruvuma in the south. The Ruvuma River forms the border between Tanzania and Mozambique, 'Portuguese East Africa' as it was then.

Masasi District covered a lot smaller area than the diocese; Masasi town was small then, but was the district headquarters. Near the town was Mtandi, with the bishop's house and the diocesan offices, as well as our beautiful cathedral, which had been built at the beginning of the 20th century. On beyond the town was Mkomaindo village, with hospital, church, and a group of small dwellings for the missionary staff, the parish priest, nursing sisters and Dr Taylor (introduced at the beginning of chapter 5).

Arriving at Mkomaindo with Dr Taylor, I wasn't allowed to hang around for long. Frances did everything fast. A quick look round the hospital, a brief visit to Mtandi to meet Bishop Trevor Huddleston, (Bishop of Masasi, 1960-1968) now well settled in, and some of the other staff, one night at Mkomaindo, giving time for a shower of pearls of wisdom, and we were off in the Land Rover. Taking the Newala road going south from Masasi, a rough road, but in fair condition, after almost 30 miles we reached Nagaga. At that time Nagaga was a tiny village, but for some obscure reason was always shown on motoring and tourist maps of Tanzania. Here we turned left, down a track which appeared to lead to nowhere, while the 'main' road climbed on south for 18 miles to Newala on the Makonde Plateau, getting steadily worse as it went!

Our track appeared to gain some confidence as it came to the first unfenced plank bridge, and we were glad to find it not washed away! Soon we came to pools and quagmires, ruts and slithery mud patches, one or two more bridges, and we reached Lulindi village – only about 3 miles from Nagaga they told me.

The village was small, but many people lived a little way out, near their fields. Houses in this area were rectangular, not round, and of local materials, with grass or palm thatched roofs. Often there was a storage hut, built separately near the house. Primary schools, separate for boys and girls, (and at a suitable distance apart), were just outside the village. Nearby was a 'duka' or roadside shop run by an Asian man and his family, and they probably ran several others in nearby villages.

Just beyond the village was a rather large church, filled on Sundays and overfilled on popular festivals, by folk coming in from all around as well as those from village, schools, hospital and nursing school. Opposite the church was the parish priest, Fr John Ley's house, which would soon be our guest house, when Fr Laurence Kasembe took over from Fr Ley. Fr Laurence was a local man and had a family house in the village with some space for growing vegetables. He would also need land nearby for his family to grow maize, beans and other crops, even if he himself hadn't much time to spare for that. Millet was another crop much used in this area.

The three nursing sisters, Helen Carpenter, Pamela Haynes and Brenda Stone, had attractive little houses nearby, with palm leaf thatched roofs, and flat stone-slab floors filled in between with beaten mud. Mine was near the church, a little bigger than at Minaki, and with a small separate room as bathroom and store. It had much more character, including window shutters, which were quite heavy and difficult to manage if I came in during a storm! It also had a small veranda on the front and the usual pit latrine down the garden path at the back.

Pamela Haynes was a nurse tutor, and as well as tutoring she ran the operating theatre – most efficiently – and was also our housekeeper. The sisters and I shared a cook and dining room, and Father Ley had some meals with us. Beyond our houses was the nursing school, and nearby was the hospital, far more compact than the very open air one at Minaki.

Frank and My New Life

Frank was a new feature in my life and soon became a friend. He was known as my driver, but he was a lot more than that. He took care of my Land Rover, as well as driving, cleaning, and doing simple repairs on it. He cleaned my house, did my washing, and helped in the kitchen. When we were out for the day, or spending time somewhere like Newala, on arrival I just stepped out of the Land Rover, washed and changed (if possible), and went to work. Frank found out where I was to stay, prepared the room or guest house, made sure I should be fed, lit lamps, saw to mosquito net, and, well anything else he could think of! He was not a very experienced driver, but had plenty of ideas. When a bridge was covered with water, one of us would wade in and stand near the parapet, while the other cautiously drove over; when the bridge was down over a shallow flood he would go and cut branches to lay across the track until we hoped I could drive over safely. When it came to getting us out of mud or sand, I made sure I had the easier job! Dear Frank – after I left Lulindi I heard that he had died, but never found out what had happened.

The Land Rover we had was a soft top, short wheelbase one, which leaked during heavy rain, but had some advantages over the heavier long wheelbase type available then. They had little resemblance to the 21st century modern Land Rover, but could cope pretty well with awkward driving conditions!

The Monthly Routine

For most of my time in Masasi Diocese Lulindi was my base and first responsibility. However, unlike at Minaki, I was mobile. During the first two years, I spent two or three days each fortnight at Newala, and one or two days I was out for the day at a dispensary. There were leprosy clinics to visit around the diocese, and later, when Frances had left, there would be the dispensary and maternity clinic run by a CSP Sister at Ngala. This was primarily for the families of those at the Theological College, which is usually called 'Rondo' now, to indicate its location on the Rondo Plateau. And I wasn't lucky enough to escape committees!

Calls from the police to give evidence were a new feature, and I was never quite sure how I escaped them at Minaki. The court was 100 miles away on the coast at Mtwara, south of Lindi. Once the police came at 2 am, saying that the magistrate wanted to ask me 'one more question'. No, I couldn't give them a written answer. I had to go with them and he wanted me there by 8 am when the court opened! I had a meeting the same day at Masasi. I paid a quick visit to the hospital to see a couple of very sick patients and tell the staff nurse on duty what was happening, seized some necessary things from the house, and was bundled into the police Land Rover, wondering how I should get to Masasi and then back home that day.

It is a tribute to the stability of our Independence period that I can't think of any time when I would have had more than a moment's anxiety about being taken off in a police car during the night!

Twice a month Frank and I and the Land Rover set off for Newala. The track out to Nagaga on the main road was the way out wherever you were going, and at Nagaga we turned left, south, for Newala and the Makonde Plateau. Newala is 18 miles on along that road, up the steep escarpment onto the 3,000 foot Makonde Plateau which looks over into Mozambique. The road is rough and rock strewn, with alarmingly sharp hairpin bends; the compensation is the superb view, changing in all weathers, sun, rain, storm and tempest, and the cloudy days with light changing all the time, and perhaps patches of mist, or just blazing, glaring sun. I didn't look much while I was at the wheel! A plain stretched out west to a horizon of mountains, and was dotted with sudden outcrops of rock, typical of that area. Brilliantly coloured wild flowers suddenly appeared all over the plain just before the rains, but how do they know?? Newala is high and cold during the winter months, especially when raining, which can be dangerous for small children.

Down here in the south the countryside was different, with its escarpments and plateaus with outcrops of rocks, from the coastal plain where I had been before. There was more cultivation around us than at Minaki, and so fewer wild animals roaming about. With longer periods without rain, which seemed more violent and intense when it came, there was a long dry dusty period before August, which was the month of epidemics, the dust being thought to spread the infecting organisms. Meningitis was common every two or three years, as in 1960, when it reached serious epidemic proportions and interfered with Bishop Huddleston's enthronement. The tribes here were the Wayao, who spread over a wide area to the west, with the Wamakua, and also the Wamakonde, whose home was Mozambique, or Portuguese East Africa as it was then. There were far fewer Muslims here and more Christians, Anglican and Roman Catholic, because of early Christian settlements as described in the old mission literature.

Many of the Wamakonde had found their way across the Ruvuma River from their own country, as under either regime they couldn't get treatment for TB or leprosy, both of which were evidently common there, as they seemed to be in all that southern part of Tanzania.

Many of the Wamakonde are wood carvers, and by the brilliant development of their carving, mainly of African ebony, they were able to stay on in Tanzania, both before and after Independence, and so get their dread diseases cured. The very long courses of treatment needed until more drugs and regimes were developed, meant that many patients failed to complete treatment, and so risked drug-resistant infection to other people, as well as making their own cure slow and unlikely.

Altogether there was a great change in my life and work. I had far more clinical work and less teaching and paperwork. I was mobile, with dispensaries and Newala to visit. I spent my days (and sometimes nights) passing from one sick patient to another, one fresh problem to the next. It was a doctor's dream as long as it didn't wear you out. But I was young then, only just over forty, whatever Tabibu Alfred may have thought of that great age!

Newala and the Sisters of the Community of the Sacred Passion

At Newala was the parish church of St Andrew. As well as the CSP, some African Sisters were starting to build up the Community of St Mary (CMM) with help from the CSP Sisters. The hospital consisted of a maternity department, with a ward, and a delivery room convertible to operating room, and a children's ward. At that time there was a small government hospital, mainly for men. The Sisters also ran a small orphanage.

The Newala visit included a visit to a dispensary, of which my main memory is of the track through fields and trees, part of which was at such an angle that I used to speculate about the angle at which a Land Rover would fall over onto its side! Thankfully it never happened to us.

On the children's ward I would do a careful round, but first the maternity department. The sister in charge might have booked a case for an operation, and I would certainly have problems to discuss with her. It would be rare to do a cold or elective (ie, non-emergency) caesarian section, as a caesarian, for whatever reason, gave problems. To start with, a young wife could be sent home, and dismissed by her husband if she didn't deliver the baby normally. Customs like that are hard to overcome. Also the next pregnancy had to be considered: the mother needed to be in or near hospital next time, and the husband and family may have wanted to make sure that there was no 'interference' with normal delivery this time.

Sometimes they delayed too long in getting the necessary help. We used caesarian section as sparingly as we considered safe. Sterilisation was also used very sparingly, but there were the few for whom it was lifesaving, or at least health-sparing. Even for such women not all would agree. I did a simple abdominal operation, under local anaesthetic, usually as an out-patient procedure.

At Newala I worked with several different CSP Sisters, all experienced nurse-midwives. Sister Jacqueline was one I enjoyed working with in four different hospitals over some 30 years, Newala, Magila, Muheza and Kwa Mkono. Sister Olive Marian was special! She was the one who called me up to Newala to deliver by abdominal operation, a full term extra-uterine (ectopic) pregnancy. The mother was brought into the hospital in advanced labour with no hope of course of a normal delivery.

A man on a bicycle carrying a note was our method of communication. The usual note calling me for a caesarian operation said, "Please come quickly doctor, the theatre will be ready. I have a lady in labour at full term, needing a caesarian operation urgently." Sometimes she would give the reason, usually obstructed labour. On this occasion it was " ......a woman in labour at full term, and the baby is extra-uterine." This means that, with the baby outside the uterus, an urgent abdominal operation is essential or serious internal bleeding would occur. With a quick thought for anything needing me urgently at Lulindi, a shout for Frank and the Land Rover, a word to tell someone what was happening, and Frank and I, the man and the bicycle, were in the Land Rover, and Frank drove us off on our 18 mile twisty stony climb to Newala. Strangely enough, I had another case later on at Lulindi.

Both babies on these momentous occasions were normal healthy infants, though with rather funny shaped heads, improving within a few days. The placenta (after-birth) is the problem. It is of course attached to all the wrong things, and attempts to remove it can easily be fatal from haemorrhage, or from damaging internal organs. It seems dreadful to leave it, but amazingly it gradually gets absorbed.

Two years later I read in the Lancet about a successful case in England with a live healthy baby, written up as an almost unique event. What a pity I hadn't the time, energy and good sense to write up our two exciting cases – the circumstances made them even more special!

It was Sister Olive Marian also who taught me to do caesarian sections under local anaesthetic. In the 1970s when I was working at Magila, she called me up at night: "Doctor, I have a lady with a prolapsed cord".

That is, the baby's umbilical cord was slipping down in front of the head and so the baby was in grave danger until the head had been delivered.

"Of course you will do the caesarian under local anaesthetic."
Quite calmly I replied, "Yes sister, if you will show me how to."

She had been assisting a Chinese doctor, who had come to the government hospital at Newala, and who always used locals. I had been reading it up in a textbook. Spinals of the type that I had been using I knew were not really safe, but I had no reliable alternative, not having a trained anaesthetist, though happily I had avoided casualties. However, I don't think I ever again used spinal anaesthetic for that purpose, and was very thankful for that night's work. Spinals were still extremely useful for other abdominal operations.

Sister Mary Joan, also a nurse-midwife, and with special training in children's nursing, looked after the busy children's ward. Our ward rounds were long and we both enjoyed them. She had good text books, and knew how to use them. We discussed the cases on the ward and their possible complications, treatment with the drugs which were available, dosage which is so very important in small children, and how to handle emergency situations. We discussed cases which Sister had been worried about, and I found I was learning a lot from her experience and observations, as so often happened with nurses with long experience, as well as those new from England and with up to date information.

Sometimes I would go to Newala with no 'homework', that is, no accounts, letters, teaching notes, etc to catch up with. I had my meals with Canon George Briggs, the parish priest of Newala, who later became the first Bishop of the Seychelles. Occasionally we had an invitation out to supper, which for me was rather a mixed blessing; I got an excellent supper, but at the cost of making up their four for bridge. It was probably worse for them!

Our return to Lulindi was normally shortly before dusk. Usually weary and perhaps anxious about problem cases at Lulindi, the scenery out to the west would take my mind off it, and I would be absorbed in the scene, in whichever of its moods it was that day, with the light picking out some feature, or the sunset colours more startling than ever. I hadn't been long there, before turning the corner at Nagaga gave me the feeling of coming home.

Lulindi Hospital and Nurses Training School

Lulindi Hospital was well built, unsurprisingly since Dr Leader Stirling had built it. (See chapter 5). Unlike Minaki, the main part was all under one roof, which was corrugated iron (none under thatch). The entrance was into an out-patient hall, with consulting rooms, stores, a laboratory, and passages leading from it. Corridors on either side led to wards, men's on the left, women's and children's on the right. At the back were isolation wards, a small chapel, and the operating theatre. The theatre was spacious, with an ingenious sterilising room leading out from it. Heat was supplied by a wood fire stoked from outside, with a long flat surface for boiling instruments, and for autoclaves like large pressure cookers for sterilising gowns, drapes and gloves. We didn't have to use expensive paraffin, and there wasn't the danger of fire when using the very inflammable ether or other inflammable anaesthetic. Nearby was a small generator, for a very small X-ray machine, and it also gave light to the theatre. I brought the spotlight from Minaki, and could use that on its own if the generator was not on. The X-ray machine gave basic pictures of fractures and chests when it was working, but we were a long way from any mechanic who could repair it, and it was long past its sell-by date. There were great rejoicings when War on Want sent us a new generator and small X-ray machine.

Another interesting feature in theatre was a 'watching window'. It was placed so that the main thing the watcher could see was the back of the anaesthetist, but relatives or close friends of the patient felt that they could see something of what was going on. From Leader Stirling's time this was found to allay some of the fears of both patient and family. Several of the African CMM Sisters needed quite major abdominal operations while I was at Lulindi. They appreciated the window, and for me as well, it was very reassuring to have one or two Sisters sitting at the window praying.

The nursing school was nearby, with accommodation for male as well as female students, and one good-sized classroom, much of the teaching being done on the wards. In 1962 when I arrived they were just adding midwifery to the three-year course for girls. This was now to be covered as part of the one course, while the boys would be doing extra TB and leprosy study. This led to the Grade B qualification. We had not yet started on the higher Grade A training, which led to nursing officer posts.

Staff and Our Work

Medical assistants at Lulindi shouldered the out-patients work. I didn't do out-patient sessions, but was called when needed. It was the staff nurses, backed up by student nurses, who ran the wards, guided by the nursing sisters, who were all expatriate so far, until we could get some Grade A Tanzanian nurses qualified for these posts. We aimed to have four male and five female staff nurses, and some of them were out-standing. Pauline Mboga stands out in my memory. After qualifying she had married, become pregnant, developed severe thyrotoxicosis, gone into heart failure, and lost the baby. She had come to the hospital at death's door. With treatment (all before my time) she had made a successful recovery and had a successful second pregnancy, and by my time was working again. She had a very special touch with sick, frightened women, as well as the tiny sick babies. Basil Mkata and Ambrosio Sijale were the outstanding male nurses. Very sadly Ambrosio died soon after I left, but Basil had administrative ability as well as actual nursing skills, and we were to meet again nearly 50 years later.

In 2008, at the time of the Lambeth Conference, various meetings were held in London and other places to give news of the diocese to its supporters and all who were interested. Basil by then was executive secretary of Masasi diocese. He with the projects officer, Geoffrey Monjesa, also from the diocesan office, gave an excellent account of what the diocese was doing in medical work, famine relief, agricultural advice, and all they could do to improve conditions for the poor and needy in the scattered villages. It was a real joy to meet them and to hear their news. [The Friends of Masasi and Newala send out a regular newsletter.]

There were three nursing sisters: Pamela Haynes, nurse tutor, took care of nursing school and operating theatre, Brenda Stone, who was Matron, coped with stores, drugs as well as all other supplies, while Helen Carpenter could be happy all day and most of the night with babies and small children, who of course needed close attention all the time. Helen and Brenda shared the adult wards, and they all helped each out so as to get some off duty time. Helen was brilliant at handing on her expertise to the nurses, and many boys as well as girls readily developed the special skill and understanding that very sick little ones need. The staff nurses became expert at giving intravenous fluids to children and even to small babies, which was very necessary, as gastroenteritis and dehydration were common problems and frequent causes of death. During the recent meningitis epidemic, the doctor had wisely taught two of the staff nurses to do lumbar punctures. This meant that children or adults admitted with suspicious signs, could have their cerebrospinal fluid examined in the laboratory, and treatment started at once, even if the doctor was out. To save life and prevent serious complications, starting specific drug treatment can be very urgent indeed.

My memory of those two children's wards after all these years, is of a caring, loving atmosphere, where every child was special and support given to distraught parents. I am sure that tears were shed by many of us when these little ones died, as so many of them couldn't be brought to us in time.

This was true too of new-borns, brought in with tetanus, after birth at home, because of general lack of hygiene and unsuitable cord ligatures. Maternity and Child Health Clinics (MCH) all over the country were working hard at immunisation and health education; tetanus anti-toxin is often too late by the time the spasms have started and the baby has reached hospital.

Our 'busyness' at Lulindi was different from Minaki. I don't remember any walks or other leisure activities at Lulindi, except the occasional visit to Ndwika (see page 121) for a service or a meal or both, with the ladies there. The sisters and I just went on from one job to the next, and it was all so interesting and varied that we only needed an occasional break. Brenda did take an hour off once a week, when she had a leisurely bath (in her tub bath) and didn't come to Compline! If I could get away from the hospital at around 6 p.m., I sometimes called in on Pamela for a cup of coffee and a small ration of Terry's bitter chocolate which a friend used to send her. It gave us a chance to discuss the teaching programme or student problems, or just to relax before Compline and supper.

After supper there was usually some desk work to do. Money matters, statistics, reports and correspondence had to be fitted in, though Brenda did some of that, and Pamela dealt with the nursing school.

Surgery

The surgical problems at Lulindi were similar to those at Minaki, but there were more of them. We usually spent two mornings a week in theatre, as well as emergencies. The common cases like hernias came in a steady stream. I was taking on more difficult cases like hare-lips, because there was no other option for them, but it was difficult to give a safe anaesthetic with no anaesthetist, little equipment and not the choice of anaesthetics that we have now. Extra digits, which were commoner than in England, could be dealt with when the child got old enough to co-operate, but joined fingers are more difficult. I should have found both these and the hare-lip a lot easier if I had had the training in plastic surgery which I had been expecting at one brief period in the past.

At the other end of the scale, on the women's side, we had the huge and difficult fibroid uterus to remove, often complicated by past infection. For men huge hernias could be bad enough, but also the elephantoid scrotum. This is caused by the parasitic infection filariasis, spread by mosquitoes. It can produce scrotal enlargement of a formidable size; I have even heard of a wheelbarrow being used for transport, but we were not faced with them quite that size.

We had fewer animal injuries, as round Lulindi it was not such good country for wild animals, and also fewer gun shot wounds. There were more fractures I think, and with our small X-ray machine they weren't such a problem. We still used chloroform anaesthetic for fractures, with a 'rag and bottle', i.e. a wire mask and gauze and dripping the chloroform on as required. How clearly I remember being told as a student, "If you are not happy about the patient's condition or breathing, take the mask off". How well I remember that returning gulp of air when it happened to us! The old methods had their risks, and keeping the rules was vital.

For fractured hips we still had to use balanced traction, with the leg resting on a Thomas's splint, and slung up from a beam. Traction was applied by bandaging long strips of a special non-stretch strapping to the leg and hanging a suitable weight from it over a pulley at the end of the bed. I can't say that the patients enjoyed it, but they got used to it, usually after a few days. After a few months, when many found they could get back to their normal activities, they were delighted. They realised that without treatment they would have been crippled for life.

For women who were taking serious risks with heart, thyroid, or other problems, or just wearing themselves out with seemingly unending pregnancies, we offered a very simple and virtually trouble-free sterilisation. This could be done as an out-patient procedure if they could stay near. Twenty minutes in theatre, a very small abdominal wound, and return for stitches out in 8 days, was all they had to face. Regular pills would cost money and could be forgotten; three-monthly injections became quite a popular alternative when they were available.

Women of the Makonde and Makua tribes had a special problem. They had a tendency to have a narrow shaped pelvis. Improved nourishment and generally better health meant their babies were often larger, and these two factors could cause delay or actual obstruction to child-birth. The need for assisted delivery became commoner, and we were thankful that sometimes a vacuum extractor could help the baby out, and so avoid the dreaded delivery by operation, with its problems for the mother afterwards. A small, but rather tricky operation, 'symphysiotomy', allows stretching of the pelvis as the baby's head passes through, but it has possible complications which make its use controversial. I found it very useful in carefully selected cases. It leaves no external scar, and makes future deliveries easier and safer.

Burns are a common problem in houses with open fires or charcoal stoves, and plenty of small children about. Skin grafts were often needed to hasten healing. A cut-throat razor worked well, if really sharp, for taking the graft; safety razor blades had the great advantage, if new, of being 'razor sharp'!

Eye surgery requires special skills and special instruments, as well as special lighting. I didn't venture into that speciality. Eye injuries I had to do my best with, and foreign bodies, like a thorn or a tiny chip of metal buried in the cornea (the front of the eye), had to be taken out. But an eye infection, common in the tropics, trachoma, caused inturning of the eye-lids, so that the lashes scratched the cornea, gradually causing ulceration and a lot of pain, and it would finally cause blindness. For that there is a fairly simple operation, which, together with a long course of tetracycline eye ointment, gives great relief, especially if done early before there is serious damage to the cornea. I had a lot of success with these small operations. Flies carry the trachoma infection, so hygienic habits reduce the incidence of the disease.

Tuberculosis and Leprosy

Similar organisms cause these two dreaded diseases, and both were commoner than they had been at Minaki. There were national schemes for treatment of both, with drugs issued, instructions about dosages and courses prescribed, in an ongoing attempt to try to eradicate both. Progress was slow, but new drug routines were giving some hope in both diseases, the very big problem being the long periods of attendance that were required. At Lulindi a number of our TB patients needed in-patient treatment for various reasons. Many when they came had other diseases or malnutrition to deal with. Others lived far from treatment centres and so they could not attend regularly, while a few were just too ill to come without some form of transport. An early need for the hospital was a TB ward for men and suitable arrangements for women and children.

We soon started raising funds for a male 12 bed ward, and had no sooner got it built and occupied than it was struck by lightning! We were doing a ward round, and there was a most dreadful crack, very alarming with the patients all lying there on their metal beds. In charge of the ward was our leprosy worker, Ronald Heald from England. He was scared stiff of thunder and lightning, and always insisted on taking off his red socks if he was wearing them, and putting on rubber soled shoes during a storm, but it was all too sudden this time! Mercifully the lightning shot down the drain-pipe off the roof, shattering the drain-cover in all directions. Giving thanks for our safety, we continued our ward round. 'Bro', as we called our leprosy worker, survived. Brother Heald was a skilled leprosy worker, caring for each leprosy sufferer just like a brother, and overseeing leprosy clinics all round the district. We might laugh about his eccentricities, but we loved and admired him too.

For women and children with TB we made good use of several small rooms at the back of the hospital, thus keeping children out of contact with patients who had drug-resistant infection. This was the great danger of irregular treatment, or stopping too soon before complete cure, in TB as well as in leprosy. Recurrence in those cases is difficult or impossible to cure, and the same is true if the infection is passed on to others. The small wards kept the children from that danger, and also from incidental infections passing between families.

Bro spent part of his time with a busy leprosy clinic at Lulindi. He also had teaching programmes for his leprosy workers and for our nursing students and he tried to give some teaching to all grades of general hospital staff. Included too were the staff of the village dispensaries who made up the front line for finding new cases and bringing them in for treatment. They could help too by teaching in the villages that leprosy was curable, and that only a few cases were infectious, and also even in those it passed off when treatment was established. The clinic at Rondo was included in Bro's rounds, as local people as well as those of the college used that as their dispensary.

Simple surgery was sometimes needed for chronic ulceration, resulting from nerve damage in leprosy. In some cases pressure on a nerve can be relieved to prevent the damage. I didn't have the opportunity to develop the skills needed for the more complicated surgery, where muscles have become seriously paralysed.

Francis Namkuwa was an RMA who had had a lot of illness himself, and also had a great interest in leprosy. Bro gave him a really good period of instruction, and Francis was an able student, with the same caring attention for his patients, and ready to give all his time and energy to the subject. Some years later, when Bro retired, Francis was well able to take over from him.

Church and Hospital Chapel

With our parish church so near, we had no difficulty in joining in parish worship. As at Minaki it was usually the daily Eucharist at 6.30 am and Compline at 6.30 pm. The custom was for men to sit on one side and women and children on the other in places of worship. I had my own place at our side, so I was easy to find if needed in a hurry. We also had our little chapel in the hospital, with a Eucharist one morning a week, which the 'walking wounded' came to, as well as some of the staff. As there were a number of TB and leprosy patients, we always received Communion by intinction, the wafer dipped into the wine and put on the tongue by the priest, to avoid any fear of infection. The chapel also gave patients and relatives somewhere to go and be quiet and pray. The parish priest was our hospital chaplain.

Ndwika Girls Secondary School and Teacher Training College

Half a mile on from our houses was Ndwika, where three lady missionary teachers lived. Helped by a staff of Tanzanian teachers, they ran an excellent training centre. Kathleen Beresford Knox, always known as KBK or K (NOT "Kay") was the principal. Verity Bode, a highly skilled domestic science teacher, and of all sorts of other things I'm sure, was also an excellent house-keeper. They had been there for ever, and one saw no reason why they should ever leave! (They did of course, and stayed with us in Dar-es-Salaam on their way to England, managing to take with them not one but two of our house keys!). Kathleen Vallins was the third, who fitted in well with them, and was replaced by other teachers later.

I was able to visit Ndwika almost twenty years after leaving Lulindi, and was very happy to find how well the tradition had continued, when in different hands. I'm not sure that they could quite produce Verity's standard of Christmas dinner!

Often we were invited up there for Christmas and Easter and other special festivals. On those occasions a feast was produced which would have been well beyond anyone else's efforts with the ingredients available. It amused us that after a really good meal, coffee was on offer, but "in case it would keep you awake", alternatives were sweet sherry, or a sweet sticky, malty sort of drink called 'Milo'. Have you heard of it? It may be excellent for night starvation, but after a hearty and very good meal? No!

The chapel at Ndwika was dedicated to the Blessed Virgin Mary, and was beautifully cared for. The girls were taught about this, and were taught to serve in the sanctuary. At that time girl servers were unheard of, at least in Tanzania however they may be viewed in later times. The Lulindi parish priest was their chaplain. He seldom had a curate, and with the hospital, Ndwika, the parish church and five outstation churches, and all those congregations to look after, his days must have been pretty full. Not much time to work on his 'shamba', but his wife would have seen to that.

Connections with America: Overseas Leave

Bishop Trevor had connections with America – Chicago, Milwaukee, Fon du Lac amongst others, and of course the Episcopal Church Centre in New York. I had my personal contacts in Flint, Michigan, where my brother Alan was now living, with wife and their two boys. So I was planning to visit them during my leave. In 1962 we were able to send two nurses to Chicago for further training, which was a great excitement for them, and also for us. One, Joyce Mchakatu, did well. She came to us at Lulindi for a short time and then worked at Mkomaindo until she married, and then unfortunately for us, moved away. The other sadly had to return almost at once as she was found to be pregnant; this was already starting to be a serious problem among our young nurses, and one which the young men so often got away with.

Our first medical students, coming for their elective period, came from America. As time went by, at our various hospitals there was a steady stream of students from England, and a few from elsewhere, coming for periods of 3 to 6 months during the latter part of their training. It was a shock to them, I think, especially for the Americans, to see how we lived, as well as our conditions for work. I was amused at one who came out with me on a dispensary visit. I produced a packet of biscuits which I had been glad to come across at a local duka; they tasted of sawdust, but were quite edible. He said, "We can't think why you eat these biscuits." The reply, "Because we're hungry", seemed to surprise him! Evidently not their usual reason for eating. However we really enjoyed having the students, and they found it a valuable and very interesting experience.

They saw tropical diseases which were quite new to them, and also familiar medical conditions in different and often worse states than they were used to. I don't think they saw any smallpox, but the meningitis continued, and many were in their final year of medical training, so it was safe to let them do lumbar punctures and other procedures under supervision. For us, it put us on our mettle, and we could pick up some tips in recent developments, even if much was irrelevant to what we could actually put into practice.

One of our male staff nurses, Ernest Ilaila, went in 1962 to Exeter, England, for a full three year nursing course. After working for a while at Mkomaindo, I heard that he had a senior post at Ndanda, on the road between Masasi and Lindi, where Roman Catholic Benedictines had quite a large and well-staffed hospital with a nurses' training school. At that time one could be sure that some hospital in the country would benefit by these special opportunity trainings that nurses had received, but at a certain amount of expense to us and inconvenience to our hospitals. With our perpetual shortage of funds it was sometimes hard to appreciate that!

A Family Feeling

Masasi diocese, being in a rather isolated part of Tanzania, had a real family feeling among the diocesan staff, and there was often someone who could 'fix' a problem for which one could find no easy solution. There was Father Ronald Cox (Ronnie) who dealt with cars and buildings; anything mechanical was his line. Fr George Faussett, the diocesan treasurer, was the one to help with money, office and even legal matters, like our load of drugs stuck at the port. The nursing sisters had plenty of opportunities to offer their care and skills and advice.

We doctors had plenty of calls. One of my rather alarming incidents was with Bishop Trevor, who had serious diabetes and was on large doses of insulin. Sensibly he carried glucose sweets round with him, but was always surrounded by children, so often the supply had run out when it was needed. Long trips round the diocese, and delays in meal times were very liable to make his blood sugar drop, causing the troublesome hypoglycaemic condition, leading to unconsciousness if not treated. His Land Rover rushed up to the hospital one day, the passenger door opened and Bishop Trevor nearly fell out. He was faint and fuddled, saying all sorts of strange things. The staff quickly got him onto a couch, and while I looked at him, a sister made some tea with lots of sugar; fortunately he was still able to drink it with some persuasion. The effect was immediate and dramatic. He was then taken to our guest room and given a much needed meal. The result was that we had him with us for a few days, for rest and re-assessment of his insulin regime, which was a rare pleasure for us.

Another call I had was at the diocesan synod, of which I was a member after Dr Taylor left. The bishop asked me, instead of attending the synod, to bring my eye testing set, and call almost all the clergy to have their eyes tested to see if they needed reading glasses. He would see that all who needed them got prescription glasses.

One of my mother's brothers, Uncle John, was a pharmacist, and pharmacists (who were usually called chemists then) did sight testing in those days. Fortunately once when I was staying with him, he had taught me simple testing which was adequate for this purpose, and I could pick out any who needed prescriptions involving astigmatism or other more serious errors, so that further action could be taken.

Not many weeks went by without a visit from Bishop Trevor, sometimes alone, often with a visitor who had come to see the diocese and its activities, sometimes to give expert advice, or discuss projects and support for them. I always appreciated his visits, and even when he was critical, he never left without giving some advice and encouragement. He was always impatient of what he saw as our lack of enterprise and progress, our apparent satisfaction with things that were behind the times and old fashioned. I couldn't help being amused at Mtandi, where all the buildings of the diocesan headquarters had been given 'permanent' roofs, while his was still thatched! It was much more attractive to look at!

Farewell to a Veteran

We were sad to say goodbye to Dr Frances Taylor after her 30 years invaluable pioneering service in Masasi diocese. She had set up the Church's medical network in the Masasi area, building Mkomaindo hospital as the centre for its work. Her pioneering gifts and determination were special, and were just what were needed at that time and place. Now increasingly it was the nursing sisters who were running the hospital. Her care and consideration for any member of staff who had special problems like a sick family in Tanzania or England were remarkable. Otherwise they and others never knew what might come out. Even David Bartlett, Warden of the Rondo College, had his tale to tell. For some unexplained reason, he was one day holding the lamp while Frances was opening a small abscess. "Hold it still, you fool" was thrown back at him ---- "Oh! It's you" soon followed. The nursing sisters had similar stories, but all both loved and respected her. I always enjoyed staying with her when on leave later on in England.

Dr Taylor's departure gave me more responsibilities, as the new doctors at Mkomaindo had hardly arrived yet, and Dr Gill was a newcomer too. Sister Susanna's dispensary at Rondo would be one of these, and I looked forward to my visits there.

A Dramatic Start at Rondo

The first visit to the Rondo dispensary was notable for bees, the fierce and quite dangerous African type. Frank and I set off on the 100 mile drive, first up onto the Makonde plateau, almost to Newala, then down towards the coast onto the plain, then up again on a rough track, the last 5 miles or so covered in rocks and stones, and with a frightening drop on one side. Our naughty colleagues at the college used to say, "Oh yes, when our visitors don't arrive we know they have gone over the edge!"

On David's first arrival at the college, the Land Rover's gears packed up on that worst bit, and he and Fupi, David's dog, made their entrance on foot. Fupi was scared stiff, as they could hear the occasional lion's roar in the distance, and eerie hyena's laugh, and anyway his legs were a bit short for such a climb, and he hadn't recovered from his horrible sea journey yet, tied to the mast with other four-footed travellers. Our valiant leprosy worker, Ronnie Heald, liked to arrange to come with me on visits to Rondo "to save petrol", and you can guess whose Land Rover we went in. Not difficult to guess too who was driving, as Frank was in the back. However, I was more used to hazardous driving now than on our momentous trip in the Penguin to Lushoto and Bumbuli.

On that first visit I was welcomed to the college guest house, which was an attractive, comfortable-looking chalet. While changing for supper, which would be in a building about 50 yards away, the bees came down on to me from the roof – a whole swarm of angry, fierce African bees. Hurrying to make myself respectable, and with long hair flying I rushed over to the dining room, calling out to the assembling mission staff of the college, "Get the bees out of my hair". It was quite a dramatic first appearance of their new visiting MO! Then we realised that David had not arrived, and the door flew open admitting a cloud of bees. David and Fupi scrambled in, he trying to get the bees off Fupi, but we saw that he was in a worse state than the dog, and someone found some brandy, while I ran for my stethoscope. Fupi got some brandy too, when we saw that he also was collapsing. David was put to bed, I went and tidied my hair, and then we sat down to supper, a bit shaken up by the episode.

We heard later that Sister Ruby CSP, who looked after the small orphanage at Newala, had suffered a similar attack, and was given an MBE for rescuing her orphans. Two Africans whom I knew were attacked by our dangerously fierce African bees, and had died of the attack.

The rest of my visit went according to plan. I was shown round the site next morning. The old chapel was still in use, with family houses for African staff loosely clustered around, giving space for vegetable gardens. Accommodation for overseas staff, who had to be single according to UMCA custom, was communal, with a pleasant dining-room and sitting room, a cook, and a gardener to work their vegetable plot. Further out were 'shamba' (fields) for the families, and the water supply system, always a worry until they could get good rainwater collection organized.

The purpose of my visit was to see Sister Susanna and the dispensary, so that occupied most of the morning. Sister showed me her facilities which were simple, but of course in perfect order. We talked about supplies, finances, workload, health of the staff and students, their families, and especially the children. Eyesight was a problem for the clergy also, as I found when I was asked to test them all at the Synod after Dr Taylor's departure. Dr Taylor had checked the students but some of their wives couldn't read, but she had apparently said that they must learn to read before she could test their eyes! I promised to bring my testing set and see what I could do for them. I would use a chart of capital 'E's with the arms of the E pointing in different directions, and in different sizes. They would show with their arms which way they were pointing. The urgent problems at Rondo were usually to do with childbirth, and then Sister would more or less commandeer the college Land Rover, and if the driver was not there, James or David found themselves going down a steep track to a Roman Catholic hospital at the bottom of the escarpment, whatever time of night or day. Soon they would be thanked profusely for being so kind as to come to the rescue.

The dispensary was open to people from the nearby village, but most of the work came from the students and their families, and being of childbearing age, Sister Susanna could really enjoy herself keeping the families healthy.

Before lunch an invitation came from James for drinks before the meal, and David had recovered from the bees and agreed to join in.

To my surprise some whisky was produced, but they evidently had no glasses, so they drank it out of tooth mugs, providing something softer for me, as well as something a bit more conventional to drink from. It was very good to see them again, with some time to talk about what had been going on since we last met. Things had changed a lot for each of us.

In the afternoon there was time for some relaxation, first a rest, and then a walk. Two or three other Sisters of the CSP lived and worked at Rondo, and an invitation to go and see them for a cup of tea came next. Sister Hazel lived near them in a tiny house on her own, living as a hermit. She had been a missionary member of diocesan office staff for many years and then felt called to live as a hermit, only seeing a few visitors, old friends, and those who came to her for spiritual advice. I came into both categories.

Evensong with staff and students came next, then back to the chalet, and mercifully no bees today. We think that the day before, several swarms were at war fighting for territory with few crops in flower just now and we just happened to get into their line of fire – and it was fire! It was a recurrent problem at Rondo, and several attempts were made to start them off in hives, but that is difficult with these fierce and uncooperative African bees. They are used to living in trees or rocks, and don't understand the advantages of being 'kept' and cared for in artificial hives.

After supper there was a better chance to get to know the other overseas staff than the night before, when we were all nursing our bee stings. Then I went back to the chalet for an early night before leaving for home after the Eucharist and breakfast next morning. It had been a useful and mostly very pleasant visit.

England and the United States Again

By 1964 I was overdue for leave in England, and really needing it. A Dr Billington, formerly a missionary in West China, was able to come to Lulindi. When he had found his way round, and we had another doctor temporarily at Newala, I was able to fly to England. It was a strange leave for me. I was expecting to divide my time there between my one remaining aunt, Elsie Savage, and some very dear family friends, Elsie and Freddie Hilliard, who were living in London. It was they who had handled Gertrude's affairs when she died suddenly. I knew that Aunt Elsie wasn't very well, so phoned as soon as I reached England, to find that she was in a nursing home in Sevenoaks. Going there first thing next morning, I found that she had died in the night. She had been a much loved aunt to us as children, known as 'the-aunt-who-could-do-a-hundred-things-at-once'. I think this was because whatever needed doing she could do it, whether it was cooking, gardening, knitting, painting, carpentry, any DIY around the house, and at least another hundred! I was sad not to get there in time, though possibly she preferred it that way.

There were the usual 'jobs' to do in England, meetings, shopping for personal needs and hospital, visiting friends, of whom some were supporters of UMCA whom I had got to know over the years. This time the only family members to visit were a doctor cousin and his wife, Frank and Billie Clouting. Frank was the only surviving first cousin, except his younger brother and sister, Jim and Grace, who at this time I hardly knew. We put that right when I was back living in England. Frank was a general practitioner at Ancaster in Lincolnshire, and we always enjoyed meeting and comparing notes about our very different jobs. It was he who had been able to lend me a rather elderly car during a previous leave. Tom Stuart-Black-Kelly was a cousin of Gertrude's on her Manx mother's side. I had never met him, but we had spoken on the phone once. He and his wife Jane lived in Bath, and they invited me there for a few days. He, also a doctor, was an eye specialist, and I really enjoyed the few days I had with them, but there was of course not enough time to learn any eye surgery!

I had my eyes thoroughly tested, and also saw for the first time, a solar powered hot water system in their house. It is encouraging that solar power is now being used much more for light as well as hot water supply in the places where I have worked. My one experience of using it in a hospital produced serious problems! The nurses thought that hot water flowing from a tap was too good to be true, and of course, it was when they left the tap running. Asbestos was unwisely used by our architect for roofing, and the heavy solar panels soon cracked and broke them! It was too expensive while I was there, to use for lighting in any general way.

By 1964, the two missionary societies, UMCA and the well-known SPG, had joined to form the United Society for the Propagation of the Gospel (USPG). So another 'job' was to visit the headquarters in Tufton Street, Westminster, to get to know the headquarters staff, and to discuss the work at Lulindi and in Masasi diocese. Next it was America. The first visit must naturally be Flint, Michigan, where Alan and Joy were living with their two boys. Jim was nine now and Martin seven and a half, and so they were both serious schoolboys. What a change it was for me to join in activities with a young American family!

The exciting and rather alarming aspect of the American visit was that the Episcopal Church had arranged for me to do a tour in places as widely separated as Portland, Oregon; Pittsburgh; and Salt Lake City, with its Mormon Temple, and impressive mountains. On my way back to England I went to New York, to visit the Episcopal Church Centre. It felt very strange to have a sheaf of air tickets, and to be welcomed, shown round and entertained, and to have a number of engagements before flying off to the next destination!

Before New York and England, I had a few more days with the family in Flint, and on my way there called in at the Benedictine Priory (later Abbey) at Three Rivers, Michigan. It was at that time a Priory of the Community at Nashdom in England of which I was by then an oblate.

One result of the America visit was a large and very valuable donation of drugs, drugs which we needed badly, expense always being the problem. Unfortunately like so many things, it was not straightforward. Freight was to be arranged by the donor, and was paid for, but when the drugs were due to arrive, there was silence. We heard nothing, our agents heard nothing and all enquiries were fruitless. One year after the drugs were due to arrive, a friend told us that the Tanzania Gazette stated that a load of drugs, addressed to me at Mkomaindo, was about to be sold by auction if not 'claimed' immediately! They had been landed at Tanga Port, instead of Dar-es-Salaam. No one was informed, and all 'claims' which we had sent were ignored, so they just sat there at the docks. We did eventually get them, but of course by then some were out of date.

We had a similar experience some years later with a Land Rover, but with a slightly different out-come. That time, as well as writing and phoning repeatedly, we had gone to the docks ourselves, and were told it had not been received. After a year we were sent a huge bill for 'demurrage' on the 'unclaimed Land Rover', but by that time we had successfully claimed insurance and bought and collected its replacement, and were using it. On that occasion I was able to hand the problem over to the Christian Council of Tanganyika. The bill for demurrage would probably have been more than the value of the vehicle, after it had stood uncared for somewhere in the Tanga docks area for a year...

A Visit to Minaki

My return to Lulindi was via Dar-es-Salaam and Minaki. Edith Horton, who had been such a valuable member of our hospital staff at Minaki, had joined us at Lulindi in 1962 while Pamela Haynes was on leave. She had taken Pamela's place in nursing school, operating theatre, and many other jobs. She stayed with us for over a year, giving time for others to have their overseas leave, and living in the thatched house next to mine. As a locum for those on leave we appreciated Edith's experience and skills, and her ability like my Aunt Elsie to turn her hand to anything. Early in 1964 Edith had married Timothy Fox, one of the new teachers who came to Minaki during the period before we had closed the hospital. He and his sister Liesel from England, and several other friends, had visited us at Lulindi, on a tour which they were doing before Timothy went to England.

By November 1964 Edith and Timothy, with their new baby Susan, (born the same month), were back at Minaki, and I had been very glad to accept the request to be Susan's godmother. The timing was fortunate, and the baptism was to take place in Minaki Chapel; they had kindly planned it to coincide with my visit. When still a medical student I had held Susan Hilliard, another god-daughter in my arms in Ely Cathedral. I had been far away in 1950 when Elizabeth Hughes' turn had come, my second god-daughter, and Susan was number three.

It was really good to see Edith and Timothy, and the lovely baby. They showed me round the new Minaki, with its many changes since I left three years before. They had one of the new staff houses and seemed happily settled, in circumstances much changed for Edith from our hospital life there. After the happy event of Susan's baptism, I flew off from Dar-es-Salaam to Mtwara, where nurse tutor Pamela, with some of her student nurses, was expected to meet me for the final lap of the journey to Lulindi.

Chapter 7
Lulindi with a Difference

A Surprising Welcome

My return to Lulindi produced some drama. Arriving this time at Mtwara air-strip, a crowd of Lulindi student nurses came down to the coast to meet the plane. They were having their annual outing. This meant that a lorry was hired, Pamela could do some essential shopping, nurses could picnic or visit relatives, and they could, on this occasion, meet their 'Mama Daktari' on return from her travels.

As the steps came out and the plane door opened, a group of nurses swarmed across the tarmac. There were hugs and kisses all round: "Welcome home Mama! What news of our staff nurses in Chicago? Habari za siku nyingi (what news of many days)?"

Time only to reply, "How lovely to see you all; all's well in Chicago", when two policemen rushed up to ask what this 'mzungu' (foreigner) was doing arriving by plane in a restricted area? With no time to reply, I was whisked off to be questioned. Happily it didn't take long when they discovered who I was and who the nurses were. It was an example of how friendly the police were on the occasions when I had any dealings with them after, as well as before, Independence.

Soon on the lorry we bumped back home up onto the Makonde Plateau to Newala, where we called in on the parish priest, still Fr George Briggs, and the hospital; then down the Lulindi side of the escarpment, and back to familiar sights and sounds and people, who soon left me with no doubt that I was back home.

Both hospitals seemed to be in good shape, and I quickly settled down to routine, after Dr Billington had told me about his time there, handed over, and gone on his way. It was soon clear that I had left things in good hands. Now two of Dr Taylor's dispensary visits would be added to my schedule, Namasakata and Rondo, both with dispensaries, and both in the hands of CSP Sisters, and so they would not need frequent visits.

Gifts and Improvements

A welcome gift to arrive soon after I got back was a new electricity generator with a small X-ray machine and equipment from Oxfam. The old ones had become unusable, and the X-ray processing equipment was equally unsatisfactory. These occasional gifts from Oxfam, UNICEF, Christian Aid and other charities , who worked so hard to help, were cheering, as well as extremely useful, as we so often needed things which we couldn't afford.

At Lulindi and the places where I worked later, a gift which came to us regularly was skimmed milk powder. Most of it came from America, and it was used at the MCH clinics to prevent and cure protein deficiency. It has a high protein content, and can be added to uji (thin porridge) after weaning. Children are usually weaned at about two years, at which time a high protein diet is needed for healthy growth, and it is often in short supply in the diet. At the same time the mother is given teaching about ways of using beans, as well as eggs and cows' and goats' milk, and other locally obtainable foods to supply protein.

Breast feeding was the normal custom among the country people who regularly attended our clinics, and of course we deplored the advertisements which were appearing from some babymilk firms, encouraging women to change to using their products. However, we were also extremely grateful to Nestles and some others who occasionally sent us free supplies of good babymilk. There were the few cases, where for illness or other reason, including the death of the mother, a starving baby was brought to the hospital. At that stage a good babymilk, which the relatives could not afford to buy, will save its life, until improvement begins and some regime can be worked out, using local supplies.

The year 1964 was a good one for gifts to the hospital. From English supporters came money to refurbish our poor little pathology laboratory. Ulcers, especially of the legs had been so common in the past that we had set aside a room as 'the ulcer dressing room'. Penicillin and better treatment methods had considerably shortened the period needed for dressing ulcers, and yaws had disappeared now that we had good supplies of penicillin. Yaws was a condition caused by a spirochete, similar to that causing syphilis, but not a sexually transmitted disease. Amongst other symptoms, intractable ulcers, mainly on the legs, were common. Before the coming of penicillin we had used the other anti-syphilis drugs, preparations of arsenic and bismuth, which had many disadvantages, so we were delighted to be able to abandon them.

Now we had a bigger room to use for the laboratory, and we could put in a work-bench with a stainless steel sink and soak-away, as well as a good supply of equipment. Our tests were still simple, but speed and accuracy were definitely improved, as well as providing a bit more comfort for the workers!

American gifts, following my visits, enabled us to get a good supply of foam mattresses and pillows. From England a consignment of good second hand hospital beds (replaced there no doubt by very superior ones!) were sent. Unfortunately we had to find the money for freight on the beds, which was a lot, but the other gifts had freight paid for by the donors. Fablon for the top of lockers, and a clock for each ward were much appreciated by the staff. These details give an idea of the financial restraints under which we worked. Priorities were always in mind. Some supplies like penicillin and the other antibiotics were sure to be given high priority. But we still had to decide whether to use them or not; and how important are new mattresses and pillows compared with petrol for dispensary visits?

A Few Happy Patients

Many of the patients and relatives were happy when they left the hospital, or even before they left, and of course sadly there were those who managed to be grateful, even if the result had not been what we all hoped for. Some of them stick in the memory. A little boy, who came dying from tuberculosis, went home still on medication, and a great deal improved in health. He was soon back after discharge, this time not for his supply of pills, but with a broken arm. No doubt he had been climbing where he shouldn't have, which at least did credit to his health and energy. He was one of these lovable pickles, and definitely accident prone!

At the next TB clinic the lad turned up, now for his plaster to be checked as well as his pills, and he looked well and fatter, and no longer frightened of the hospital. At the same clinic an old man who had fractured his femur and had been slung up from a frame for 8 weeks, was reported to be walking on both legs without even a crutch. This was somewhat surprising, as on many of his nights in hospital he had cut all the strings which held his splint up. As well as renewing them, on some days the leg had needed straightening again – painful for him and a nuisance for us!

Another example of a happy result was an incident at a crowded TB clinic, when I was reviewing some of the patients near the end of their treatment. I was aware of a hand gently feeling for my pocket. Looking down, I saw an elderly hand trying to put two small eggs into the pocket.

Progress at Mkomaindo

In 1965, plans for developing Mkomaindo hospital at Masasi were being put into action. From early 1966, Dr David Gill was based there, and was made district medical officer from January 1967. Dr Bill Murdoch with his wife Pauline and a flock of children had been holding the fort there. When David took over, Bill was free to move to Newala to take charge of the Government hospital and develop it. He took charge of our hospital too, which relieved one of our problems.

Plans for the new nursing school were being drawn up in 1965, and building was to start next year, so that the move could start with the new intake of students early in 1967. Three doctors who had a link with the Society of St Francis (SSF), Anglican Franciscans, in England, were expected during 1967 and 1968, of whom I had met one while in England in 1964. Frank Johnson had taken me to the Franciscan Friary in Alnmouth, Northumbria, so that we could have a talk, as well as meeting some of the Brothers. Sadly it was a day of heavy sea fog, so I couldn't see the view out over the sea, which I can imagine is really special, but the day was special anyway. Meeting the Brothers was a pleasure, and we were to see more of SSF in Tanzania later on. It was also an excellent chance to discuss the Mkomaindo plans with Frank, who had already been briefed by Dr Taylor and by Bishop Trevor.

The other two doctors of the group had wives and families and I for one was really pleased that we should have some families among the expatriate staff. Of course it produced a few problems, including salary, but for once it was not my problem, so I made no enquiries! Up to that time the missionaries received minimal pocket money. We didn't need much, as the housekeeper had an allowance which paid our board and lodging requirements, and there wasn't much else to spend money on. The system gradually faded out as our conditions of work altered, and we became responsible for our own food and home expenses. Then the diocese, using grants from our missionary society, provided housing and furniture if we hadn't got our own, and a suitable living allowance.

During 1966 the improvements to buildings at Mkomaindo were progressing well. A new and well planned maternity block had been built, and alterations made to the outpatient department and stores. Some covered ways were built, and temporary private rooms made out of existing buildings which were not in use. The nursing school, a two storey building very unlike ours at Lulindi, was almost ready for use.

At this stage a sort of semi-official 'opening' took place. Mkomaindo Nursing School had to wait for its completion, and they then had the great honour of Mwalimu Julius Nyerere, the President himself, to perform the full ceremony. On this occasion we had a junior minister from the Ministry of Health, supported by representatives from the Masasi district headquarters and local authority, and of course priests and others from the diocesan headquarters at Mtandi. Speeches were made, the nursing school was declared 'open', and the Minister headed for his limousine. His chauffeur, with suitable deference and bows, saw him into his seat. He then rushed round to me: "Oh thank you doctor, thank you very much; twelve years ago you cured my hernia, and then I could work again, thank you". With that he seized my hand, rushed round to the driving seat, and started the engine. It was all done so quickly that his boss probably didn't notice. It meant more to him and to me just then, than opening half a dozen new nursing schools!

Special Dispensary Visits

Early in 1966, Brother Heald and I paid a visit to Namasakata, the home of the theological college before it moved to Rondo. It was fun doing a long distance dispensary visit as Bro's guest. For one thing one's bodily needs were well provided for, including early morning tea, sent round by one of his minions if there was no 6.30 eucharist that day. We drove to Masasi, and then west to Tunduru, then left, south, along a rather perilous track six or eight miles, (it seemed like 10 or 15 miles) to Namasakata. The weather was good, but the track was inevitably different during the rains, and quite often impassable.

We called in at Mindu on the way, with just a few patients to see there next morning. Mindu has a special ethos about it, partly I'm sure because of the CSP presence there for many years, as well as a very holy, but I gather rather eccentric priest. It is also in a very interesting situation with what one can only describe as a 'little mountain' behind it. I liked the name of the little place where we had to turn off the main road to find Mindu – Nakapanya. I was with the Sisters for two nights there, one of whom looked after the dispensary, and the other was kept busy in the parish.

Bro was driving this time, in his Land Rover, which was surprising in view of his problems over difficulties on the road. Namasakata seemed strange without the college, but CSP Sisters were still there overseeing the dispensary, and busy with various projects in the villages around. Bro had a busy leprosy clinic staffed by a dresser with long experience, and had arranged for me to see a few patients, and I spent some time with the dresser, but on the whole the trip was more like a few days holiday for me.

The Rondo visit I did on my own this time, just with Frank, and no bees attacking us I am thankful to say. I had again taken another day off, but the first day was for Sister Susanna and the dispensary. The staff and students' wives came in turn for their eye testing. It was straightforward testing those who could read or at least knew their letters. Though some needed reading glasses, I didn't find any who had serious problems. Using a chart of the letter 'E' of different sizes, the illiterate ones could show the direction in which the short lines of the 'E' were pointing, and they were the ones among whom I found people with more difficulties. These had presumably hampered their attempts at mastering the art of reading before. Some I could help, but some needed expert testing. We had quite a bit of fun with it, and most were keen to get suitable glasses and go ahead with learning to read. I had an assortment of reading glasses which had been sent out from England, so a few wives went home with high hopes for the future.

The CSP Sister and I discussed not only the usual things like staff, supplies, funds, and daily problems, but also her difficult maternity cases and others, especially the children. We could compare notes on successes and also the times when we wished we could have done better, and how to cope with limited facilities. I valued these discussions, and learnt a lot from them. We both had our problems from time to time with expatriates, especially with newcomers struggling with unfamiliar climate, diet, circumstances far from home, and perhaps tropical diseases.

By teatime the other Sisters were expecting me. Sister Marina, a north country sister, always had some secret ingredients hidden away, which appeared on these occasions in the form of a special tea, and we had plenty to talk about as well. There was time for a walk before Evening Prayer and supper, and an early night in the comfortable chalet.

Morning Coffee with a Difference

In the morning Sister Hazel, the hermit, was expecting me, and it was David's turn to invite me to morning coffee. James wasn't there, and the coffee was made in a rather alarming way on a primus stove, roaring away in a cupboard! However there was no explosion, and no clothes caught fire. The roaring stopped, David handed me the coffee, and with hardly time to take a breath he said, "Will you marry me?"

Is it surprising that I spilt the coffee? In later years he remembered the spilt coffee, while I remember that I said, "David, how can I?" It came as a complete shock. We were both attached to our jobs, mainly because we felt that God had called us to them, and also we knew how vital the work was. I couldn't join him at Rondo, and he, as far as I could see, couldn't come to Lulindi, or to any other place with a hospital that would need me when Lulindi became a rural health centre. We were expecting that to be the right future for Lulindi when the nursing school moved to Mkomaindo.

After clearing up the coffee and giving me some more, we talked. It was some years since I had contemplated the possibility of marriage, so I didn't think of people in those terms: admirable, yes – clever, sensible, fun, all sorts of adjectives, and of course all the opposite ones, but not in terms of a possible husband! David said that he had always wondered how he would know if God wanted him to get married, and now he did know. But I needed to go away and think and pray. Before going I managed to say how much his friendship had come to mean to me, and that whatever happened I didn't want to lose that. Most of David's students were away on placements in parishes or on holiday, so he was not so busy as usual and I should be able to go back later in the day.

Returning in the afternoon, I was ready to hear the plan which David had in mind, knowing that by the end of the following year, 1967, I should no longer be needed at Lulindi, and nothing had yet been planned for my future. He told me that he had been out of parish life for ten years now, and felt that he needed a break from full time teaching and to get back into a parish. He had thought a lot about possible plans, especially as James Potts would be ready and willing to take on the warden's duties. I realised that there was nothing I should like more than to be able to cancel "How can I?", and to say a very positive "Yes". When we thought about it in practical terms, we realised we would want to be married here in our diocese, although both of us had reasons for going briefly to England. David was due for a short overseas leave; I had developed 'carpel tunnel syndrome', with pain in wrists and hands, making operating difficult amongst other things, and needing an operation, as injections had not done any good. My instructions from the USPG doctor in England had just arrived: "Come to England at once to get them put right".

After a while we parted, with the deep joy and happiness of being privately committed. Bishop Trevor was in America and discussion would be needed with him as well as USPG, who would no doubt agree if he did. David had evidently thought it all out, and would get things moving as quickly as possible, and would find ways to keep me informed. "If you sort out your hands, I will sort the rest out", he said, and I was happy to accept that. Next morning I went home to Lulindi, rather dazed, hardly believing what had happened. Soon I was so absorbed in my fascinating occupations that time didn't drag before our news could be told.

David's Background

David's family home had always been in Salisbury diocese, where his father, Canon Lindsay Bartlett, had served in different parishes during his long ministry. He and Margaret, his wife, now lived in Salisbury Close, almost next door to Sarum College, and I got the impression that their home, 23 The Close, was well known for friendliness and hospitality. I had met them twice. The first time was when they visited David at Minaki, and I had taken David to the airport to meet them; we had also had some meals together.

Later we happened to be on leave at the same time, and I was staying near Salisbury with Juliette Mullins, who had been at Minaki, a very useful member of our nursing staff. We took the opportunity of combining a visit to David and his parents, and to Salisbury Cathedral. It was one of those days when everything went well! Perfect weather, the beautiful cathedral in its lovely open surroundings, and the welcome by David and his parents, not forgetting the excellent lunch which they gave us.

David was the middle one of three brothers. Edward, a teacher, was married and had four daughters; Robin, the younger, was married but with no family yet. Both David and Edward had been educated at Sherborne School, Dorset. David was 15 at the beginning of World War Two, and joined the army on leaving school two years later. He joined the Inns of Court Regiment, driving tanks and armoured cars and doing radio work.

He was accepted as a candidate for ordination while still in the army. Fortunate in getting his release from the army as soon as the war ended, he went up to Selwyn College Cambridge in January 1946 to read theology, and then on to Sarum College Salisbury, and was made deacon in 1951. His curacy was in Yorkshire, at Brighouse, in Wakefield Diocese, and he was ordained priest in Wakefield Cathedral in 1952.

During this time Africa was in David's mind, thinking of the South Africa Railway Mission, but during his curacy he felt an increasing interest in theological education, and was keen to give some years to it at the start of his ministry. When he knew the UMCA (Universities Mission to Central Africa) was looking for just such a person, he was soon booked to come to Zanzibar Diocese. He started in a parish near Korogwe in 1954, and interestingly the parish priest was Father Yohana Jumaa, who 15 years later became the first Tanzanian bishop of Zanzibar Diocese. Two years in Tanganyikan parish life gave him the experience of country and customs, which he needed, and time for language study. After a short spell in England, he joined the small staff at Namasakata Theological College in Masasi Diocese. St. Cyprian's Namasakata served the dioceses supported by UMCA, Zanzibar, Masasi and Nyasaland as they were then. Later they were divided and the names changed. David's short spells at Minaki were times when he could be spared from the college to fill gaps, first in the very temporary theology teaching at Kalole, and later as chaplain to St Andrew's College, Minaki.

A Break in Our Silence

David was able to come over to Lulindi after he had made some of the arrangements about our plans and the wedding. He came over to see two of his students, Basil Sambano and Tito Mhando, who were doing a month's placement in our parish under Fr Lawrence Kasembe, by then our parish priest. We were able to meet at Newala, calling to see Bill and Pauline Murdoch and the children, Bill now at the Government hospital there. Our wedding was being planned for early August and that was only 5 or 6 weeks away, so we decided we could tell them the news. After suitable excitement and congratulations, it came out that they happened to have a finger gauge, so we could measure my finger, and David had one of his problems solved!

We managed only one other meeting before the wedding. Sister Marina provided David with a picnic lunch, very special of course as David had whispered our news in her ear. We met at the post office in Lindi, and were relieved that the ring had arrived! A picnic in a shady spot near the sea was all we had time for, and there was shopping to do to justify this break in normal routines. We also exchanged one or two letters by post, and one or two by hand. The friendly Asian with the 'duka' (village shop) brought one. With a suitable expression, and in a suitable tone of voice, he said, "It comes from Pottsi", which was evidently what they called James Potts. James would have been amused.

It was a relief when plans were fixed, and the uneasy silence could be broken. The date for the wedding was to be Thursday 11th August 1966. The bishop wanted it in the cathedral; he himself would celebrate the nuptial mass and also give the reception, and would invite everyone! At least, that is what it seemed like when I heard that, as well as missionaries, priests, the teachers and medical staff of the diocese, nursing students, Rondo students and many others were on the list. Fr Ronnie Cox offered to make the cake, and Canon George Faussett, the diocesan treasurer would give the bride away – most appropriate I thought. I suppose I had some say in all this, but perhaps only to agree, and anyway my chief feeling was gratitude to so many people for being so kind and helpful. Neither David nor I would have expected all this, but we were each well known in this diocese because of our jobs, and it would give a great deal of pleasure to people who had a lot of work and duties in their lives, and not much to relieve the daily round. Most would not have seen 'wazungu' getting married, and certainly not missionaries in the cathedral!

David was inviting a teacher, Paul Mhina from Minaki, whom we both knew well, to come down with his wife Grace; Paul was to be his best man. The Sisters from Newala were of course invited, but would be in retreat at that time, so Sister Marina would come to represent them, and would bring an orange blossom bouquet for me from their garden.

The plan was that after the wedding and a short time in England, David should join me at Lulindi for the year that I should still be needed there. He would be working with Fr Lawrence Kasembe, our parish priest; David would have a motorcycle, and would look after the five outstations in the villages round Lulindi, as well as helping with Fr Lawrence's other duties.

When I told Brenda that we were to be married she said, "You're joking!" But they were all excited when they took it in, and very pleased to hear that David would be at Lulindi for a year. The local tribe, the Wayao, were a matrilineal tribe so the custom after marriage was for the husband to move to the wife's village. So we were following local custom! In Western eyes it no doubt seemed strange for him to move from head of a college to curate in a rural parish! It was just what David wanted, to get him back into parish life.

Now that the news was out I could write to the USPG doctor, Margery Moncrieff, giving her our dates in England, and asking her to make arrangements for the operations on my hands during that time. My one remaining problem was what to wear. I had to give it some thought, as I always wore a very simple style of cotton dress and sandals. Fortunately I had a meeting to go to in Dar-es-Salaam before August, and should be staying with Lucy Crole-Rees, a musical friend, who lived in Dar-es-Salaam and worked with other musicians, singers, concert players, and anyone interested in music, to develop more musical activity in the town. She took me shopping, and we found some lovely turquoise Chinese silk, and started to make a dress. Soon she agreed to come to the wedding, to stay with us for a few days, and my share of making the dress became minimal!

A Diocesan Event

The day came, and with blazing sun as usual in August. Lucy's help had been invaluable. A cup of tea was all we could have before the mid-morning nuptial mass. The Lulindi contingent piled into the Land Rover, and I had to keep calm to drive safely the thirty miles to Masasi, with a stop half way there at Chiungutwa to pick up the mail. On arrival at Mtandi I changed into the dress, put on the headpiece which Lucy had cleverly made, changed shoes but forgot the stockings, and gladly clasped Canon Faussett's arm to proceed up the seemingly endless nave of our great cathedral.

The Swahili nuptial mass is beautiful, and of course the promises are the same as in English. The singing was hearty, unaccompanied as usual, and well known by the large congregation. Bishop Trevor and his assistants made sure that everything went smoothly, and then I found myself clasping David's arm on our way back to the west door of the cathedral. In Tanzania the custom is for the congregation to come out before the bride and bridegroom, so that they are ready to welcome them at the church door. As we appeared on the steps at the great west door of the cathedral the 'vigelegele' (spontaneous dance of joy) started, the women dancing and yodelling to celebrate the occasion. Photographs were taken, but the 'expert' who had kindly offered to use my camera, had no success. The pictures he took were all hazy and blurred! Others had done somewhat better.

It was now about 1 pm, so we were glad to be whisked off for breakfast, and to find that Ronnie Cox had produced a hearty bacon and egg, toast and marmalade spread with coffee, a rare treat, and just what we needed!

Out in the sun again, we found the guests seated round little tables, and being given sandwiches and snacks and soft drinks, so we wandered round talking to as many as we could. Called to join the Bishop and others, we were astonished when a real two-tier wedding cake was brought in. Father Cox had made it himself, and also supplied the pillars, 'building materials', bought on one of his expeditions to Dar-es-Salaam to get supplies for the diocese. Verity Bode, the domestic science expert at Ndwika, had done a truly professional job on the icing. Perhaps a few items like icing sugar had been included on the 'building material' expedition list. Speeches were not too long, the crowd dispersed, and we could relax.

Before leaving we had to make sure that plans for our time in England were complete, and especially for our return, which we hoped would be five weeks later. Also David made quite sure that we had marriage certificates which would be valid in England with both Church and State. For one thing I wanted to get my name changed, as in our circumstances there was no need for me to keep my maiden name. We were to spend the night at the theological college, before flying off for England from Lindi next morning. The Rondo Land Rover drew up, goodbyes were said, and we were off – but – clanking tins tied on at the back by the kindly James had to come off first! Soon we had to make a second stop for the driver and his mate to buy coconuts, or was it sacks of charcoal? Then we were really on our way.

A Honeymoon with Some Extras

First things first. My close family in England consisted of three first cousins, only one of whom I had had the opportunity to get to know at that time. So it was David's Uncle Blandford and Aunt Ina who came to Heathrow airport to meet us, bringing David's parents, elderly, and not able to drive so far as that. On our way to Salisbury, to 23 The Close which was still their home, Uncle Blandford was so busy teasing the 'newly weds', that he turned the wrong way into a one way street, and David was asked to take over!

Soon after our arrival, there was what seemed to me a huge family gathering of uncles, aunts, brothers and their families and cousins: just the sort of get-together that David's parents excelled at. How would I ever get to know who was who, except Gillian, cousin Franey's wife? She had a riding accident two years before, broke her spine, and was paralysed from the waist down. She was brought back to life and health at the marvellous rehabilitation unit at East Grinstead in Sussex, set up by the plastic surgeon Archibald McIndoe especially for the airmen who suffered terrible burns and other injuries during the Second World War. Gillian appeared for the first time in her wheelchair at a family gathering, so we were sharing the celebration. Many civilians have had reason to be exceedingly thankful that the East Grinstead unit has continued as one of many to develop this good work.

After a few brief family visits, we stayed in London with my friends Elsie and Freddie Hilliard for two or three days and got one of my carpel tunnels dealt with. Then we went on to the Hilliards' cottage in Norfolk for a week really on our own. My second hand was dealt with at the Norfolk and Norwich hospital where I had worked in 1944/5, but it was a second attempt. The first time I was turned back on the way to the theatre, because there was a scare about gas gangrene in the previous operation and I had to go back a week later.

Our return journey to Lulindi was via Geneva. A Swiss friend of David and his family gave us a weekend at a posh hotel in Geneva as a wedding present, and took us sight-seeing in town and countryside. I was glad of the opportunity to deliver by hand an application which was to go via the World Council of Churches to 'Bread for the World'. This was for support for a re-building project at our hospital in Newala, but sadly they were not able to help us. It was a relief that my hands were healed up and ready for action by the time we reached Lulindi. I did make a mental note to advise any young friends not to plan an operation on their hands during their honeymoon if they could help it!

Lulindi Again

How different life at Lulindi was now, even though it was the same place and the same job to be done. My little house was quite adequate; David had our guest house to use as an office, as we had few visitors. We had our main meals with the nursing sisters, and breakfast and tea on our veranda. David spent most daylight hours out in the villages, or at his other duties nearer home. These included hospital visiting, which staff as well as patients appreciated, and which he enjoyed. On Sundays I often went out with him to a village church. I soon got used to the back of his motorcycle, clinging on through fields and tracks through the bush, enjoying the outings and seeing the places from which our patients came.

Christmas was very special that year. It always is of course, and particularly in our hospitals, where I found that Muslims often felt free to join us in celebrating the new baby who meant so much to us. David celebrated the Midnight Mass at Nagaga, where their first church was nearly completed, and alright to use as long as it didn't start raining. It was a clear night so far, but it had a feeling of approaching storm, and a motorcycle can be a very wet form of transport! Carols were being sung when we arrived, mostly Swahili versions of our well known English ones, which Tanzanian congregations really loved. The worship had all the joy of Christmas, with a packed church and everyone in good voice.

As we came out, the clouds looked ominous, and was that a spot of rain? The vigelegele had started, and the women were dancing and yodelling, so we had to pause and enjoy it. When we did set off they danced after us. How David kept going and how I stayed on the back, I don't know, but we did. We arrived just as the first huge drops of rain were splashing down. We were very thankful to get under our thick cosy thatch, and get a few hours sleep before we were back in church for the early Communion service. Then I was back in the hospital seeing those who needed me and joining in the celebrations there, while David was out sharing Father Lawrence's many activities.

The evening was the time for some social life, with the customary invitation from Ndwika for one of Verity Bode's feasts. It was such an enjoyable evening that we managed to stay awake, but were thankful there were no hospital or other emergencies, and also that we could come away quite early. We didn't need any of Verity's special Milo drink to make sure we slept well!

Traditional Celebrations

A very different celebration six months later caused some anxiety. It was the time of the 'Jando', the traditional celebration of 'rites of passage' for the boys, their passing from boyhood to manhood. An enclosure was made in the forest in which the boys stayed for a month. During this time teaching was given and circumcision performed. An early bishop, Vincent Lucas, had taken a lot of trouble to study the teaching and ceremonies, and the meaning of it all, and then to create a Christianised version of ceremonies and teaching which would satisfy the village elders as a valid form of the rite, while excluding words and customs which could not be accepted by a Christian.

One morning as David and I were having our breakfast on our veranda, a very worried looking medical assistant came along. His problem was that some of the boys had developed a rash which he thought looked very much like smallpox. David was very aware of the problem this caused, as he and Father Lawrence had taken part in the teaching and the rites, and knew that the Jando was at an end. Within a few days, everyone from the surrounding villages would be coming for the final celebrations. Looking over to our guest house, I saw five little heads bobbing up over the low wall in front, behind which they were hiding. Going over there I found five little boys, wrapped in black cloths, shy and crouching down, peeping up from time to time to see what was going to happen. And what was going to happen seemed to be my problem!

Sure enough the rash was typical, similar to chickenpox, but larger in severe cases, and a lot on hands, feet and on the palate, which distinguishes it. To my relief it was the less severe form, variola minor, and the boys were not really ill. However an epidemic could start and evolve into the severe form, variola major, a dangerous disease even now with no satisfactory treatment.

The diagnosis confirmed, we were able to take advantage of the situation, turning it into a very effective vaccination campaign. We sent out notices via the local authority to all the surrounding villages, and to those running the Jando. It said, "Yes, go ahead with all your celebrations, with everyone welcome as usual, but every person coming through the gate will be vaccinated". Fortunately we had plenty of vaccine, and in those days all medical assistants and dressers and some nurses knew how to vaccinate, as it was routine for all babies at the MCH clinics, and for many others. All travellers by sea or air had to be done, and we ourselves always kept our certificates up to date. When in 1979 the World Health Organisation announced that smallpox had been completely eradicated we just couldn't believe it, but it seems to have been true.

Sadly it was not uncommon for epidemics of the minor form to progress to variola major, and we had two, or rather three fatal examples of that. A pregnant woman developed variola major shortly before delivery. The baby was covered from head to foot with the rash, and both died. She had not been vaccinated, but one of our staff nurses whose vaccination appeared to have taken well, also died, which was very disturbing. These in 1967 were the last cases of smallpox which I saw.

Our little thatched house was a haven of peace, that is, apart from the puss cat. She was called Frisby, because the American students had brought a frisbee to play about with, and I didn't know how to spell it. She had a will of her own. When she came to me as a kitten I used to carry her over to meals with me. When she grew up I stopped doing this which made her cross. One day when it had been raining, she agreed to go and ran ahead, scrambled up a small tree, and shook it all over me as I went underneath. When David came, unsurprisingly we used to sit together on the small settee, with comfortable room for two, but not for three. She would rush around, jumping on and off the furniture, and growl or whine until we made room for her – between us of course.

What of the Future?

The year was passing rapidly, and in the back of our minds was, "What next"? Would there be a place in Tanzania where we should both be useful? Or perhaps in another nearby country, though language would then be a problem at least for me? Could we know before going on leave, which was planned for August 1967 when the changes would take place in the hospital, and David would have had the year he wanted before being in charge of a parish in Africa? We just had to pray and wait, feeling sure that we should get the right answer.

By now the diocese of Dar-es-Salaam had been divided off from Zanzibar Diocese. It consisted of the town of Dar-es-Salaam and the surrounding area. John Sepeku, whom we both knew, was its first bishop. He wrote to ask David to go to Dar-es-Salaam as priest in charge of St Alban's Church and parish. St Alban's was the Anglican church in the centre of the town, which was at that time the capital of Tanzania until Dodoma took on that function. It catered for both English and Swahili speaking congregations, and also for the many Malayalam Christians from Kerala in South India.

The Malayalam Christians were enthusiastic members of the English speaking congregation, and they also had visits from their own pastor every month or so, with services in their own language and rite. As a branch of the Mar Thoma Church, they were believed to have been founded by St Thomas, when the Apostles spread far and wide to preach the Gospel.

St Nicholas' Church was being built on the western edge of the town, an area known as Buguruni, and was expected to be the cathedral, though some years later St Alban's took on that function. The diocesan centre was at Buguruni, with the bishop living nearby at that time, and also some CSP Sisters.

Bishop John had been asking some questions and wanted me to accept a post as surgeon at the 1,000 bed Government hospital, the Muhimbili hospital, which he felt sure I would be offered, as he thought that this could be a good witness to the co-operation between Government and Church, and I had always regarded that as important.

What a change this would be for us if we agreed. St Alban's was a large town parish, and included all the government offices, the embassies and high commissions, with their residences and the presidential palace. In the past the social life would have been too much for us, but it was dying down now. The university was flourishing, and there were schools and training schools, and the hospital with all its staff, students and patients. George Briggs had come up from the south two or three years ago as priest in charge and Father Paul Hardy had come from England fairly recently as chaplain at the university.

For me it would be almost too much of a change to come suddenly from being 'Jack of all trades' in a bush hospital, to turning back into a surgeon. The idea was good, and it had the added interest that the 1968 students would be the first to take their medical degree at the newly formed medical faculty of Dar-es-Salaam University. Previously Tanzanian students had studied at Makerere University in Kampala, Uganda. Now Tanzania would be giving its own MD, and I should be taking part in their final year's teaching.

After much thought we decided to accept the bishop's suggestion, and I put in an application for the job at the Muhimbili hospital. We should leave Lulindi in August 1967, go on leave until early in the New Year, and be ready to start work again by the end of January 1968.

We were thoroughly enjoying the year together at Lulindi. Next year would be very different. How should we get on as 'townees'? It would be a very interesting change to be at the centre of things, with many different nationalities around, and many visitors. We should have a big house in the centre of the town. What could be more convenient for a stopping off place for missionaries in transit or for visitors, especially visitors to the diocese? And so it turned out. We would need different transport too, two cars instead of a motorcycle and a Land Rover.

Meanwhile there was plenty for us to do at Lulindi, and at Mkomaindo things were moving forward. David and I had met Dr Bevis and Ann Cubey during our brief stay in England, and they would come early in the New Year (1967) with their two little children. Bevis had passed his FRCS. Frank Johnson, who had taken me to Alnmouth SSF Friary, was working for the equivalent in obstetrics and gynaecology, and so he would come six months later. Brian Wheatley and family couldn't come until early in 1968. The building work was progressing well, and the new intake of students were hard at work in the new nursing school.

It was sad to think that Lulindi's nursing school and hospital had to wind down, but I had to remind myself very firmly of what we had learnt at Minaki, that some good things have done their job, and then have to make way for something else. Here at Lulindi a health service would continue in the form of a rural health centre, run by medical assistants. The leprosy service would continue unchanged, with Francis Namkuwa in charge, as Brother Heald was leaving next year. Brenda wanted to stay on to run the maternity and child clinics, training others in that very important work.

The diocese planned also to use some of the hospital buildings to start a school for children needing special teaching because of disability of body or mind, limbs or brains. Up till then nothing had been done in this area of medicine. If these projects worked out well we should have no doubt that the hospital was being put to good use.

Good-bye Lulindi

I have always found it difficult to say good-bye to people, places, jobs, and the time at Lulindi was no exception, with the staff and the 'special' patients. Violet was one, the tiny baby with her birth fracture of femur, and the two amazing extra-uterine babies who did so well; the old man with the broken hip who used to cut all his strings down at night, but was reported to be walking well after only a few months out of hospital; and the chauffeur, who rushed round the car to thank me for his hernia repair twelve years before, not forgetting the elderly TB patient who tried to put two eggs into my pocket, when of course he would have done well to cook and eat them himself. Most of the names fade out, but the injury or disease, its problems and the patient's reaction to it, and the face or voice of some little thing they said, make them memorable and loved. It was a great joy for me and for the other hospital staff to have such a close relationship with many of our patients. To me it seemed a special characteristic of Lulindi hospital, and I hoped I could carry something of it on with me to the next place where I worked.

David had settled in quickly, although he was only at Lulindi for one year. The hospital staff appreciated his readiness to come to the hospital whenever we wanted him, or just to stroll round and talk to patients, and no-one ever objected to that in our hospitals, except perhaps the staff if their work was delayed!

The year of our wedding came to an end. With the usual round of parties, speeches, services, presents, some tears shed and promises to keep in touch exchanged, we set off for overseas leave. It would be England first to David's family, and then the United States. David would meet my close family, Alan and Joy and the two boys, Jim and Martin, for the first time. Bishop Trevor also had something of a programme for us on that side of the Atlantic.

Pamela Haynes, sister tutor, Lulindi Hospital.
Edith Shelley 1930-43 initiated leprosy care in Masasi diocese.

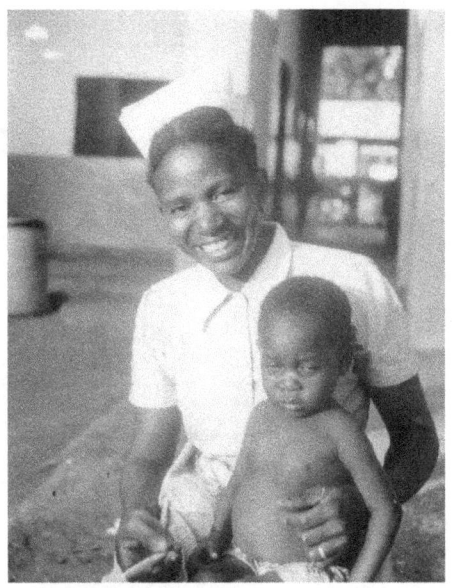

Staff Nurse Pauline with Edward recovering well from TB

*Brother Ronald Heald ('Bro') at Luatala dispensary,
clearing up after tornado, 1965*

Our wedding with Bishop Trevor, Paul and Grace Mhina

After the wedding at the Rondo

In Chicago, with a Lulindi-trained nurse doing an upgrading course

Bishop Trevor at St Alban's Rectory, Dar es Salaam. The crucifix was our wedding present from the RC Abbot Bishop of Ndanda

Canon Robin Lamburn and Mary Peake

*Dar es Salaam: Harbour with Lutheran Church;
St Alban's, now Dar es Salaam Cathedral*

Chapter 8
A Taste of Town Life

Home to Salisbury Close

Before starting at St. Alban's Dar-es-Salaam in January 1968, came our leave in England and America. Our arrival in England was less dramatic than the previous year, when our wedding had been only 36 hours before. Twenty-three, The Close was now really 'home' to me as well as to David. I was soon introduced to friends in the Close, including Harold Smith, then Warden of Sarum Theological College, which was almost next door. Harold was an excellent cook, as well as his many other assets, and I remember a delicious dinner there one evening in his attractive dining room furnished in deep purple and green.

But the horror for me was, that of all occasions, it was at Sarum College, when David was due to talk to the students about our work in Tanzania, that his back, which gave him a lot of trouble for most of his life, completely prevented him from getting up off his bed. Somehow I had to take his place, and by showing transparencies of our work in parish and hospital I averted total disaster, and the students were polite enough not to go to sleep or walk out!

I gradually got to know some of David's family, and we spent a few enjoyable days with Uncle Blandford and Aunt Ina in their country house near Salisbury. I also got to know Salisbury, the city itself and especially the cathedral, which we looked out on from our windows.

Soon our leave started to follow the usual pattern, visiting friends, visiting parishes to tell them about the work they were supporting in Tanzania. Plenty of sermons for David, kind hosts and hostesses, and perhaps too many occasions for cups of tea or coffee and biscuits!

Fred and Elsie Hilliard were now living in the country house near Norwich where my mother had been with them just before she died. It was during a later leave that we stayed with them in their holiday cottage also in Norfolk, when their daughter Sue, my god-daughter, married Anthony Hansell in the tiny local church. It was a brilliant August day, and the reception was on the lawn, among ripening corn fields.

That cottage has many happy memories for me, the outstanding ones being the days there during our honeymoon, then for Sue's wedding and three years later playing croquet on the lawn, with Freddie among the 'audience' holding little Peter, Sue and Anthony's first baby, on his lap. On another occasion David and I had stayed there on our own in winter, when the pump got too cold to work, so our water supply depended on smashing the ice on the water butt outside the back door. The equivalent in Tanzania, I suppose was that in one place our daily water supply came from an underground tank, and we had to dip it out with a tin on a string!

America

Then we were off to the United States, to Flint, Michigan, where Joy and Alan and their two boys, Jim and Martin were still living. It was high time for them to get to know my husband, and we really enjoyed that first meeting. They all cracked jokes when Alan passed me a handful of dollars, and I handed them straight on to David!

During the days in Flint we met various friends of the family and had some good outings, one to a nearby fruit farm which had a 'cyder press'. American 'cyder' is what we English call 'apple juice', and the boys had a great time pressing their own cyder to drink there and to take home.

From Flint David and I went on to Chicago to see our two nurses from Lulindi, who were doing up-grading courses there. This was one way in which American sponsors were supporting the work of the Church in Masasi Diocese, for which we were very grateful.

From there we went on to Wisconsin, Milwaukee and Fon de Lac Dioceses, spending time in Madison. During David's period at St Cyprian's Rondo they had received help from volunteers from these dioceses, and also from a group of secondary school boys, who came for a week or two and did some building work for the college. It was a help to St Cyprian's, and also a great experience for the boys. It also had its problems, like a trip to Lindi, that hazardous drive down the escarpment, for a ragwort injection, or even for an 'urgent' phone call – to a girl friend! There were plenty of people to meet who wanted to hear news of Masasi diocese. David had a succession of talks and sermons to give, and my transparencies came in useful. It was before the time when everyone expected more sophisticated ways of passing on news!

On our way back to Flint for a few days with the family, we visited the Benedictine Priory of St Gregory at Three Rivers. I had stayed there on a previous visit because of their link with Nashdom Abbey in England. Our last calls were to New York and Princeton.

In New York we had the pleasure of staying at the General Seminary, where a Tanzanian priest, Martin Mbwana, was a post graduate student. We both knew Martin well: David as a student at St Cyprian's for a short time; I when he came to Lulindi to have a small hernia dealt with before going to America. After Martin completed his diploma at the General Seminary he returned to Dar-es-Salaam, and was Warden of St Mark's Theological College. Soon he moved to England to take up a post with the Anglican Consultative Council (ACC). He and his wife Jane with their five (yes 5) daughters came to live in London, Kennington. Jane was a qualified teacher and was soon able to start work. Very sadly, before long Martin developed cancer and died after quite a brief illness. We loved and admired Martin, and he was someone who might have gone on to give a truly Tanzanian contribution to the ACC and to the Anglican Communion. Jane and the girls stayed on in England.

Our time in New York included Thanksgiving Day, and we were invited to Princeton by a young teacher, Barbara Huber, who had taught at Ndwika, near Lulindi, and was now living with her mother near Princeton. We travelled by train, and were met and taken to their home. Arriving at about 12 noon, we were not surprised when lots of drinks appeared, and also a lot of small snacks. Expecting a meal within an hour or so, I spun out my first drink as long as I could. Time passed, and gradually the afternoon went by. At around 4 pm we were ushered into a car, and heard that the festive meal was to be with friends, and we were expected at about 5 pm. It was a good thing that David's diabetes had not made its sudden appearance until almost 20 years later! The friends welcomed us to their lovely home; more drinks were offered; the phone rang from a party: "On the way"; more phone calls – "Getting nearer" – and finally the front door bell! At around 7 pm we sat down at a very long table. At each end was a huge turkey, and I was to see for the first time an electric carving knife doing its work. The table was laden, including large bowls of different varieties of cranberry sauce, and many other delicacies. English as well as American plenty continued to be something of a 'culture shock' to us, though it was not until later (at Kwa Mkono) that we ourselves were faced with real shortages of basic supplies. The shock on that evening continued when apple pies and pumpkin pies appeared, and plenty more besides.

A late train took us back to New York and the seminary. Next day we saw more of Martin Mbwana and went on to the Episcopal Church Centre, to talk about the links which were being made between them and some of our dioceses and projects in Tanzania. A brief visit to the cathedral was all we had time for before our flight back to England.

Our leave was passing quickly, and soon we had to be on our way back to Dar-es-Salaam and our new work. There were still a few jobs to do and people to see, and we had to have some time at home in Salisbury. We had already bought a Volkswagen Beetle, which James Potts had been using while on leave. He sent it off, hoping it would arrive not long after us. I should need it for work or David would waste a lot of time taking me back and forth. There were no mobile phones by then, and no doctor could keep to set 'working hours'. Dad was elderly and unwell when we left, and very sadly he died quite soon after we had settled into our new home. As we were kissed and hugged and sent off to our plane, Dad had stuffed my pockets with sweets, and David's with cigars!

Starting Our New Venture

St Alban's Rectory, near the church, was an attractive building to look at, but as a home it was awkward! A two storey building, it had a covered way along the front, with four doors leading into the building. First on the right the door led into the kitchen; the second led to quite a large dining room; the next led to the parish office/David's study; then came our front door to the stairs up to our home area. There were four bedrooms in a row along the back, a bathroom at each end, and a long space along the front. This was closed in with criss-cross burglar wire only, and was our sitting-room area. Outside was an inconveniently shaped four-way road crossing, which added noise and dust to the wind and rain which entered freely. We realised that taking the last bedroom with bathroom, which could be curtained off, was our best hope of privacy.

With our two large bedrooms available, and the smaller third if needed, we were a haven for travellers, which made life interesting, and justified having our cooking and housework done for us; we seldom sat down for a meal on our own, and afternoon tea soon became 'open house'. Missionary visitors came to town for a few days shopping or meetings or just passing through, as well as visitors to the diocese, and 'youth' were starting to back-pack round the world at that time. We did sometimes heave a sigh if we saw several large back-packs approaching the house, especially if all we were feeling like was supper and sleep! One back-packer was Colin Galloway whom David knew, and he had earned his ride from Zambia on a lorry carrying copper for export through our harbour and docks. He had shared the driving of this huge vehicle on the long and hazardous road, and we were secretly relieved that his parents knew nothing about it until he arrived safely, and could phone them to say he had reached friends. The TANZAM (Tanzania-Zambia) railway was being built by the Chinese during our three years in Dar-es-Salaam, so before long he would not have had that opportunity. The railway gave Zambia much needed access to a sea port, and Tanzania a source of income.

'Government Surgeon': Will it Last?

The Muhimbili hospital in Dar-es-Salaam was built in the 1950's to replace the old Sewa Haji hospital named after the Arab who had built it. Opened by Princess Margaret, the hospital was named after her, but naturally that was changed after Independence. It was a thousand-bed hospital, well staffed by local standards and developed further over the years, with more beds and more facilities introduced. In retrospect I think it was mainly a PR exercise in co-operation between Church and Government. Bishop John Sepeku, soon to be Archbishop of Tanzania, was a much respected leader, and his suggestion, perhaps request, that Church and State should work together in this way would not easily be ignored.

I enjoyed the experience of working in a large hospital with staff of very mixed nationalities, and also seeing something of how Government ran its institutions. Being surrounded by final year medical students on ward rounds, in operating theatre, classroom and outpatients was enjoyable, and made especially interesting by the fact that they were the first final year students who would receive an MD from Dar-es-Salaam University. Previously there was no medical faculty at Dar-es-Salaam, and most of the students for medicine went to Makerere University in Kampala, Uganda.

My post at Muhimbili lasted only a year. It was a period of intense africanisation, when those without Tanzanian citizenship were being, quite understandably, replaced by those who had, if they were available. Unfortunately it led to some nonsenses! The newly appointed first African matron of the Muhimbili had her appointment cancelled, as did her husband, a doctor at Medical Headquarters, because they were Malawians (previously Nyasaland) and had not taken Tanzanian citizenship. I was replaced by a dark faced Indian, born and brought up in England, who had never been out of England, or so I was told. Happily he was a good surgeon. I had several times been invited to join one of the few general practices in the town, so I accepted an offer from a Scotsman with his partner, a nice young Pakistani doctor. The Scot soon returned to the UK, and the two of us could cover the work.

I was able to keep my hand in by doing some simple surgery at the Aga Khan hospital once a week, which was an expensive private hospital, catering mostly for Asians. The practice which I had joined did sessions on contract for the dock workers, so most of my work there was repairing dock workers' hernias. Standards were high in that hospital, and I enjoyed working there.

The period of general practice was an interesting experience. I met people of many different nationalities, mostly from the Embassy staff and their families. The aid agencies often had their own medical care arranged. A few of our patients were 'old boys' of St Andrew's College Minaki, who had done well and were in good jobs, and greeted me with surprise as "Dr Phillips". One exclaimed, "I know who you are, you're Dr Phillips and you are married to Father Bartlett". Anyone who had worked at Minaki for 12 years would be recognised by teachers, medical workers and others from all over the country.

I took my turn for being on call for the practice, so I had to learn my way round the town, or at least the 'better parts' of it, where people could afford to call out private doctors. A number of our patients were Indians and Pakistanis, working as clerks, teachers and shop-keepers, the latter being the well-off ones. I had no control of course on the amount which we charged. Dar-es-Salaam diocese had no medical work at that time, or no doubt I should have been offered to join that.

The Parish

My time got pretty full, as I was also learning to be a housewife, hostess and rector's wife! David's responsibilities in the central parish of the capital city were of great interest to both of us. There were many nationalities and many religions, representing aid agencies, embassies, traders, professionals and others, as well as all the local people. It was also a time of refugees from all around us. Ruanda and Burundi were in turmoil, South West Africa (now Namibia) was hoping for Independence, ANC (African National Congress) members from South Africa were having to get out of the country to make their plans. Added to this the Biafran war in Nigeria affected us. A number of Nigerians on both sides were working in Tanzanian towns, and they, as well as Biafrans studying in places like Russia, and elsewhere in Europe couldn't go back home, so they stayed on or came to Tanzania until the war 'at home' was over. The Chinese, men only, were a very noticeable presence, working on the Tan-Zam railway, and also helping Nyerere's plans in medical and various other work. Much of what they did must have been of value to developments in the country.

Our contact with staff and students from the University and Hospital was mainly with those who worshipped at St Albans on Sundays. We had an 8 a.m. English Eucharist, with the main mid-morning Sung Eucharist in Swahili at 11 a.m., which was well attended, with a full church and a very mixed congregation. Evensong was in English, with hymns and other singing if we could get someone to play the organ. Swahili has no such problem and responses, psalms and hymns are sung heartily with or without organ, drums, band or whatever. When a diocesan synod debated whether local instruments should be used in worship, the Tanzanian priests voted 'no', the Europeans voted 'yes', and this included drums. My feeling was that local people connected local music, especially drums, with old customs which they didn't want brought into church.

The Malayalam Christians (from Kerala, South West India) came to the English services, and were keen Sunday school workers.

Dorothy Barlow was the only white face seen regularly at the Swahili services, and she sang in the choir. She had a secretarial job, and was in some way not bound by regulations, communicating with her relations in South Africa and even travelling there when the border was closed. She lived out her time after retirement in her little house in Buguruni, near St Nicholas' church.

Marriage Laws

During our time at St Alban's, local African women were beginning to get into higher education, and a few into responsible jobs, mainly I think in Government service. In the home I fear that few had any sense of 'equality', and women were becoming more conscious of this. As the marriage laws were being debated in Parliament it was a time for demonstration through the streets. Leader Stirling was in Parliament by then, and he and his young Tanzanian wife, Regina, with their toddler son, Kaspar, were staying with us. Regina had friends in high places, including Government. At least one of these joined the demonstrators, carrying a banner, 'One Man One Wife', and she was was one of a Government Minister's two wives. Regina was making anxious phone calls, hoping that her friends wouldn't get into trouble.

The marriage laws were passed, with a good outcome. Now marriage certificates had to state unequivocally whether the marriage was polygamous or monogamous. It seemed to us the best that could be expected in a country with people of different religious beliefs about marriage. We didn't hear of trouble for Regina's friends when they got home; did they hide the banner, or did they keep it on view?

Sadly Regina died of cancer not long after. Then a close Tanzanian friend of Leader's got killed; he jumped off the back of a Land Rover when it stopped and it backed into him. After a few months his widow, Anna, and Leader were married. Anna was a complete contrast to Regina, older, and a stately lady whom Leader treated with suitable deference and they were just right for each other. Leader and Anna stayed on with Anna's extended family until

Leader was well over ninety. They were ardent Roman Catholics and Leader's funeral was on a national scale in the Roman Catholic Cathedral in Dar-es-Salaam. As well as Government and other dignitaries, priests, monks and nuns came from all over the country to honour this remarkable doctor.

An International Celebration

Soon after we settled in at St. Alban's came the news of Martin Luther King's death. St. Alban's was the place for a memorial service, so David had to work out a Swahili/English celebration, drawing in as many people as possible. It was Saturday, and the service was to be on Sunday afternoon; service sheets were needed, and some of us would be getting our hands stained with purple, running off copies by hand on the duplicator. The problem was, no paper. As I was not on call, I was the obvious person to go out and look for some, with some money, ours I guess, in my hand. I searched the town with no success. However I saw a very good bargain in curtain material in a shop, and we badly needed a large cheerful curtain to give some privacy between our long thin sitting-room area and our bedroom and bathroom. So I was really in luck; to my relief some paper turned up from somewhere, and the service sheets got printed.

The memorial service for Martin Luther King, celebrating his life given to equality and freedom, was the first of the great gatherings during our three years in Dar-es-Salaam. Everyone wanted to be there. Tanzania's relationship with the United States was delicate during that period. They were not best pleased with us for being so friendly with China. Nyerere's policy was to get ideas, advice, and in some cases help from many different countries, with their different policies. His aim was to build an African socialism, suitable for Tanzania. He always stuck to his Catholic Faith, and that would keep him from going too far in the Communist direction, which the Americans feared. A senior diplomat at the American Embassy had taken the trouble to learn some Swahili, and he used it by taking part in the service, which helped the truly international atmosphere of the gathering.

It was in 1970 that Tanzania, formerly part of the Province of East Africa became an autonomous province of the Anglican Communion and our Bishop, John Sepeku became our first Archbishop. That great ceremony and gathering took place at St Nicholas' Church, outside the West door, with 'everybody' there, including President Nyerere. I was sitting just behind him, and David, of course, was robed and involved in the ceremonies. Archbishop John was a great leader for the new Province of Tanzania.

The provincial headquarters was set up at Dodoma, 300 miles inland, and soon to become the capital of the country. Dodoma was also the headquarters of the diocese of Central Tanganyika, which during the coming years was divided into many smaller dioceses. All this inland area was supported by the Church Missionary Society (CMS). Becoming a separate province would give the Church some new freedom in development and also encourage closer co-operation between the areas supported by our Mission (now 'USPG') and CMS.

Some International Experiences

Dar-es-Salaam was hot, humid yet often dusty, noisy and crowded, but our life there was extremely interesting, and we much enjoyed having the opportunity to meet people of so many different races. At church, the Malayalam Christians were always well represented. Keen, friendly Bible Christians is my memory of them. Among the Nigerians and Biafrans (as they preferred to call themselves at least while the war was on), some preferred English worship, while others enjoyed the choral Swahili services. Europeans and others from the University usually preferred English, either the 8 a.m. Eucharist or the English Evensong, which needed an organist, because 'Wazungu' for some reason can't sing unaccompanied in church. Embassy people and those from aid agencies had the choice of the Roman Catholic Cathedral of St Joseph or a very attractive Lutheran church which looked out over the harbour.

At the hospital we had staff of many different nationalities. At one rather notable night emergency when I was on call, my registrar was Egyptian, the anaesthetist Polish, the house surgeon, a Biafran trained in Russia. The patient was a casualty among the Chinese railway workers who were at that time building the TANZAM railway from Tanzania to Zambia. He had a neck injury causing complete paralysis from the neck downwards so he needed urgent relief. The Chinese Embassy at first refused the operation, but later in the night agreed, provided that the Tanzanian senior surgeon was present in the theatre. Why didn't I go back to bed and leave it to him? But the Medical Superintendent said, "No, your team must do it, you are on duty!"

For me, with China so prominent in my background, it was tantalising that we had no opportunity to get to know any of the Chinese. Even a Chinese patient was not allowed to speak to a white person except through an interpreter. It was the Chinese authorities who prevented it, and it was a rare opportunity missed for showing friendliness.

On our first Christmas day in Dar-es-Salaam we had an international lunch party, all refugees. From South Africa was an African National Union (ANU) member, who had been in trouble there. From South West Africa, (now Namibia) was a student fresh from studies in the United States, who complained in a rather snooty accent, "These flies, don't they bring disease?" I wondered how he would get on when he could go home. My Biafran house surgeon couldn't go home until the Biafran war for independence from Nigeria was over. He knew Russian but no English or Swahili, and practically no surgery; it seems that Russian medical trainings vary enormously, as a Rwandan medical registrar trained in Russia was very well thought of; he came to lunch bringing his Russian wife who was an engineer. She kindly offered to help with the washing up.

The conversation during and after lunch between these young people from different countries, each in the middle of its political turmoil, was quite encouraging. They were enjoying the opportunity of talking freely together about problems and possibilities in a calm and reasoned way, and not put off by ourselves. They were clearly really looking for solutions which could bring peace and prosperity to their countries, and it was well worth listening to.

We did our best with the social life which David's position required, and managed to give the occasional fairly formal dinner party. Most of our full tables were friends and fellow missionaries, visitors to the diocese or parish, and others for whom no formality, just a good meal, was needed. Conversation was varied and never lacking. At tea time the dining-room door was never shut, and there were always plenty of cups put out, and scones or cake while they lasted. I got some amusement from our male visitors, especially missionary clergy. Many would say, "Oh I never eat tea, just a cup if I happen to be in". It was remarkable how often they were in, or 'just passing', and how quickly the scones disappeared! Friends from the town or university also called in so we tried to see that at least one of us was around at tea time.

Robin Lamburn and the Kindwitwi Village Project

Canon Lamburn was one of the really special Masasi veterans; David knew him already, and I got to know him while at St Alban's. His long period in Masasi had included St Cyprian's College, Namasakata, where he had taught and been responsible for the curriculum and teaching methods in the past, as well as time at the headquarters at Mtandi. For a time he had been Chief Scout for the country as had Leader Stirling. When we reached Dar-es-Salaam in 1968, Robin was 100 miles inland from Dar-es-Salaam in the Uluguru Mountains, doing something in the scouting world. However as well as a priest, he was a bacteriologist, and took a great interest in leprosy, both from the compassionate and the medical point of view. He was now taking an active part in its prevention and treatment, and the welfare of sufferers from this dreaded disease.

The border between Dar-es-Salaam and Masasi Diocese is the great Rufiji River with its formidable delta. Kindwitwi is a village just south of that river, not far inland, with an old style leprosy settlement for those who were not wanted by their family and home village. Utete District Headquarters was not far away, and gave them some minimal support, and the District hospital would supply what drugs were available while they needed them.

Father Lamburn had his eye on this village, and, retiring from Masasi Diocese and from USPG soon after I arrived in the diocese in 1962, he gave the rest of his life to developing that village as a centre for leprosy work in the difficult delta area of the Rufiji. In 1968 Robin moved to Kindwitwi and settled there, with sufficient funds available to take over the village and get started. The aim was to give people who came to stay there sufficient funds to get a house built, plant some crops and make it their home, becoming independent as far as their condition would allow them to. For some their stay might be temporary, but for many it would be their home for life.

Twenty-five years on, when he died in harness at Kindwitwi in 1993, the village was flourishing, with a small hospital for the few really sick patients, and a village with better facilities than many others. In 1993 a support system was set up, the Rufiji Leprosy Trust (RLT), based in England and also active in Tanzania. Many volunteers, including young people from overseas, have spent time there, and thoroughly enjoyed giving help with development projects, including building, teaching, especially English, setting up a library, helping and advising about physiotherapy. There is also close co-operation with the district hospital and its leprosy programme. It is encouraging that the International School in Dar-es-Salaam has always been a strong supporter of Kindwitwi Village.

The Outreach Team

Outreach to this whole area is an essential part of the work which Fr Lamburn took on. Many of those who have started leprosy treatment at Kindwitwi can later go home to continue their regular tablets and other care if their family and village agree. So clinics must be set up and visited regularly by a team of leprosy workers. The first duty of the team will be to teach everyone, old and young in the whole area:-

i) That this dreaded and feared disease can be cured if sufferers attend early for diagnosis, followed by regular treatment.

ii) That the common skin patch type is not infectious: the nodular type, normally on the nose and face, is infectious through close contact, but not after treatment is established.

iii) Everyone's confidence must be won, so that people with suggestive signs do not hide or get hidden away, or even worse expelled from their village. Instead they should be encouraged to come quickly for diagnosis and treatment.

Because of loss of feeling in hands and feet, great care must be taken to avoid injuries, and every day the hands and feet should be examined for injuries which would not have been felt, especially after what can be dangerous occupations like cooking or using a sharp knife for the hands, and walking with or without shoes, and even rats nibbling the toes at night if not well covered. The team must include provision of special well-fitting footwear, made individually, usually from old motor tyres.

Early recognition and treatment is the only way to complete cure, and all this work is done in close co-operation with the District Medical Officer as part of the Nationwide Leprosy Project. It is particularly hard work in the Rufiji Delta area, where during and after the rainy seasons the journeys are done by canoe and foot, rather than bicycle and Land Rover.

Although he was a keen boy scout, Fr Lamburn couldn't swim, but that didn't stop him from canoe travel; this would have been worrying, especially at his age, if there had been time to think about it!

Kindwitwi has always seemed part of my life, although we never found an opportunity for a visit. I think there were two reasons. The first was Robin himself, with his wonderful vision and dynamic personality, put into action in the long post-retirement stage of his life. Rufiji was a largely Islamic area, and the village and all its work was open equally to people of both religions, as was all our medical work, but here it affected the organisation of village and social life. Second was my great medical interest in the disease itself, and the fear and dread and cruelty that surrounds it. The progress from the witch-doctor's efforts, through rubbing with chalmougra oil, to modern drugs and research, and also modern surgery when required, was quite remarkable. How long before we could say, "No more leprosy!"?

Visitors

Robin was a fairly frequent visitor to us at St Alban's; others from our Masasi days included Kathleen Beresford-Knox and Verity Bode from Ndwika on their way to the UK, Maurice Sosileje, who was Assistant Bishop of Masasi at that time, and taught at St Cyprian's, and on the first page of our visitors' book I see the names of the two St Cyprian's students, now ordained, who had been at Lulindi during our secret engagement period. Basil Sambano was later made Bishop of Dar-es-Salaam, and Tito Mhando was one we kept up with until his retirement to his home in Kideleko. Bishop Trevor's name appears three times during 1968, the last on his retirement to the UK.

Leader and Regina Stirling appeared quite frequently with or without their son Kaspar, and a couple whom we got to know well doing leprosy work in Government service, Harold and Pat Wheate. Harold was running Chazi Leprosy settlement, about half way between Morogoro and Korogwe. Harold ran it on thoroughly good lines, but without the freedom to make it a long term project for those who needed a home. They retired before we did, after a spell at the great leprosy centre in Addis Abbaba. They were extremely kind to us later, meeting our plane at Heathrow and taking us to their home near London for a few days when we arrived on leave with no family members in England who could do the welcoming.

James Potts is a name that recurs over the years, and other well-loved priests, nurses and teachers from Masasi diocese, like George Briggs, Ronald Cox and George Faussett, and Brenda Stone, who had stayed on at Lulindi after it became a Health Centre. I must also mention Franciscans from Hilfield in England, CR Fathers from South Africa and Mirfield, as well as the occasional CSP Sister who was not staying with the Sisters at their house near St Nicholas' Church.

St. Mark's Theological College

It was during our time in Dar-es-Salaam that the Theological College moved from Rondo in Masasi diocese (where David and I had made our momentous decision) to Dar-es-Salaam, to a site in Buguruni near St Nicholas' Church and the diocesan headquarters. Our friend James Potts had the job of organising the move, the reasons being related to the site on the Rondo Plateau, a lovely place, but rather far from everywhere else! It was complicated and expensive moving students from their homes with their wives, families and possessions to St Cyprian's. The site moreover was in the middle of a Roman Catholic area, and so it was not suitable for students to get experience of parish work without another move. Another reason for moving to Dar-es-Salaam was to be near to the University, with the possibility of co-operation, and for experience of town ministry, most students coming from rural situations.

With James Potts as its first Warden, St Mark's Theological College Dar-es-Salaam came into being. However, the need was seen by Bishop Huddleston for continuing theological training at St Cyprian's, Rondo, especially for students from Masasi Diocese and from the old Nyasaland Diocese, now being divided into several others. So St Cyprian's has continued on a smaller scale. Now a 'Junior Seminary' or Boys Secondary School has been set up there, to which some Community of St Mary (CMM) Sisters have also been admitted. A collection, taken up at the installation of a window at Lancing College Chapel, Sussex, dedicated to the memory of Bishop Trevor Huddleston, helped to fund the CMM Sisters.

What Would Come Next?

David and I had always felt that our time working in Dar-es-Salaam was short term and that our place was somewhere rural. Some quite experienced missionaries were saying that the time for 'wazungu' in villages was over, now that many Tanzanian priests were available, but we saw the value of a scattering of expatriates within a diocese, and found that at least some Tanzanians, including the bishops, felt this too.

Naturally I was keen to get back into church medical work. At Magila hospital in Zanzibar Diocese (now called 'Zanzibar and Tanga') Dr Ursula Hay was in charge, the doctor who had welcomed me to her hospital at Liuli on Lake Nyasa (Malawi) and even to her operating theatre. She had spent 10 years running Liuli hospital with outreach to the hilly and difficult country near the Lake, then moved to Kideleko and Handeni, and on to Magila. There she had a busy maternity department, a larger general hospital with more surgery than she wanted, a nursing school, and still no second doctor. Added to all this there was a major project in hand to build a much more up-to-date hospital and nursing school at Muheza, the market town and District Centre 3 miles from Magila. This hospital would replace both Magila Church hospital and Muheza Government hospital under the new 'Designated District Hospital' agreement with Government, which basically said, "You do the work and we will provide the money, but first you get it built". Clearly Ursula needed another doctor if she was going to do all that.

Magila was the place where, in the early days of UMCA, the Church in Zanzibar had sent a mission to carry the Gospel to Tanganyika, making a base to spread over a very wide area. The hospital and nursing school buildings were old; repair and modernisation were not options because of limited space and problems with sanitation. The parable of putting new cloth into old garments came to mind; also the market town of Muheza was far more accessible to the district than Magila. Muheza Government hospital had similar problems, though 'only' 40 years old, but put up then as a temporary building.

Magila had grown from an initial dispensary towards the end of the 19th century, and was gradually built up to its present form under the care of the Community of Sacred Passion (CSP). The first professions to the Community were made in Zanzibar in 1911. In 1923 the Community moved its Mother House to Msalabani, Magila, and took over the dispensary and its developments. Working with them was usually a doctor, at one time Dr Walters, skilled in leprosy work, and later Dr Dulcie Adkins who was there during much of my time at Minaki. The bishop of that diocese was Yohana Jumaa, who had been David's parish priest when he came to Zanzibar Diocese in 1954. He wanted to divide Magila parish, making a new 'Muheza parish' centred on the market town and district headquarters.

At a meeting of the Diocesan Finance Board, of which Ursula was a member, someone said, "What we need is a priest married to a doctor," and Ursula responded, "Bartletts".

"Bartletts" were quite excited when they received Bishop Yohana's letter of invitation. It sounded just right to us, and the more we thought about it the happier we were. We felt that we should really enjoy taking part in these developments. It would give David the chance to put ideas, built up over his period of teaching, into action and it was a challenge which I think he felt ready for. I too was happy, assuming that Ursula would be in charge, now that I had the added responsibility of home and marriage, especially as it was to a parish priest. When the time came we settled happily at Muheza and got to work, for me developing the surgical side of things, as well as sharing in other departments, and taking some strain off Ursula; for David buying a motorcycle and exploring his future parish area. But soon after our arrival early in 1971 Ursula dropped a bombshell; she was planning to move out of clinical medicine and had accepted an administrative job in Dar-es-Salaam.

The Tanganyika Christian Medical Association (TCMA)

In my early days in Tanganyika I had been very much involved in the Mission Medical Committee (MMC) and its activities. This developed into the TCMA, which was a more formal body, better able to act on behalf of the different Missions and Churches in the country, including Roman Catholics. Ursula would be full-time secretary, and the office would be in St Alban's Rectory, when various alterations were made there! It was hard for me to see how someone could move from clinical medicine to administration. I was always fascinated by the structure and function of the human body, and its amazing struggle to put itself right in illness and injury. We struggle to help it, backed up by others with their ideas and research. Also God is with us, even though often we can't understand how he acts, or why he sometimes allows 'everything to go wrong' however hard we try. Let us hope that we understand and do our best in the part each of us has in treatment of the sick and injured, and in keeping people healthy.

People

There is so much more one can say about Dar-es-Salaam, with its traffic, noise and bustle, people and nationalities, religions and social life. Here we met and got to know many 'wazungu', especially those who came to the English services; elsewhere there had been few white faces, and later, when we white people rode past on our motorcycles, the children would stand on the bank by the roadside and call, "Wazungu, wazungu ...".

Josephine and Robert Sharpe were a couple of 'wazungu', whom we kept up with in England, where he was involved with the

Thames Water Barrier System. Another Public Works couple, in the Electrical department, moved to Hale, a small village between Muheza and Korogwe when we were at Muheza. At Hale there was a very important hydro-electric plant, and as manager it must have been promotion for him, though to a very isolated place, unknown until the use of its river made it known far beyond Tanzania. The river ran a long way underground, with a lot of rock above it.

We were soon invited to dinner there, and as we still had the car we could go reasonably well dressed, David in his long white kansu, the cotton garment which Muslim and Christian clergy wore. Imagine our surprise when after an extremely good meal, we were offered, no, not liqueurs and coffee, but to see round the works!

We were led out to a building where there was a lift and not much else. In the lift we went down and down, and kept on going down. Eventually we got out into a huge chamber carved out of the rock. Around the walls were pipes and cables, flow meters and electric meters, and much other paraphernalia (as I remember it from nearly 40 years ago), and sitting in one corner was a little man making himself a cup of tea with his electric kettle. We were then taken to the entrance to a tunnel in the rock, along which we crawled and scrambled (but how did David control his long garment?) not very many yards until by crouching over an opening at the end, we were looking down into a raging torrent, the river. Evidently they had not yet heard of 'Health and Safety', and fortunately I had no posh dress, but motorcycle garb would have been more suitable. It made an interesting and quite unusual evening.

I was reminded of an event in childhood, when Alan and I were taken on a tour of the Gas Works in Norwich, near our home in Norfolk. I must have been small, as climbing round a huge noisy building on hot metal stairways (don't tell Health & Safety about that either) I was scared, though of course not able to show it because the manager who was taking us round was our great friend Mr Austin. My other memories of Mr & Mrs Austin are delicious tea parties round their log fire at Christmas, and in summer, picnics of the same very high standard on the Norfolk beach.

Among the many Tanzanians we got to know in Dar-es-Salaam was Dr Sam Ndimbo, who had replaced Ursula Hay at Liuli. He was studying obstetrics and gynaecology at the Muhimbili hospital. Later he was ordained priest while still in charge of Liuli hospital and outlying medical work. Augustine Ramadhani, a nephew of John Ramadhani (who was later to be our Bishop and then Archbishop and personal friend), was studying law at Makerere University, Kampala. He soared high in the legal profession, and was Attorney General Zanzibar in 1980 when we went over for the centenary of the Cathedral, and later Chief Justice of the Republic. We knew him first as an almost self-taught organist, having a few lessons in Kampala, and practising on the organ at St Albans during his vacations. Later we met him in Zanzibar, where he came whenever he could to play for services in the Cathedral.

Stanley Lichinga, another of our Zanzibar contacts, tells me that David baptised him in Dar-es-Salaam while we were there. In Zanzibar he appeared as a highly intelligent and conscientious, and rather hyperactive catechist. If a bicycle dashed past our open front door and seconds later a voice called "hodi" (may I come), to which the automatic reply was "karibu" (come), it was sure to be Stanley. I met him again in 2008, in Hereford, where he had come for meetings at the time of the Lambeth Conference, to which I had also been invited, because two priests from the Tanga area whom I knew would be there. To my surprise there was Stanley, now a priest, and representing St Mark's College, as the warden was unable to come. We were both staying with the kind and hospitable Hazel and Walter Gould, who were very much involved in the links between Hereford Diocese and the Tanzanian Church in the areas where I had worked.

There were of course many others, but I must mention a Biafran couple, Mr & Mrs Ajamagobia, employed in some high up United Nations capacity. They had lost many members of their family during the Biafran struggle for independence from Nigeria, their home being in the border area, where they were attacked from both sides. This couple were keen to enter into everything that was going on, and their eldest son and daughter came to David for teaching before confirmation. Their mother insisted on helping at a parish jumble sale, not realising what she was letting herself in for. Being put on 'the gate', this stately well-dressed lady was to be seen struggling with the mob of people who were trying to get out with their arms full of clothes, while she tried to see if they had any receipts!

Later we were invited by the Ajamagobias to a dinner party, and this time we too had to be well-dressed, David in his wedding cassock. At dinner a huge fish was served, and the service was supervised by the eldest son, with several waiters in attendance. After dinner the men were shown into the sitting-room, while the ladies were invited by our hostess to her smaller sitting-room. After a while the teenage son appeared and said politely, "May I join you Mother?" There we struggled in a mixture of Swahili and English (some guests knew neither) and time passed. We continued to struggle and time continued to pass. Was this a Biafran custom? What would happen next? Who had to make the move?

Finally suggestive sounds came from the men, polite good-byes were said, and with obvious relief the ladies followed suit. On the way home I heard that the senior guest, who was no less than the Tanzanian Ambassador to China, had fallen asleep, and clearly no-one would think of waking him up. I realised too that this was no other than Eliya, the very intelligent student at Minaki, who when asked by Miss Fisher in class, "Are there any questions?" had replied, "Miss Fisher I have not understood a word you have said".

Farewell St Albans

Now we had to pack up and fly to England for leave. It was only our personal things, some for England and some for Muheza when we returned, as until then we had not had to buy our own household things or furniture. As I had had an income, though relatively small, we should be able to get those when we got a house to put them in, and somewhere to build it in the new parish of Muheza. My relative wealth would allow us also to build a very comfortable little house, including the essential small guest room and a study/office for David.

By the time we returned and stayed with Paul Hardy at St. Alban's, the house as well as ourselves had had some changes. Paul Hardy was parish priest, and his kitchen was at the top of the stairs where the guests' bathroom used to be, with the dining-room taking over that end of the sitting-room. A shower was put into the first guest room; then Paul had the other guest room as his bedroom, and 'our' bedroom as his study. So the downstairs rooms were available for use as offices, including the TCMA office. When time allowed during our visits to Dar-es-Salaam, I was happy to do a turn in Paul's fairly modern kitchen! But home leave was the next thing on our agenda.

England and our Families Again

Leave was the usual round of visits, meetings, sermons, shopping, and also a chance to get a bit of time on our own. Much as we had enjoyed the busy town life, the people we met, and the activities of St. Alban's, and our activities while on leave, it was good to get away from it all sometimes. The Hilliards' cottage in Norfolk gave us just such a break, as did Sue and Anthony's house in Norwich on another occasion.

On reaching England we went straight to Somerton in Dorset, as David's mother had moved there when his father died in 1968. She was sharing an attractive cottage with Robin, David's younger brother, and his wife and their little daughter Tamsin. Gladys, Mum's long term trusty helper, had come with her so we knew that she was well looked after.

Next we had to go on to Uncle Blandford and Aunt Ina, those who had brought the welcoming party to Heathrow Airport to meet us after our wedding. Theirs was a lovely country house not far from Salisbury, with golden pheasants and peacocks strutting round in the grounds. Others of the family were not far away, so we went on to Auntie Gladys in Mere, and cousins scattered in the country around. On our last leave we had called in to see Edward, David's elder brother, and his wife Susan and their four daughters living in Ely, the girls I think all still at school. This time their home was at Ibberton, Dorset and the girls rapidly growing up.

Instead of visiting America this leave, Alan and Joy had arranged to come to England to see us, and to go on to see cousins and various of their friends. We booked bed and breakfast for them at the pub in Somerton for a few nights, so that they could meet as many as possible of David's family, and specially his mother and brothers. We had bought a second-hand, rather large and unwieldy Ford car for use while in England, so we could take them round a bit, and then on to their next destination. For us the car was useful for our list of parishes to be visited, and among those visits, to make sure we saw friends like Fred and Elsie Hilliard, and Timothy and Edith Fox.

We were glad this time to have a few days with Frank Clouting, my General Practitioner cousin, and his wife Billie, in Ancaster, Lincolnshire. As well as medicine Frank and I shared a great interest in the flora and fauna around us. Billie was an excellent hostess and cook. During the war, when Frank and I were medical students in London (he several years ahead of me) we used to meet at his father's house (my Uncle Charlie) in Kew. After a good lunch we would go off to Kew Gardens. For a few pence we spent hours roaming round the gardens, with their fresh air, green grass, an enormous variety of trees, shrubs and flowers, birds in the trees, and on the various stretches of water. Always more to see next time, like the greenhouses and what lived in the water, which was Frank's special interest.

Frank's father, the architect, working in Edinburgh at the time, had lost his wife in childbirth when Jim and Grace were small. A lovely Scottish lady, Miss Hunter took over care of the children, and soon became known to all as 'Wee Mum'; she continued to look after the children in Scotland during the war, when Uncle Charlie's job brought him back to the danger zone of London. Because of this his eldest sister, Aunt Minnie came from her Sevenoaks flat to housekeep for him, and her flat was available for my mother when our house in Norwich was bomb-damaged. That is how the flat in Sevenoaks was available as a bunk hole for me during the London blitz, for an occasional weekend, and longer when we were firebombed out of the School of Medicine and awaiting re-location to Exeter. Just some of the complications so common in wartime.

Jim joined the Merchant Navy in his teens, and was at sea at times when I might have met him; Grace, the youngest, was doing research into grasses for animal feed when I next had a chance to meet her briefly in Cambridge. It was not until Jim had retired and settled in a cottage in Cornwall, and Grace was cattle farming on Dartmoor, Devon, that I got to know them.

Time to Return

Knowing that we could leave Mum in caring and capable hands, David and I now had to turn our thoughts back to Magila and Muheza, parish and hospital, and building projects for them both. We knew that at first we should be living in a disused, semi-furnished house in Muheza. It turned out to be two: first a small and rather over-furnished one, and then a large empty-looking one, both intended for the research team working on malaria in Amani on the hill above Muheza. I should have our Volkswagen Beetle to get to Magila, while David would enjoy equipping himself with a motorcycle to get round the parish. With the usual mixed feelings, sadness at the farewells, especially to Mum, but quite a touch of excitement about our new ventures, we set off for Heathrow, and our flight back to Dar-es-Salaam.

Chapter 9
Magila and Muheza

Another New Venture

Our plane landed in Dar-es-Salaam in May 1971, and we were soon off to St Alban's after a few formalities at the airport. There were a few necessary visits to make, especially to discuss with Archbishop John Sepeku the jobs which we had been asked to do in Magila and Muheza. For one thing we needed his support with the application for suitable land on which to build Muheza Church Centre, and also for the new hospital complex and nursing school, including enough space for future developments.

Soon we were packing our things into the VW Beetle, filling the tank and spare cans with petrol, and setting off for the 200 mile drive on a reasonably good road, part dirt, part tarmac, to Muheza. Ten years before when two nursing sisters and I were leaving Minaki, it would have been 400 miles via Morogoro, Handeni and Korogwe. An old switchback road which I had rather unwisely travelled once before, had recently been opened up between Chalinze and Segera. Lack of funds for upkeep had been as usual the problem.

The beautiful country around Magila and Muheza I have described in Chapter 3 when Paddy Shiel and I did a tour of the medical work in this diocese. The tribes we were most aware of here were the Washambaa from the mountains, and the Wabondei in the lush farming area in the valley. To the south, round Kideleko and Handeni are the Wazigua, cattle people, with miles of bush and low trees, and clearings between them for their crops. All this is within Tanga Region and in this diocese, now named 'Zanzibar and

Tanga', formerly just 'Zanzibar'. Shortly after we retired from Tanzania, Tanga and Zanzibar became separate dioceses.

On reaching Muheza we turned left (north) off the Tanga road, and leaving Muheza market town on our left, we passed what we hoped would be the new hospital and church sites on our right, and the old Government hospital on the left. Going on about 3 miles up the sandy, rocky track we reached Magila. I was glad that David was driving the VW over those stones. I soon got very tired of driving over them, often several times a day, or night, and he sympathised with me wanting to be 'promoted' to a motor-cycle. In a car it was almost impossible to avoid hitting the bottom. A few years later my kind brother provided me with the money to buy a neat little Honda motor-cycle. On David's advice the diocese was using the Japanese Honda and Suzuki Trail type motor-cycles, higher off the ground and so easier to manoeuvre on rough ground, and with plenty of gears. The Honda was a good friend until once again I no longer needed daily transport to work.

As we entered Magila village, on a hill on our right was Hegongo. This used to be the diocesan headquarters until that moved to Korogwe. Now Archdeacon Michael lived at Hegongo, and also some of the hospital staff. Later it became dormitory accommodation for a boys' secondary school which took over redundant buildings when the hospital and convent moved away. Looking out over Magila village and the main part of Magila hospital from Hegongo hill gave an impressive view of Magila parish church and the convent of the Community of the Sacred Passion (CSP) silhouetted against a back-drop of the Usambara mountains. Both are attractive stone buildings, the church with a large crucifix in front, as its dedication is 'Msalabani' – the Place of the Cross. The convent was the original mother house of the Community when the sisters moved here in 1923, and is a two-storey building with cloisters, built round a well kept garden bright with flowers.

Beyond the convent, and seven minutes walk from the main hospital was the maternity hospital. Communication between the two was a nurse with a note, and I was soon comparing it in my mind with that between Newala and Lulindi (see Ch. 6). There it was a man on a bicycle, 18 miles of escarpment and then sandy or muddy lanes, with the Land Rover to take us all back to Newala.

The nursing school classroom and hostel were tucked in between the convent and the track to maternity. Just one classroom was needed as most nursing and midwifery were taught in wards, operating theatre and other parts of the hospital. The nursing school, like both sides of the hospital was feeling its age, which of course was why we wanted to re-build at Muheza. Little did they know what beautiful new quarters they would have when eventually that great day came.

On arrival at Magila we soon found Dr Ursula Hay and were welcomed by her and the CSP Sisters, and also by Archdeacon Michael. He was an elderly priest, looking forward to retirement to his home not far off and his 'shamba' (fields). This came about not long after, when in this area rural deans, later called 'area deans', took on the duties of archdeacons, and David was made rural dean of Magila area. This included Magila and Muheza and four or five other parishes and their out-stations. We already knew many names of these, and of missionaries and Tanzanian priests who had worked there in the past.

Settling In

Returning to Muheza we found the house which had been rented for us near Muheza district hospital, and settled in, grateful for some supplies already on the shelves. The house had been used by research staff of the very active Malaria Research Centre at Amani, in the foothills of the Usambaras, just above Muheza.

Our temporary home was conveniently situated, only five minutes from the old church or 'synagogue', as we called these tiny out-station places of worship. It was on one side of the market place. By road David took five minutes on the motor-cycle. There was also a footpath which crossed a valley and the railway line which linked Tanga and Moshi and passed on into Kenya. So by foot it took no longer to reach the synagogue and market place. (When my American nephew visited us he was fascinated by our steam trains.)

David would spend a lot of time on his motor-cycle on roads and tracks through field and forest in parish and deanery. The VW Beetle did its best to stand up to my bumpy three mile journey by day or night, until I was able to borrow a simple bicycle type Honda 90 which had no clutch and therefore easy to learn on. The town had a marvellous market, which supplied many of our needs, but it was soon to be reconstructed, and our little church replaced by a bus stand, making a new church somewhat urgent. We spent most of our first year living in Muheza. Then a new house built at Magila for a medical assistant, was available for us to live in for 6 months, giving us time to get ours built at the new church centre.

Magila Hospital

The life of a doctor in different Christian hospitals in the same country has many similarities in the daily round and in its aims. High medical standards as far as circumstances will allow are of course at the centre, and also to show God's care for all. This includes patients and their families, staff, students and all workers of whatever race, tribe or religion, and especially the helpless and derelict. Here at Magila there would be differences for me from my previous hospitals. With different surroundings and local customs, different climate and crops, different students and staff, there would be plenty that was new, and this would be so too for David in the parish and deanery. We both needed to get settled in quickly and get to work.

Magila hospital had always been run by nursing sisters of the CSP, and their nursing standards and devotion to the job were marvellous. Many of the sisters at Magila had long experience, especially of midwifery, often being able to teach a doctor a thing or two, for which this doctor was often grateful. In our situation we doctors were expected to have all the answers, from "Does this patient need an urgent operation?" to "The Land Rover tyres are worn out, where can we get new ones?" Tanga 25 miles away was our shopping centre, but shortages were serious at that time and even a trip of 200 miles to Dar-es-Salaam might not be successful.

Naturally I compared Magila with Lulindi. I soon realised that neither I nor the CSP Sisters could spend such ridiculously long hours in the hospital, which I took for granted at Lulindi, as did Brenda and Pamela, and Helen with her beloved babies and small children. The Sisters had their convent duties, and I lived three miles from the hospital, and had a husband and home to consider. Of course there were plenty of emergencies taking precedence over all our other activities.

The hospital was well planned and well built in its time, though parts were wearing out with age. It was however divided into two parts, general and maternity, with the convent in between. To call the doctor to an urgent maternity case, when she was doing a round in a general ward took a nurse with a note seven minutes, and for the doctor, when found, ten minutes or so to change jobs. Ursula gave me a warning: never refuse an offer of a cup of tea, coffee or whatever, on the grounds that you are going for your lunch. If you do you will get stopped on the way and called to do an urgent job, perhaps a long one, on the other side of the hospital.

Ursula's New Job

This advice was perhaps a warning of Ursula's bomb-shell soon after our arrival. She had accepted the offer of an administrative job in Dar-es-Salaam, starting almost at once. Was she tired of the stresses and strains of routine clinical work, or of the responsibility of running a hospital, where shortage of funds was not the only problem? When I heard what the job was I realised that it was one which she couldn't refuse. She had been asked to accept the post of secretary of the newly formed Tanganyika Christian Medical Association (TCMA).

Ursula and I were both well aware of the importance of the Association, which would now be responsible for liaison between Churches and Government in planning and policy, staffing and financing of medical work all over the country. (Medical services in

Zanzibar and Pemba were under different administration.) This would be a paid job, but would give her time for other useful activities including membership of the Nurses Examination Board, which set standards and a policy for the various nursing courses. She would also be on the leprosy co-ordination committee dealing with national leprosy policy, and co-operation with world-wide leprosy missions, and projects like Kindwitwi village set up by Robin Lamburn and his supporters.

With twenty years experience in Tanzania, ten of them right inland on the eastern shore of Lake Malawi (Nyasa), and ten in the Tanga Region, Ursula was very well equipped for the job. Even I had to admit that losing her from Magila was justified by the importance of maintaining the close co-operation which we had always had between the churches' medical work and that of the health ministry. The old Mission Medical Committee had done such a good job under the early leadership of Dr Mary Gibbons and Dr Leader Stirling to create and encourage this relationship. I too had been deeply involved in it ever since I arrived in Minaki over twenty years previously.

But for me it certainly was a bomb-shell. When David and I had received the invitation from Bishop Yohana Jumaa (see chapter 8), both jobs had to me sounded just right. For a priest in mid-life who had been training priests in Tanzania for ten years, what could be better than to have a new parish to develop together with the possibility of doing more training, and for us both to have a new church to plan and build?

For me too it had seemed just right. Some of the pressure would be off. While keeping up my clinical medicine there would be the opportunity to develop the surgical side, and this seemed to be much in demand at Magila. So we had accepted Bishop Yohana Jumaa's offer with enthusiasm. We thought that we had made my position clear, realising that being slightly older than Ursula and with longer service in Tanzania, I would be considered 'senior' to Ursula, and so would want to be in charge. (See chapter 8, 'What would come next?) Now I should find myself in that position. Our new bishop had a favourite saying on such occasions – "God moves in a mysterious way" – but I was not sure that it was relevant here.

Surgery, Gynaecology and Obstetrics

I enjoyed my surgical work at Magila in a well set up theatre, and with Sister Jacqueline in charge much of the time, with several very competent staff nurses taught by her. S/N George Kimweri was prominent among those, and later had the opportunity of 'upgrading', making him eligible for promotion to nursing officer by the time we moved to Muheza. 'Kimweri' was a prominent name in tribal leadership in the area, so leadership in hospital would easily be accepted by local staff and patients and also, I was sure, by people from other areas.

I sometimes felt that 'obstetrician' would have been a more suitable qualification for me than 'surgeon', especially at Magila. Ruptured ectopic pregnancies were prominent in our operation register, as were hysterectomies for alarmingly large uterine fibroid tumours. On the midwifery side were the caesarian sections, which for some reason so often turn up as night emergencies!

A rather alarming day was when not one but two women were brought in who had a ruptured uterus during a delayed labour. This is always sad as the baby dies and the mother is at very severe risk, especially in our circumstances. Distances and delay in getting transport and the difficulty in getting blood for transfusion always make it seem miraculous when the mother survives. To our great relief both these women survived a difficult hysterectomy in spite of their severe shock.

Another day a woman was brought in who had bled so much during an obstructed labour that neither she nor the baby had any pulse on admission. We couldn't get any improvement in her condition, so I had to operate, and somehow she survived a caesarian, though of course with no hope for the baby.

Not long after this we had a day when I really didn't know how our system survived and kept producing what was needed next. We had a small staff, all sterilization had to be in little autoclaves on primus stoves, and the supply of instruments, gowns, gloves and drapes (sterile towels) was limited – to put it mildly! Somehow Sister Jacqueline managed to see that the two nurses who would assist were ready, one to assist me, one to look after the instruments, and that we had what we needed when we needed it. The morning brought a poor blind lady who knew little Swahili, and had with some persuasion from her relatives come for the removal of a huge fibroid uterus. It was an ordeal for her under spinal anaesthetic and hard work for us. A few small booked items followed.

Before long came first one and then a second ruptured ectopic pregnancy, with alarming internal bleeding. These as usual produced some dramatic moments, one going into heart failure on her way back to the ward. We always collected the patients' own blood from the abdomen and transfused it back into a vein, which supplemented any donor blood we could get, and this I'm sure made a big difference to the patient's recovery and to our survival rate.

That may not sound like a heavy day to you for surgeon or theatre staff, but remember the conditions: it's hot, there's no air conditioning, the lighting is quite good but not excellent, attentive nurses are the surgeon's assistant and scrub nurse, but there is no other doctor in sight or on call, and the surgeon is expected to be a specialist in whatever problem turns up.

I for one often felt far outside my comfort zone. There were plenty of sad times when situations were beyond our means, but also we had the thrill of sending many home, well on their way back to health.

A small but popular operation was the repair of in-turned eye-lids. These were the result of long untreated trachoma eye-lid infection, which scars the inside of the lids so that the lashes turn inwards and scratch the cornea of the eye. This caused a lot of pain and gradual loss of sight. Prevention is by cleanliness and fly control, and by early and persistent treatment with tetracycline eye ointment if the trachoma gets started. A simple operation is possible under local anaesthetic, which can be relied on to give a good result, but there is often residual damage to the cornea causing some permanent interference with vision.

Communications

When we got our own house in Muheza, the 'phone was put in at once so that I could get calls from Magila hospital while we were still working there. It was a great blessing, especially at night. The Muheza telephone exchange was a tiny room at the post office, staffed from 8 a.m. to 8 p.m. by a girl who sat there pushing plugs into the wall. At 8 p.m., if she remembered, she connected our line to Magila hospital, so we could just lift the receiver and talk. That covered calling me to go, as well as asking advice or reporting on progress of very sick medical cases and especially very sick children, and was often used when I was the only doctor. Of course if the girl forgot it would again be a man on a bicycle with a note.

When my transport was a motor-cycle some of the sisters became anxious about my safety at night, but I took the attitude that most people around Muheza knew that I was 'Mama Daktari' and if anything happened to me they lost their doctor!

On one late evening call when a caesarian operation was needed, but fortunately not a very urgent one, I arrived to find the theatre full of white ants. There had been a flight of them, and our windows were evidently not ant-proof. The poor mother lay on the operating table for almost an hour while we all struggled to clear the place and get started. Fortunately she was not distressed, and the baby came out kicking and screaming to the relief of all. As I came out of the building I found the relatives, excited and happy of course to hear the good news of mother and baby. They were sitting on the steps roasting the white ants for their supper – a delicious smell, but I didn't try one.

Men as Well as Women

Men were not neglected. Hernias were the commonest item in our operation register, mostly men, and the men's medical ward was always crowded. Waterworks problems were common involving prostate enlargement as well as urethral strictures. For prostates I had to use the old method for a variety of reasons. It was the method which I had learnt at my first job in Norwich. Even so the success-rate was reasonably good. Men were going home happy and advising their friends to 'give it a try'. Lack of transport or money and anxieties about the treatment were some of the reasons for serious delays in turning up at hospital. Blood donors were difficult to come by, and might well be needed, and plenty of things could go wrong. Many of these patients were Muslims. A conversation at the bedside when they understood the dangers, might end with them saying to me, "Tuombeane" – Let us pray for one another. The often repeated saying, "Mungu ni Mmoja", God is one, could often mean: We Muslims believe in the One God, while you infidels pray to three gods. Here I felt sure that they meant, "Let us both pray to the One God whom we both worship".

Hernias came in all shapes and sizes. The very large ones were always a bit daunting, and the small ones too could have their complications. One such patient gave us a surprise. He had developed sudden and very severe pain more than 24 hours previously, but distance and transport difficulties caused the long delay, by which time this otherwise strong healthy young man was very sick. We were able to have him quickly on the operating table, and a spinal anaesthetic at once relieved his pain. As the operation progressed I thought that the tense bulging hernia sac felt 'funny'. Pressure needed to be released quickly, and I could see that the bowel inside was gangrenous and would need resecting. Great care was needed not to let it rupture first.

For a Jack-of-all-trades surgeon, a gut resection is quite a challenge, but to my relief it went well, and the man returned to the ward in good form. Good nursing care is then vital, with careful control of fluid intake, and very gradual return to anything solid by mouth, but with no setbacks he was on his way home before long. In opening the sac after the operation we found that the funny feeling was because the sac was full of little hard things, similar we thought to damson or sloe stones. Then the story came out. Thirty-six hours before we saw him, the patient had been out in the forest with a hunting party. They were hungry, and a fully laden zambarau tree gave them the chance of a refreshing snack. Zambarau fruit is very like damson or wild plum. The hungry hunters didn't bother to spit out the stones, just swallowing it all, and with no problems except for this unfortunate fellow.

Just one more story of night calls, and one with unusual features: I was still using the car, and it was away for repairs, so when the customary call came in the night from maternity, David soon had his trusty steed ready for action. Half way to Magila we found that our dog Sally was trailing us to find out what her master was up to. Reaching the hospital, David and Sally went to the office which had an examination couch where David settled down. I didn't know what Sally got up to. Over in maternity we got on with bringing another baby safely into the world under a local anaesthetic of course, and with a happy mother I'm glad to say. Then David and Sally and I set off for home.

Not far out we met a taxi, a very rare event at Magila. We dismounted and found that it was carrying a man with waterworks problems. Hoping that the medical assistant on duty would be able to cope with this problem, we continued on our way. But not far on Sally decided that she was too tired to go on, so she got a lift on my lap, somehow sharing it with my medical bag, and neither was exactly small!

Reaching home, and just as David was putting his motor-cycle into the garage (his office) the phone rang: "Please would you come and see a patient who has just come in with retention of urine?" We left Sally firmly locked into the house this time, and we got home just in time for David to get ready for the 6.30 Eucharist.

Relevant to all the midwifery stories, you may remember that it was at Magila that I launched out into doing caesarian sections under local anaesthesia, thanks to Sister Olive Marian and the Chinese Doctors at Newala. (See chapter 6.) It saved us a lot of anxiety in the busy maternity department at Magila.

A Rather Hyperactive Children's Ward

Lulindi was not the only hospital to have a happy and very active children's ward. Staff nurse Judith Mnkondo was special on the nursing side. A degree in nursing would have been quite beyond her, but her love and care of the little ones was something in itself to teach and inspire the young student nurses. An equally caring CSP Sister had general charge of the ward.

Chest and tummy complaints and malaria were the conditions which threatened many lives of the infants and toddlers at Magila. Meningitis occurred of course, but nowhere near as commonly as at Lulindi. Malnutrition was I think not such a problem as at other places where I worked. Steam tents for babies with severe coughs were popular at the time, though somewhat dangerous, as a charcoal stove and kettle were often the source of steam. Small boys (and even girls) climb trees, so fractures were not uncommon. The ward could look quite interesting with 2 or 3 make-shift tents in place for the bronchitis and other chest cases, and legs slung up from beams or 'gallows' for several broken legs. Soon we benefited enormously when Dr Ken Wilkinson and his wife Barbara joined us for two years. Ken was a paediatrician par excellence, never so happy as when bringing a dying baby back to life and health. He was also a highly-skilled and willing handyman, ready to come at a moments notice to 'fix it'. Whatever 'it' was, bent, broken or just not working, the answer was "Call Ken".

When we heard that Barbara was a Spanish teacher, we thought, "Oh dear!" but soon realised how wrong we were. Barbara too was multi-skilled and willing. Amongst other things, the student nurses needed help with their English, struggling with our difficult language in text books and in national exams. Barbara's English classes were of great value for them. She was also often to be found in surprising places doing something really useful, and certainly not limited to Spanish or even to teaching.

Other doctors came and went, giving a few months or up to two years of very useful service with their different skills. One such was Elspeth Martin, who gave two very good years. She could turn her hand to most things, specially to children's and medical wards. She needed a bit of help and encouragement at first when called for surgical or midwifery problems. Later came Gillian Webster, older, and with a lot of useful experience. She also enjoyed the children's ward, and was a specialist on the medical side, so I was really glad of her particular skills. Gillian was a Methodist, with missionary vision guiding her life. After two very useful years with us, she went on to a Methodist hospital in West Africa before continuing similar work in England in London.

Dr Stanford and His Wife

By June 1972 Dr Andrew Stanford (who died in 2011) and his wife Margaret, a newly qualified nurse, arrived from England. They came by sea, with plenty of luggage, which was a good sign that they intended to stay, and stay they did for five years. During that time Margaret put in some periods as a staff nurse, but was also occupied in starting their family. Mark and then Salome arrived safely with the help of the CSP maternity service, and to the joy of all around.

Andrew was active in all departments of the hospital. Skilled at giving anaesthetics, he was also eager to pass on his skills to other members of staff, if spinal or local anaesthetics were not suitable. For me that was a great relief, and of even greater value was his willingness to take charge of the hospital after about six months getting used to us.

The Muheza Hospital Project

By 1973 Sister Greta, who had already retired from nursing, came back to the hospital as administrator, and settled in to a newly set up office. Andrew was taking over as doctor in charge so while still active in the hospital I could give time to our big project. This as described briefly in the last chapter was a further step in co-operation between Church and State medical services, made possible by the new agreement between the two sides. Some districts in the country had no district hospital, and in others like Muheza, the existing one urgently needed replacement. With Magila and Muheza only three miles apart, it was clearly a more economical use of resources to build and run one new hospital than two. In most places where a church or mission took advantage of the agreement, it was simply, "You (the church) provide the building, and we will provide running costs". In our case the government would also supply one quarter of the building costs. We should take on all the duties of the district hospital including out-reach to the district, and for this the district medical officer (DMO) would join our staff, as well as some of the staff from his old hospital.

To find the remaining three quarters of the building costs, Ursula with the help of the Christian Council of Tanganyika had applied to organisations known to us as ICCO and EZE, of Holland and Germany respectively. They were responsible for distribution of the church tax in those countries, which was used to support overseas aid projects. ICCO and EZE had agreed to our project, pending the approval of their respective governments, and both seemed confident of getting that if our government agreed to take it on.

Knowing that our bishop as well as the CSP Sisters was really keen on the new hospital, the health ministry was the final hurdle, and from them there was silence. We were all becoming very aware of shortages in the country, and rapid devaluation of the currency was causing plenty of problems for the government as well as everyone else. Ursula in her new capacity would represent all church medical work, ours as well as that of everyone else, in discussions with the health ministry. She would be aware of the desperate need in isolated parts of the country for better medical services. Perhaps the time was not ripe for our project; perhaps the two old hospitals would have to struggle on for a bit longer. We might need the much used word 'bado', not yet.

Then suddenly the anxiously awaited agreement from the Ministry arrived, including an intimation of the piece of land which would be ours. This was to be a sizable piece of an old sisal estate just across a stream and a stretch of waste ground from the new Muheza church centre. Relief, excitement, and thank goodness Andrew had settled in so quickly and was prepared to take charge at Magila.

Muheza Parish Church of Christ the King

During this anxious time in hospital plans, those of the parish were moving on. In 1972, when David and I were living at Magila for six months, he received permission to go ahead and develop the piece of land quite near the old Muheza hospital, as a church centre. The church would be three or four hundred yards up a slope from the main road, and there would be plenty of land, part of an old grapefruit estate. We made good use of the crop which it still provided while we were living there. Our first job was to plan the site and build a house for ourselves, as the one at Magila would soon be needed for a new medical assistant. A local mason and carpenter would build ours pretty quickly, while a firm from Tanga would be needed for the church and church hall.

It was quite exciting to be planning and building the first house which would be our own, with our own furniture and fittings. Built by local people, it needed just a ground plan and agreement about height of walls, windows and doors, and building materials. The choice for these was between cement blocks and mud bricks dried in the sun which were cheap but not so hardy. Later we learnt of a compressed brick made of sand, soil and lime, and this, if the proportions were right, was hard and long-lasting. It was very useful for later projects at Kwa Mkono, near Handeni in Zigualand, when cement was becoming very expensive.

Our house was built in a few months, but even so we had to move in with the front door held in place with a large box (hinges put on next day) and with the gas cooker in the living room, as the kitchen was still under construction.

Our plan worked well. At the front were our living room and David's study, with a tiny veranda, soon to become home to Sally the dog. We should have a telephone in the study and a hatch passing through to my bedside. A small guest room, with two beds and a chair and not much room for anything else and a tiny bathroom completed the picture. Guests had to be warned to pick up the rubber bath mat before opening the door after their bath; it would stick on the mat if they forgot as it opened inwards, and they would be locked in. The tub bath was emptied onto the slightly sloping floor, and the water passed out through a pipe set in the wall. A few paces outside the back door there was a small kitchen, for which I managed to get a sink with draining board. Water was from a tap outside. When we moved to Kwa Mkono ten years later we took with us everything including the kitchen sink! We had the luxury of electricity laid on, so we could use an electric fridge instead of the usual temperamental paraffin (kerosene) one; we also had a small gas cooker, as we could get gas cylinders quite regularly.

Our house would be used by the new priest-in-charge when we moved on, until a larger family house could be built for him. During my 43 years living in Tanzania, 12 years in Muheza was my record for having electricity laid on, water out of a tap, and the use of the telephone. While still living at Magila we had the joy of sitting down after supper to plan the church, church office, vestry and parish hall, feeling it to be a privilege as well as a responsibility. From our new home we should be able to watch this being built, and later see across to the new hospital and nursing school.

In her Will my mother had left me most of what she had as I was considered to be the needy one of the family. She would have been delighted to know that our 'need' was to build the Church of Christ the King at Muheza. With our plan worked out, we discussed it with a recommended building firm in Tanga. Soon they were in action on the chosen site, already cleared by some enthusiasts from the parish.

The building was 'U' shaped, the church 60 feet long on one side, the parish hall 30 feet and narrower on the other, and vestry and office forming the base. Thirty years later the church needed enlarging; Sylvester Chizazi, by then ordained deacon and still in charge of the nursing school, was one of those involved in planning the enlargement and raising funds. During those years a small village had grown up between the church centre and the road, including some of those working at the hospital. In 1972 my mother's £10,000 had paid for the whole building. By the turn of the century, more than that would be needed just to enlarge the church.

David celebrated the first eucharist in the new church on Palm Sunday 1973, with a painter at one window getting his job finished as we processed round with our palm branches. A week or two later Archbishop John Sepeku came from Dar-es-Salaam to bless the whole church centre including two houses now finished, ours and one for a future curate. Now the second house would be used by Christopher and his wife and two children. They were Masasi people, and joined us in Dar-es-Salaam, where our flow of visitors kept him busy with the housework. Here Christopher would be 'cook general', including the marketing and local shopping.

The archbishop was from a family of our area, and had at one time been parish priest of Magila, and later a suffragan bishop. He had come on the Saturday afternoon to bless the whole church centre, including the two houses. Fortunately it was fine and many parishioners joined in the celebration, processing round and singing hymns, following the archbishop, priests and servers, all fully robed. On the Sunday, when, as well as consecrating the church, a large confirmation was planned, some of the candidates lived too far away to come in the tropical deluges we had at that time of year. Crowds did come, delighted to have a new church and to have Archbishop John, a popular figure, to bless the church – although some people would have to wait now for a new confirmation date. The excitement of having our new home, planned by ourselves, and built by a mason and a carpenter whom we knew, sank into the background after these big events.

A Hospital and Nursing School to Build

Looking back at my balmy childhood days of country vicarage life, the garden with its flowers and fruit, the farm activities especially riding the huge farm horses, who would then have believed that I should be faced with building a 200 bed hospital with nursing school, staff housing, kitchens and all accessories? I certainly wouldn't and my brother Alan would have laughed! Now in 1973, married and after 24 years in Tanzania, I realised what an enormous difference it would make having David's help and support. Our two projects, parish and hospital were closely related: parish life, with its prayer, worship and activities, supplemented by the service and witness of the hospital with out-reach to the area and its training of the young.

Now that we had the Government's official agreement we had to go into action. Our first move was to visit Dar-es-Salaam to see the general secretary of the Christian Council of Tanganyika (CCT). It was he who had negotiated with ICCO and EZE when Ursula started to work on the projects, and could now advise about architect and builders. But before we even got to see him our car was broken into in Dar-es-Salaam, and it was in the 'good old days' when one didn't expect cars to be attacked in public in broad daylight. As well as the spare wheel, my brief case was taken with all the early correspondence in it about the project, which by then I had hardly had time to look at! That was the first of many disasters.

Reaching the CCT office we found that the recommended architect as well as the general secretary were expecting us. We took this as a way to save time and trouble, but with more experience we should have recognised hints in the conversation to show a red light. Later we discovered that the architect who had been chosen for us was well known for his skill at making money for himself and his friends from his clients. We had made it clear that, as is well known for such projects, money would be in short supply. We needed plans for strong buildings, convenient for staff and patients, not expensive fancy ones for show, but found that the opposite was being done. The pleasant and helpful Indian architect of the firm who was put on the job knew nothing of medical planning or of special needs like taps as a simple example. In operating theatres and other places, taps are needed under which hands and forearms can be washed without touching anything and with water neither too hot nor too cold. Anyone who knew anything about hospitals must know this, but it had to be explained several times. Once grasped, tall mixing taps appeared everywhere including the smallest handbasin in staff and student accommodation! Sad to say it seemed that this was an early example of the corruption which was creeping in, and here it was among the Christian community.

I soon realised that I should need to make a trip to Dar-es-Salaam to watch progress every two weeks or so. It emerged that the draughtsman who was doing the drawings was a well-known schizophrenic who was making irregularities in his drawings; wards would have windows of varying sizes, again increasing the costs unless they could be corrected. Before long he had a complete breakdown, and treatment was difficult to get. My experience in 'bush hospitals' was not going to be very useful in designing a modern hospital, and having an uncle who was an architect wasn't much help either.

So far we had not been given a map to show the area allocated to us for this medical centre, and no-one seemed to know where we could get one. The health ministry couldn't supply one and nor could the district office. We couldn't find detailed maps of the area in shops, so we went to the office of the Department of Lands and Mines in Tanga. Surely they would know which bit of their land was to become our property. "Oh no", they said, "we have no map, but if you bring us one we will show you where to build." "Could they tell us where to buy a map?" "Sorry, we don't know", was the reply.

The following Sunday afternoon David and I and Sally our dog set off to the area which we wanted and thought had been allocated, any previously supplied information having of course been lost with my briefcase. We paced round, counting out loud, hoping that if we met anyone, "Arobaini na sita" (forty-six) would sound like a friendly greeting. As we went I kept some sort of record, and sketched out a map when we got home. Presenting my sketch-map at the Lands and Mines Office next day it was accepted, and they drew out their version from it which we could pass on to architect, builders and others. A number of years and much correspondence later, when the buildings were nearly complete, a survey was done, and rather nervously we awaited the result. To our great relief our map fitted pretty well with theirs, the final area including the stream and rough ground between hospital and church sites.

The year 1973 was an eventful one for us. Muheza had a new church centre; the Church of Christ the King was in use with a very mixed congregation ranging from babies in arms or on backs, to the elderly and frail tottering up the track from the main road or getting a lift on the back of a bicycle or the occasional scooter or motor-cycle. Gifts to the church included a beautiful black ebony Makonde carved crucifix, a tabernacle for the Blessed Sacrament and a small Makonde crib set. Because no others were available, I made a set of Stations of the Cross, line drawings and mostly modifications of illustrations from the Good News Bible. Gradually we were able to collect what was needed for church, vestry and parish hall to make it a useful centre for parish life and worship.

We knew at last that the Muheza hospital project must go ahead. We had a site to build on and the necessary signatures of agreement for support and finance, and plans actually being drawn. Now David and I had a family visit to look forward to in October.

Martin and Rob

Back in the old days when David was doing a spell of chaplaincy duty for St Andrew's College, Minaki, his parents had visited him at Christmas time. I had got involved from day one, as I was the one with a car, the black and white van which we called 'The Penguin', so I could take David to meet them at the airport. Of course I saw more of them during their visit. Now it was my turn; we had a memorable three month visit from my nephew Martin Phillips from Flint, Michigan, age not quite seventeen. A few days before his arrival I had a rare phone call from America. I had to go to the tiny telephone exchange at an arranged time to take it, and wait while the operator pulled plugs in and out, having snatches of conversation with various places. Finally Martin's voice came through: "May I bring a friend?"

"Yes of course", was the automatic answer. What else could I say to a much loved and rarely seen nephew, and I knew that David would say the same. But what about food and our tiny guest room? How would we keep an unknown friend, Rob by name, as well as Martin occupied and content for three months including Christmas? Also would there be room in our VW Beetle for four of us and two lots of American luggage for the 200 mile drive on quite rough roads from Dar-es-Salaam airport to Muheza?

The day came; the luggage wasn't too formidable; we all piled into the car for the journey home for what turned into a very successful visit. Only a few minor problems developed, and mostly for Rob, the friend, which was understandable, as he was among complete strangers. Also we heard later that he was a rather disturbed teenager, so he was not likely to show the signs of enjoyment that Martin did. They both pitched into useful jobs, first in our house, painting window frames, and making shelves and cupboards and then similar jobs in the hospital and nursing school. The Land Rover which was used for visiting village clinics was an interest, especially for Martin, who became very friendly with the driver John Barabara. Martin already knew a lot about different vehicles and as well as helping him, learnt quite a lot more from John. They also had fun teaching each other Swahili and English respectively.

John soon had to give up driving as his blood pressure became dangerously high, so imagine our surprise when, on visiting the diocese in 1996, David and I found that the driver lent to us for visits to Kwa Mkono and Muheza was John Barabara. He was then driver for the Mothers Union, and with no sign of his former hypertensive problems. It was good to give him news of Martin, by then, sixteen years later, an experienced doctor.

Rob and Martin remained well while with us and were very conscientious about taking their anti-malaria pills. Mild tummy upsets were the only health problem they had, so imagine the surprise to us all, when six months after leaving the tropics they each had short sharp attacks of high fever, confidently diagnosed as malaria. No later attacks occurred and there were no long term effects.

Christmas 1973 was very special with our two visitors. Shortages of various foods like sugar, fats including margarine and even wheat flour had begun, and dried fruit for pudding and cake must have been a gift from England, or perhaps from Joy in Martin's luggage! So cake and Christmas pudding were made, and the main courses of Christmas dinner were supplied with chicken, not turkey of course. 'Brandy sauce' was I thought the triumph of invention, but I'm not saying what was in it or you might try it. We had a wonderful crop of tomatoes, so the visitors made very good tomato juice as a starter. All went well until the pudding came in, which I thought was the triumph of the day. At that Martin's face fell, "No custard!" Apparently English Christmas pudding to Martin meant English custard, made from Birds custard powder which they couldn't get in America – and nor could we!

The sayings of Martin on that visit were memorable. On our frequent drives up the narrow sandy rocky track to Magila, he would say when we met any vehicle, "We need only half the road, but we like it all on the same side". Of David riding an old style Honda 90, for which the gear change needs no clutch, he would say that David was the only person he knew who could double declutch to change gear on a vehicle which had no clutch!

After Christmas the boys were leaving from Kilimanjaro airport, which is some 250 miles north west of Muheza, between Moshi and Arusha. Quite near is the Arusha game park, a small one where visitors can drive round in their own cars. We spent a day there giving them a chance to see a number of different animals, as well as great flocks of the much loved pink flamingoes on a lake. Cameras were in action, especially of the elderly and rather frail rhinoceros who lived in a fenced field near the road so that visitors could see and photograph him at quite close quarters while he managed to stay alive. We were sad to see their plane depart, but they had more to do in their gap year before both were due to read medicine at Ann Arbor University in Michigan.

Healing Mission

Early in 1974 we had a healing mission at Muheza, and neither David nor I had previous experience of an event on such a scale. We were both always aware that all healing comes from God, whether of body, mind or spirit. The human part is in prayer for the sick, and for ourselves as we use all the skills given to us by God. This includes scientists, researchers, doctors, nurses and other medical workers, and many more who in any way contribute to prevention and cure of sickness and promotion of good health. It is not 'either/or', but of using God's gifts to us with thankfulness, and for the relief of suffering and promotion of good health.

News went round a wide area and crowds came, including many of the clergy, though the bishop was not able to come. Shelters were built for those who needed them on ground near the church. The healing team arrived, led by Edmund John, a brother of Archbishop John Sepeku. They fasted and prayed and read the bible, asking us to do the same, they themselves continuing all through the night in the church. The team had only one meal a day which we provided, but Edmund John, the healer, was never seen except when blessing the site or conducting worship and healing sessions. Cyprian Salu, a gentle and prayerful little man, was an assistant, who gave his life to healing and the follow up of healing missions, and to evangelism. During each day the team and our clergy and others were in the church praying; the sick were brought up one by one for prayer and the laying on of hands. David was involved all the time, and it was much in my thoughts, and I was meeting the team each evening at their meal, but not their leader.

Many of the sick came for deliverance from evil spirits, and as would be expected they had intense emotional reactions. They screamed and shouted, shaking and throwing themselves onto the floor. I think it was a standardised reaction, probably varying with their tribal background. Many felt a great sense of release: something was being done, people cared, they were the centre of attention. Prayer and the laying on of hands had made a wonderful start for them. Now the prayers of the local church and of people like Cyprian would be needed for them and their family, whether or not it was literally an evil spirit which had possessed the sufferer.

Similar emotional reactions were shown by those with other ills; crutches and sticks were thrown down, praise was given for improved sight and hearing and many other ills. Neither David nor I felt that we had seen any actual physical healing, although it had been reported by responsible people at other missions. I was sad that a bed-ridden patient from Magila hospital, brought down on a stretcher, was reported 'healed' and to have walked out of the church, whereas I had seen him carried out on his stretcher, physically unchanged.

Edmund John and the team had planned to spend the week with us, but sadly, exhausted no doubt by fasting and lack of sleep, they left with two days to go, and many still waiting to be called into the church. Cyprian Salu stayed, but not as leader. Our clergy after consulting with the bishop decided they must continue and asked David to lead the healing sessions. Working together they followed the same routine as before, with similar positive responses among the patients.

Sad of course that the healing team had left early, David's report on the mission was very positive. He saw that it had brought awareness to the parishes that the church has a place and responsibility for healing the sick, and that all of us, lay people as well as clergy, and medical workers had this responsibility. Cyprian would follow this up, and he also helped some to start house groups for prayer, bible study and fellowship. As well as healing in its widest sense coming to many who had been prayed for, renewed life and enthusiasm had come to the parishes, and so to the whole diocese.

Later in 1974 David and I were quite ready for some time in England, and also another visit to North America, as Alan and Joy had invited us to stay with them again.

Overseas Activities Again

Another event during our eventful start to life at Muheza had been a diocesan visit from Cleveland, Ohio in the United States in 1972. Among a party of about a dozen there were two black priests, whom we enjoyed having as house guests for a few days. Father Austin Cooper was truly American, while Father Anthony Coleman was from Canada. Their visit was enjoyed by all, and our visit to America in 1974 gave us the chance to return the visits.

Our leave followed the usual pattern. David's mother, still in Somerton, but soon to move to Gillingham, Dorset, was our first destination, and our base during this leave. Moving to Dorset would make her nearer the family, and Gladys, who had been with the family for many years, would continue with her faithful care. Then it was USPG headquarters, getting our health sorted out and visiting friends and family; for me talks and showing slides in supporting parishes, and plenty of sermons for David.

One unusual event was that USPG had found a young man, Jim Flood, whom they sent down to Somerton to see us. They suggested that perhaps he could relieve me of much of the strain of trying to oversee the building of Muheza hospital along with my activities still at Magila. Although not medical, and not wanting to sign on as a missionary, Jim was quite willing to work with us, understanding that 'us' included the CSP Sisters. We were lucky to have an offer from such an enthusiastic person who would I felt be sure to have more knowledge of buildings, and of roofs, drains, plumbing and power supplies than I did! Jim paid us a visit at Magila later that year and joined us 6 months later.

Our visit to Alan and Joy in America that leave included a very interesting and enjoyable few days in Ohio diocese. We stayed for a few days each with the Coopers and the Colemans, and saw many of the others who had come to Tanzania including the bishop and his wife. Fred Lambert was another priest who had spent some time teaching at St Mark's Theological College in Dar-es-Salaam and we had met him on several occasions. Thanks to generous friends in the United States as well as England, I was able to put in some very useful orders for the hospital on our return to England.

Time was running out when we returned to England, but we were glad to find Mum comfortably installed in her new home, and to spend some days with her. It was never so difficult to drag oneself away from England when there was so much to go back to at the other end.

Muheza Hospital Plans

David and I were both happy that things had been well looked after while we were away. A retired priest, Ernest Barabara, who lived near us, and grew fruit trees, citrus grafted onto lemon stock, as well as helping in the parish, had looked after things for David. Andrew Stanford was thoroughly settled at Magila, and I could leave the administration side to him after we got back. When Jim Flood joined us he soon learned a lot about the building project, and got to know the Sisters, and the other hospital staff. He was also taking on jobs gradually in the hospital and learning Swahili, mostly from the staff and the young people of the village, and interested too in local customs and farming.

The problems with our architect and his assistant soon made it necessary for me to spend two days every 2 to 3 weeks in Dar-es-Salaam poring over plans, explaining the special needs of hospitals, and looking out for unnecessary expenditure. Jim became a great help at these sessions. I couldn't expect to do the 200 mile drive on my own, and David couldn't always make good use of the time. Our routine was to leave after lunch on Sunday – a late lunch when David was coming – and return Tuesday evening. We stayed at St

Mark's Theological College, with Mary Peake, a long time teacher in Masasi diocese, who taught English at St Mark's right into old age. We became known as 'those Muheza people, always hungry' because when asked at table, "Either…or?" we nearly always replied, "Both please!" Jim took a lot of weight off my shoulders, both with checking the plans, and with overseeing the construction when the building started to go up.

Progress with the project moved very slowly with complications all round. The country was short of foreign exchange; delay in devaluing our currency made complications for us. Petrol was in short supply and to get vouchers for it meant a 50 mile round trip, and even then special permission for filling cans as well as tanks was hard to come by. Then came cholera.

A Serious Epidemic

By 1978 the country was seriously affected by its first cholera epidemic. District medical officers round us were quick off the mark. Lives are saved by fluids – given by mouth if possible, otherwise into the veins. Centres for urgent intensive treatment were set up, intravenous fluids and equipment obtained somehow, and a nurse or paramedic put in charge. Central management must have been very difficult, but was also very questionable. Road blocks, known as 'gates', were set up on all main roads and some side roads and tracks, with police or army controlling them. A cholera certificate was needed to pass the gate and it required two injections at intervals of one to two weeks, and in our district these could be issued only by the DMO and myself. It seemed that the gate keepers had no discretion to allow a seriously ill baby to be taken past. For ourselves these restrictions were annoying and time consuming. But to my dismay, admissions to our busy children's ward fell sharply, and we assumed that a number of expected admissions to that ward each week would have died at home, as we knew that a number of admissions, especially babies, would have died without urgent treatment.

In lighter vein (for us) was a Saturday afternoon incident, when I actually had the day off after what seemed like a 9 or 10 day week. I was in the kitchen doing some baking. A Roman Catholic brother turned up almost in tears; David comforted him and called me, I would be sure to have a solution! The unfortunate brother had filled his freezer van with chickens from his freezing plant in Tanga, refilled the freezer, and set out for Moshi, some 300 miles away. Passing Muheza he was stopped at a 'gate', and had no cholera certificate, and it was Saturday afternoon with the district medical officer off duty. I had all I needed to give the injections and issue a certificate, but could give only one injection at a time, so not the certificate. The only alternative I could offer was for him to swallow, there and then, 17 tetracycline capsules (why 17?) with me watching him. This was the rule if he wanted to travel that day. Fortunately there was no water shortage just then. Handing him a duly signed and stamped certificate I rushed back to my oven, while David took the smiling young brother back to his van. Minutes later David was back carrying aloft a big round cheese. We hadn't seen cheese for months. It was usually out of stock or ridiculously expensive. How sensible of the brother to give it as he drove away; it would have been an almost irresistible bribe. We needed light relief. Most of the control was in army hands, and they were not used to being gentle, and probably not polite either.

Andrew Stanford had completed his 5 years with us, so I was in charge of Magila hospital again, and I put one annoying occasion to good use. Uniformed high-ups of the army came to inspect the hospital to see whether we were taking all the right precautions to prevent the spread of cholera. I took them through the disinfected doorways of our isolation wards and around the hospital, where I was quite at home and they were not. As we went I gave them a dissertation on the dysenteries, cholera, gastroenteritis, and other intestinal infections. I explained that there were many similarities in these, including their methods of spread, and of the ways in which we were co-operating with the Local Authority (LA) all the time to prevent them. In my experience the LA had always worked hard to encourage the digging and use of pit latrines where waterborne sanitation was not available. Hookworm infestation had been reduced very noticeably by this, and it also played a major part in preventing the spread of infections like cholera. The officials were polite to me, but we realised that the army were sometimes really cruel to local people who failed to respond to their orders.

Mercifully the acute petrol shortage eased off, and the cholera epidemic gradually came to an end, leaving us with occasional sporadic cases and a few small local outbreaks. After the cholera came increasing problems of food shortages.

Uganda

The neighbouring country of Uganda always seemed six steps in front of us in development until the disastrous Idi Amin period in the 1970s with all its sad results including the death of the Archbishop Janani Luwum in 1977. Tanzania watched things carefully and became desperate when civil war broke out. The final straw was when it appeared that Amin planned to march down through Tanzania, occupying the strip of land to the port of Tanga in order to give Uganda access to the coast. We had instructions to dig trenches, as we at Muheza were on that route.

Very soon we heard that Tanzania had daringly sent an army into Uganda. Rightly or wrongly their action was successful. Our digging could stop and Uganda could start to put itself together again.

Staff for Muheza New Hospital

At the beginning of 1977, building Muheza Designated District Hospital (DDH) actually got started. We moved on April 1st 1980. It was time to make plans about the staff we should need, some from Magila employed by the diocese, others government employees. We would have a mixed race staff, with Muslims as well as Christians. It was felt that, at least to start with, the administrator should be a local person, and also a Christian. Who could it be? Could we find a local Christian with ability, experience and enthusiasm who would enjoy the challenge of unifying such a mixed staff?

Then Clement Mdoe came to mind. Do you remember him in Chapter 2 at Minaki? He was a really good medical assistant, who sadly had been forced to leave by serious and repeated threats of witchcraft. Such threats are extremely hard to resist, especially if you are away from your home village and support; also physical violence may follow if not 'successful'. Clement's home was at Lewa, near Korogwe. We heard that he had retired and also that he was wanting advice about possible training to become a priest.

David and I set off for Lewa on the trusty motor-cycle on the next Sunday afternoon, and met Clement on the track leading to his home. It was a happy meeting, starting of course with "Habari za siku nyingi" (what news of many days?) repeated several times, with the inevitable reply that news was all excellent (to begin with). "Lakini" (but) came next and then all the real news could be told. Clement's work over the years with local authorities had given him good administrative experience, as well as on the medical side. David was already giving teaching to a mature student, a teacher, Harold Mhando, and would welcome another to come to our house for teaching. Clement was really keen to join us, and was soon at Magila starting work there.

The prospect looked quite cheerful for doctors. Dr Habil Kasoyaga MD from Masasi diocese had started as one of my rural medical aid (RMA) students at Minaki. Clearly a 'bright boy' this had been recognised when he went into Government service, and he had been given the chance to progress up the professional ladder. He had recently completed the MD at Dar-es-Salaam University. At his own request he would be seconded to us at Muheza DDH.

Dr Elizabeth Hills MD, FRCP was being sent by USPG. She was a consultant physician in her forties, who had not been able to leave England before because of family commitments. Ten years were mentioned, but after considerably longer than that at Muheza, much of the progress of the hospital over the next 25 years or more resulted from her work and her influence. She became a lifelong friend to me as well as a much admired and respected colleague.

Felix Mhina, another RMA from Minaki, had progressed to MA, and now had a place at Kilimanjaro Christian Medical Centre (KCMC) in Moshi to go on to assistant medical officer (AMO). KCMC was the project which I had discussed with Dr Jensen at Bumbuli in 1951 during my first visit there (see Chapter 2). It had become a flourishing medical centre with many specialist medical facilities, as well as medical, nursing and auxiliary trainings.

The district medical officer (DMO) in charge of the old Muheza hospital and all the district work was Vincent Gongwe, an AMO who also started as a bright MA student at Minaki. He would be on our staff, and his district work would be largely based on the MCH clinic. It was always a pleasure to meet old Minaki students years later and to find them doing a good job.

Dr Gongwe retired very soon, and his successor, Dr John Kifua, was keen on surgery. He took a short course in eye surgery when he got the chance, and that was useful. Jane Gongwe, Vincent's wife, was a nurse midwife, who took a tutoring course, giving her a place at once in the nursing school, which of course trained midwives as well as nurses, male and female.

Sylvester Chizazi is the next character to mention, in charge of the nursing school at the time of the move. He trained as a nurse at Lulindi, and came to us at Magila in 1972 after further training, first at Exeter, and then a short tutoring course in London. With five years experience at Magila, this course, though short, was recognised in Tanzania in 1977, enabling him to be registered as a tutor and to be put in charge of our nursing school. He continued with devotion and enthusiasm, through thick and thin, over the next 30 years to send out well-trained midwives and nurses to hospitals and other health work in the hands of different churches and other organisations all over the country.

Sylvester was also a strong supporter of the Church of Christ the King Muheza, and was later ordained as a deacon. His wife, Agnes, was a teacher in a local primary school, and a daughter, Claire, trained to be hospital administrator in later years.

Nursing officers (NOs) and medical assistants would be a mixture from the two hospitals, and we should miss the CSP Sisters. They were not coming with us apart from Sister Jacqueline and Sister Gillian Mary, who ran the new midwifery department for the first three months. NO Salehe was one from the Government side who will always remain in my memory as a good nurse and a good man. He was a sincere Muslim, but also had an understanding of Christianity. I was told that, although he couldn't himself consider making the change, he was happy for Amina, his daughter, to follow her conscience and become a baptised Christian. She came to England and trained as a nurse, and stayed on, later marrying a Yorkshireman, and starting a family.

Another key position to fill would be the Matron. We were fortunate that a Lutheran, Sebastian Kayamba, who trained at Bumbuli, accepted that post. Perhaps he would find some other good Lutherans to join us. Staff nurses would be a more routine matter when the time came.

Muheza DDH: Layout

The new hospital was about half a mile from the centre of Muheza town, on a quarter-mile approach road from the road to Magila. This led into a large square parking area, with the original offices facing you. The wards, separate buildings, led off from a central covered way, with operating theatres half way along one side, and midwifery department opposite them. The main wards were the Nightingale type, which I remember describing at Minaki as "rows of beds, small lockers, and not much else"; here we should have far more accessories. At the far end of the central covered way were isolation wards, including those needed for the TB and leprosy patients who need admission.

At the front, as you entered the hospital, on the right of the parking area were the outpatient department and emergency, and the pathology department. On the left were the central Maternity and Child Health (MCH) clinic, from which the village clinics were serviced and also the pharmacy. On the Usambara (north) side at a little distance was the kitchen, trusting that it would prove to be on the right side for the prevailing wind!

There would be many extensions and additions as the hospital grew and took on new responsibilities like research. It also developed a very active centre for all aspects of the HIV/AIDS problem when this came on the scene, giving special attention to pregnancy and childbirth, with healthy babies high on the agenda.

Passing through the hospital and on beyond along the ridge was the nursing school, giving a superb view of the Usambara mountains, with the Church of Christ the King just across the valley.

There was plenty of room for staff houses near the hospital, but of course not plenty of money to build them. We planned some family houses and some for unmarried staff. These latter each had six good sized rooms, a kitchen and a living room, intended for six nurses. Sadly we had reached a time when these were out-dated, as good useful nurses quite often had their own babies or toddlers, and needed a little helper, perhaps a niece, living with them. One room was not quite what they wanted. Some of the houses at the old Muheza hospital could be used, and more houses were built when funds were available.

Initially the hospital had 200 beds but once it was up and running, patients came from all sides and plans were soon being made for extensions. Later the nursing school had to add to and improve its buildings and equipment, as approval to train Grade A nurses would depend on this. Way back in 1961 there had been a gathering of bishops and doctors from the five dioceses which were supported by the UMCA (see chapter 5). We discussed medical planning, with the possibility of combining to set up a medical centre, with a specialist hospital including training facilities for nurses, MAs, RMAs, laboratory assistants and others. This would provide staff for our own hospitals, and also we hoped for others. Mkomaindo hospital was thought of as a possible venue for this, though after working for six years in Masasi diocese I realised how unsuitable this would have been. A much more central place with better access would be needed for students from different parts of the country. Here at Muheza something similar might develop. Even by 1980 no diocese was training Grade A nurses, although in Grade B training of both nurses and midwives, Magila and Lulindi (Masasi) had been pioneers. Muheza DDH seemed to me to be a much more hopeful project!

Bishops

At the end of 1979 we sadly said goodbye to Bishop Yohana Jumaa as our diocesan bishop, and he died not long after. He and his wife Salome had been dear to our hearts, and he had been a really good first Tanzanian bishop for the diocese. On Sundays he usually went out to different parish churches, taking with him Mama Salome, and also Muriel Newton, his secretary. They used a rather unsuitable car, often somewhat overloaded, on the rough country lanes, with a driver who was both tolerant and resourceful. Whenever possible they would call on us for a cup of tea on their way home. Muriel had come first to the diocese as a nurse, and then returned as a very informal and helpful secretary to Bishop Yohana, who with very bad eyesight needed rather special help.

One Sunday happened to be Bishop Yohana's birthday, so I made him a cake, with icing and attempts at decorations. He exclaimed, "I have never had a birthday cake before, I must go and put on my vestments again." He soon returned fully robed, and it was the best appreciation he could give! We would miss him and the Sunday visits of this friendly trio.

All were anxious as to who would take Bishop Yohana's place. We and many others were really pleased when we heard that John Ramadhani, whom many of us knew, had been chosen. In our circumstances with fewer parishes in a diocese, though often spread more widely, we were more intimate with our bishops I think than is possible where populations are dense, and dioceses larger in that sense.

John Ramadhani was from Zanzibar, and was someone whom David and I had known at St Andrew's College Minaki, first as student and then as teacher. From teaching he soon went on to a position at the Ministry of Education, where he gave some ten years of valuable service. However a strong sense of vocation to the ordained ministry took him in 1973 to Queen's College Birmingham to study for this. On returning to Tanganyika in 1976 he was made deacon in St Augustine's Church, Tanga and ordained priest in Zanzibar Cathedral later that year. After a short while in a parish he was needed at St Mark's Theological College Dar-es-Salaam as Warden. In 1980 he was consecrated Bishop in Tanga, and became the new bishop of the diocese of Zanzibar and Tanga.

Our diocese at this time was still called 'the Diocese of Zanzibar and Tanga'. Its cathedral was on the island, in the town of Zanzibar. Later the diocese was divided; the mainland part became 'Tanga Diocese', with St Michael's parish church at Korogwe its Cathedral. 'Zanzibar Diocese' then consisted of just the Island of Zanzibar with Pemba Island, where mission work had started in 1897. Bishop John's consecration was in St Augustine's Church, Tanga and the enthronement in Zanzibar Cathedral. David was glad to be able to go to both, which were early in 1980. Soon after this Bishop John visited the Church of Christ the King, Muheza for confirmations, a joyful Sung Eucharist, and a welcoming parish tea party.

A Sudden Farewell

A word here about Jim Flood: Jim gave us five valuable years of work, turning his hand to anything, and playing a major part in getting Muheza hospital literally off the ground. Sadly his stay was terminated abruptly in March 1980, hardly a month before the move. Jim was an excellent worker himself, but not entirely easy to work with. Inevitably there was trouble between him and those responsible for faulty work on drains, septic tanks and soakage pits, and various other areas of poor workmanship.

However that was not the big problem. He was very friendly with the local youth, joining them at the local equivalent of evenings at the pub, and wanting to join their youth club. This was felt by some to be intrusive. Perhaps they felt it was a case of the white man wanting to patronize them. Jim's motives were just interest and friendliness, but in some ways too friendly I suppose. Many VSOs and other volunteers were in the area then, and it was good to see how they fitted in and got to know people. But in Jim's case it was felt that he was not quite so sensitive to their feelings and he was officially asked to leave.

This was in March 1980, just before the move, and we had relied on him to organize that. Moreover I knew that some things in the buildings were not finished: complete handover would be in six months time, and somehow Clement and I would have to cope with that last 6 months while working out how to run this new type of hospital. Jim knew the problems in the building work, and there was little time for him to put others in the picture. Really grateful for his work, we were sad to see him go.

Equipment: SIMAVI

With invaluable help from Jim Flood before his sudden departure, the buildings were nearly complete by the planned opening day. To be ready for use a lot of equipment was needed; things as varied as beds and buckets, X-ray machines and centrifuges, scissors and dressing forceps, cooking stoves and cups and plates, and lots more. Some came from Magila and some from the old Muheza hospital. A lot could be obtained on the local market, and the Government medical store could supply many basic things, but outside help was also needed.

We were introduced to another generous German organisation, SIMAVI, who could not only give expert advice, but also arrange delivery, and give some financial help. Initially I met their representative in Dar-es-Salaam, which was invaluable. During several leaves in England I had crossed the channel to see EZE and ICCO about the buildings and plans. In 1981, when we were up and running, and I knew some of the problems and shortages, I paid a very memorable visit to SIMAVI headquarters in Hamburg. We had expected to go together, but David developed pneumonia at the last minute and had to stay on in London at the flat of my kind nursing friend from Minaki days, Joyce Townsend.

Reaching Hamburg I was really overwhelmed by the friendliness and kind hospitality which I received. Home comforts over-night and an ample breakfast preceded a long and intense morning in the office. We discussed everything from dissecting forceps to X-ray machines, sustained by a continuous supply of very good black coffee! Many problems were resolved, and such was their expertise that I was reminded of important things which could easily have been left out. Sight seeing round the town and the harbour filled the afternoon, and then more work. An ample lunch was fitted in, and also 'tea' which would have satisfied any Yorkshireman, so imagine my surprise later on to go out to dinner at a Japanese restaurant! Our recent food shortages made it all the more surprising. Back in London David was on the platform to meet me.

The Move, April 1980

The opening date of Muheza Designated District Hospital, 'Hospitali Teule Muheza', was fixed rather ironically for April 1st. Some details were not finished, but there was nothing to stop us moving in and starting work. The move itself was a nightmare, open lorries went back and forth from Magila to Muheza, loaded with equipment and furniture from all departments, and to get things undamaged to the right department was almost impossible to control. My experience of packing up Minaki hospital in 1961 with the two medical assistants Anthony and Alfred, and nursing sisters Joyce and Edith, was not very much help. However it didn't rain, and we got there, and so did the contingent from the government hospital. We were open for business on April 1st, and the patients were not slow in coming!

All of us were determined to make this partnership between Government and Church work. During my 30 years so far in Tanzania, among all the other things that were going on, I had kept in view the importance of co-operation between church and state, as well as between different churches and different faiths, and here was a great opportunity to put it into action.

Elizabeth Hills arrived towards the end of March, and stayed with us while getting her house near the hospital ready for use. Soon she was at work, and it was an enormous help to have someone with her skills and experience to take so much off my shoulders. With true Christian commitment to the work and friendliness to go with it, the nurses soon loved and valued Elizabeth, even though she moved too fast for them, and they often couldn't read her writing! I think that our many imperfections shocked and amazed Elizabeth at first, but she didn't waste time on that before getting some of them put right. Our new hospital was very far from perfect but gradually solutions would be found, and Elizabeth would be in the forefront of finding them. It didn't take her long to discover how difficult things could be.

I am sure that the Lord was with us in the hospital from day one, and in any case it was built as his hospital. So our next big event was a visit from Bishop John to bless the hospital, nursing school, staff houses and other buildings, in fact the whole site. Staff, students and many others followed the fully robed bishop, priests and servers all round as the bishop blessed and said prayers. At intervals we sang hymns, and patients and staff on duty in the wards and departments joined in as far as they could. It was a very meaningful event: a new hospital, a new bishop, and in a sense a new staff as we were mixed in so many ways. It was a church hospital, but staffed part by diocese and part from the government; some Muslim, some Christian; most were Tanzanian but of different tribes; some were from overseas, usually British, but potentially from Europe or America or anywhere else. Financial and prayer support would come from all over the place, starting with the local Church. It was up to us to work together to develop a hospital with not only high medical and nursing standards, but also a reputation for care and understanding and real service to the people of town and village all around. I had great faith that some of those I have mentioned could make this happen.

Future Support

Years later I was thrilled at the way Elizabeth and others had forged ahead. Gradually a specialist staff was built up and the necessary equipment added. A comprehensive HIV/AIDS programme was set up, with special attention to expectant mothers and healthy babies, and care for the children with problems resulting from the disease. Research was taken on in co-operation with the Amani malaria research centre, already well known in our time.

To enable all this progress the hospital and nursing school had received support in cash, personnel, specialist visits and advice, and exchange of staff from various sources. Special mention must be made of three of these in England: 'Medicines for Muheza' was set up by Doctors John and Jeanette Meadway to supply far more than medicines; 'Hereford-Muheza Link Society', with Dr John Wood as its secretary, and the support of the Hereford NHS Trust and Hereford Diocese; and that of USPG continuing their background support and personnel.

The prayers of the Church both in Tanzania and overseas have been and still are vital to the whole enterprise, from day one of the planning to the April 1st opening, and without doubt into the future. It is still a Church hospital, made responsible by the health ministry for the medical care of Muheza district, hence its title 'Muheza Designated District Hospital' (DDH) or 'Hospitali Teule Muheza', shortened in English to 'Teule Hospital'. The government ministry continues to supply funds and staff.

David and I were quite due for overseas leave by April 1980, but clearly it was not the time for me to go until the following year when I felt that Elizabeth would be willing and well able to take over. David's mother was getting old and frail, so he spent 3 weeks in England in May. It was a good decision as she died at the end of the year. It was very sad for me not to see her again, but she would understand.

The Chapel

The cost of a chapel could not be included in the plan covered by funding from the Tanzania Government and from ICCO and EZE. However David and I had managed to raise enough money to include a small chapel at one side of the hospital, where morning prayers were said, and a priest came for a Eucharist on Sundays and one day during the week. It was available too for bible studies, prayer meetings or discussions for the nurses. Often it was the priest at the parish church or his assistant who was chaplain, but a retired priest who would enjoy the job was sometimes available. Denis Mhina, one of the Minaki medical assistants who had been ordained priest, was one of those who did this, and Maria his wife would be helping in whatever way she could.

Roman Catholics and Lutherans shared in the use of the chapel. Although the local Muslims were very friendly, they would not want to use the chapel. David got on well with them, and I had done one or two operations for them. When we visited Muheza some years later they welcomed us like long lost family members, literally grabbing us by the hand as we were walking through the town, to insist that we went in to see them all.

The chapel was well placed, and had a small very temporary X-ray room and staff rest room attached, though the latter was temporarily used as a physiotherapy room. We hoped that both would soon be provided for elsewhere, and their original purpose would be restored, to provide a bit of comfort for the hard worked staff.

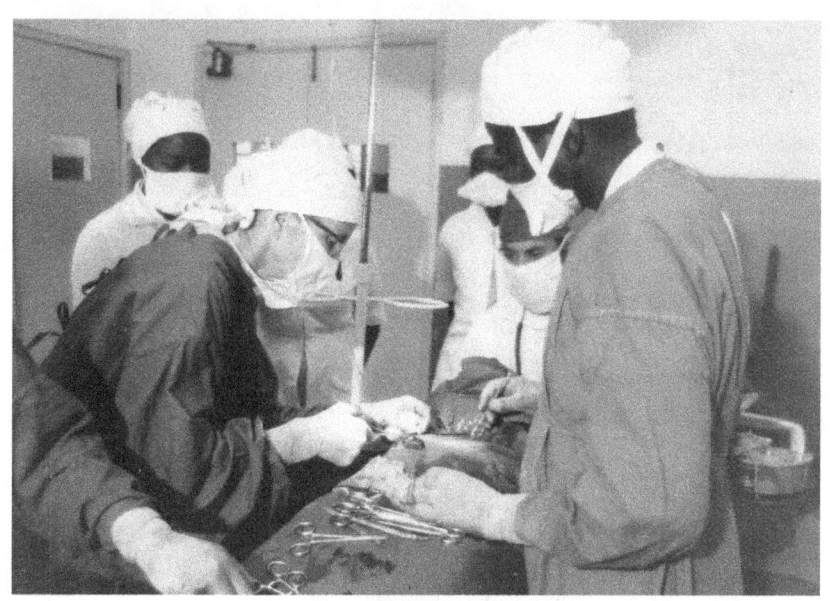
Hernia operation at Magila assisted by S/N Ernest

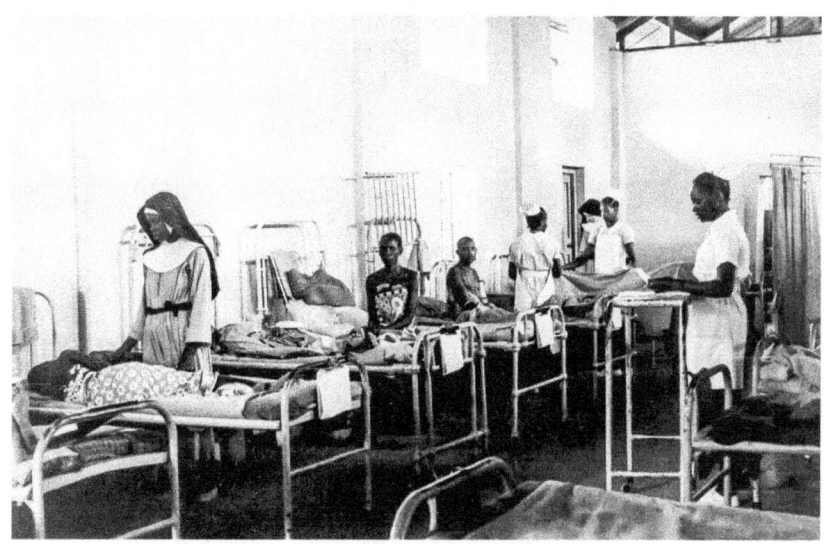
Women's ward, St Augustine's Magila

New ambulance: students admitting expectant mother at Magila

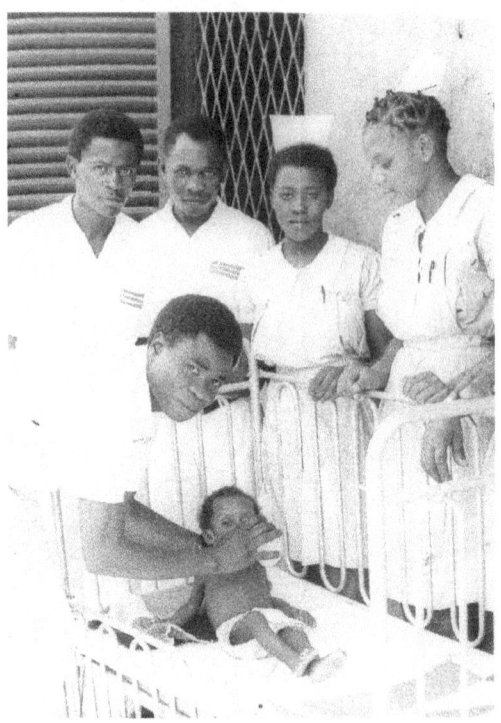
S/N George Kimweri teaching students to feed marasmic baby

Eucharist at Church of Christ the King, Muheza

Congregation outside the church and parish hall

Blessing a new house at Muheza Church Centre with Fr Clement Mdoe, hospital administrator

Muheza Hospital

Nurses singing at graduation ceremony at Muheza Training School

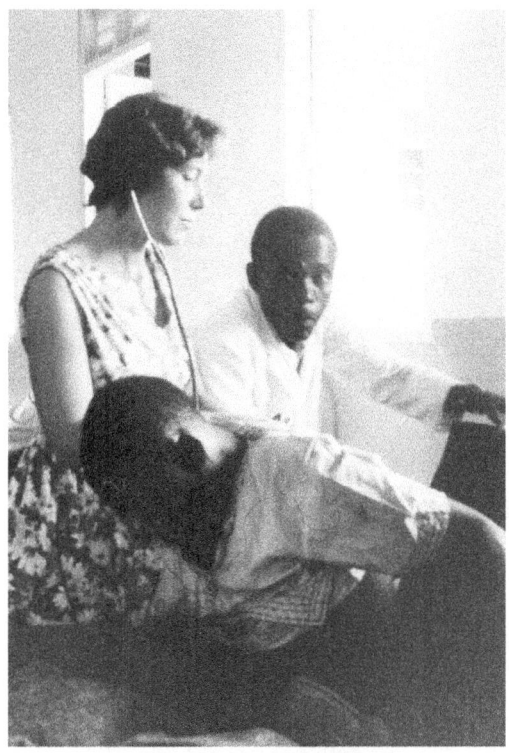
Dr Elizabeth Hills

Chapter 10
A Dream Come True?

Early Days at Muheza DDH

Has the dream really come true or is that wishful thinking? We would be finding out more about that by this time next year. There had apparently been a dream about a hospital of this type at Muheza long before Ursula Hay or David and I had come on the scene. No scheme had been thought out for it, and no money found, so I guess there was no real will to get it done. It was in Ursula's time that pressures developed in both hospitals due to their old buildings, and for Magila major problems with both sanitation and water supply; there were similar on-going problems at Muheza too but I guess with more hope that solutions could be found. The new agreement between Government and churches whereby a church hospital could be funded to take the place of a district hospital, becoming the Designated District Hospital (DDH), had come into place. Ursula with the help of the Christian Council of Tanganyika (CCT) had started the project for Muheza.

The hospital was under a board of governors, of which the Diocesan Bishop was chairman, with membership from the diocese, the District Authority and local residents, and from the Ministry of Health. As Medical Superintendent I was responsible to the Board now, instead of directly to the Bishop, and at Magila to the Community of the Sacred Passion. The financial position was very complicated; it was not just one of us, doctor or nurse, who did the accounts, but an official accountant with some training for the job. As Superintendent I realised that I couldn't now have bright ideas over-night and put them into action next morning!

New situations and new challenges are always exciting, and I enjoyed this one, at least when there weren't too many things going wrong. Leaking roofs, faulty drains, complaints about taps and other structural defects caused plenty of headaches, as did sudden failures of electric or water supply in a hospital modern enough to be dependent on both.

Having other doctors to work with was a thing which I enjoyed at Magila, and even more here. Dr Elizabeth Hills, the medical consultant sent from England by USPG, with her specialist skills in diseases of heart and lungs, was a great addition to this. She also picked up new skills at an extremely useful speed; I wondered how many medical consultants in an English hospital would, after a few months in a strange hospital in very unfamiliar circumstances, be doing emergency Caesarian sections and operating on hernias with urgent complications on their nights on call.

It was soon clear that Elizabeth would be the doctor to take charge when I was away on leave next year, so I was soon discussing plans and problems with her. Among our nursing officers, staff nurses, medical assistants many were new to me and I realised that before long we would have to decide which of them to recommend as suitable for up-grading when opportunities occurred, decisions very important for the hospital as well as the staff themselves.

My New Job

May, the month after the move, was made stranger for me by David's absence. But as the days passed it became increasingly clear that in moving to Muheza DDH I had moved to a new job. As Superintendent of the DDH there were other doctors, and more qualified staff of different categories, and on different pay rolls, as well as various other staff including cooks, as we now provided food for the patients. (Magila was one of the church hospitals where the relatives provide the food). There were board of governors' meetings to attend, not just the diocesan medical committee.

The other part of my job was surgeon with responsibility for surgical wards and theatres. Theoretically I went to the other wards only if called, as someone else was responsible for these patients, but at first our staff was incomplete, and also doctors, like everyone else, do have holidays, and even days off if they are lucky.

Different Buildings and Staff

Surgery at the DDH was very different from my other places of work. The main theatre was larger, with more equipment, good over-head lighting and spotlights, and air conditioning when the main electricity supply was working. We had a better supply of instruments and more of them, and a better supply of gowns and drapes so that there wasn't the same danger of running out on extra busy days. Operating lists were longer, so nurses (as well as surgeons!) got more practice.

Several of the medical assistants had attended short anaesthetic courses, so could act as semi-skilled anaesthetists when needed, but I continued with spinals and locals where possible. I couldn't help laughing at the MA usually on duty for anaesthetics. Being a Seventh Day Adventist he had Saturday as his regular day off. One day when I asked him to come on Sunday he replied: "Oh no! Saturday is my praying day and Sunday is my shopping day." It was as simple as that. He was good at giving anaesthetics!

An AMO or other doctor might come to theatre as learner-assistant, or even be called if help was needed. At another hospital, where the nearest doctor would be 30 miles away, I had become faint towards the end of a long operation. I lay on the concrete floor until I could see and hear again, and then, hoping for the best, got up, re-scrubbed, donned clean gown, gloves etc, and was relieved that no more problems occurred for me or for the patient. She incidentally was the least bothered by the incident and made a good recovery.

In the theatre block, as well as the main theatre, we had a small one for minor cases, and there was a small one in the out-patient area. Caesarian operations came to the main theatre, and were increasing in number as the hospital became widely known, and noticeably more popular. Also mothers and their families were becoming less averse to assisted deliveries of their babies, and modern teaching favoured earlier operation.

I foresaw that there might soon be dangerous delays for the Caesarians, as the small theatre would be too cramped, with baby to look after as well as mother. The maternity department would soon need its own operating theatre.

The labour wards were cubicles, open-ended to the daylight, so very convenient for day-time deliveries, and with good lighting for our 12 hour period from dusk to dawn throughout the year. The less serious complications could be handled there, but anything really serious had to be whisked over to the theatre.

My little theatre office was a useful bunk-hole where I wasn't usually disturbed except for something urgent. Operating lists, supplies, staff and other problems could be discussed there over a cup of coffee – no cold drinks I'm afraid as no fridge!

All the regular sterile supplies were packed and sterilised by the theatre staff. Sterile dressing packs and other necessities were supplied regularly to the wards and to out-patients and emergency. It was a lot of work to do in a small space, and by a relatively small staff.

A Different Routine

We followed official government hours of work from 7.30 am until 3 pm, except for the nursing staff with their rotas. For me it was rather inconvenient, as those hours easily got filled up in clinical work, and at around 3 pm I was wanting to see office staff just as they were going off home. Also I needed more than just a couple of bananas to see me through until I could get home, and food was very difficult over that period. Wheat flour was hardly ever seen in shops, and often no bread and no butter or spreads, and seldom any cooking fat, so a packed lunch gave problems. Cassava flour and maize meal appeared in the market, but they didn't give me any useful ideas, until our avocado pear tree produced its first lavish useful crop. David got on well with these, but was away in May; I liked them but they did not like me, and made me feel really ill! But in desperation I tried cooking them. I kneaded them up with cassava flour and a little salt, and baked them as biscuits (their own fat making it possible) and to my surprise baking had removed whatever usually upset me.

Working in the new wards was a lot easier than at Lulindi or Magila, as they were larger, lighter, and with more space between the beds. Magila hospital had grown gradually as money became available, so most wards were small, with plenty of doorways and steps. The children's ward was much larger, with plenty of space when not overcrowded in one of its common busy periods. Nursing area in all wards had been minimal, and for ease of work the new long Nightingale type ones, with sluices and duty area for the nurses, was a great improvement. The windows gave good light to work in, having given us headaches during the planning period.

I always enjoyed having reason to go to the children's wards. We had one, like the adult wards, for all non-infectious cases, malaria, anaemia, malnutrition and some chest problems, fractures and other urgent surgical cases. We did not take on children's surgery, unless it was urgent until the anaesthetist service was better covered. The ward for infectious cases was made up of cubicles with space for mother and child in each.

Even with more space we were often overcrowded. I remember one boy of five or six, who had fallen out of a tree, and had broken one leg and an arm in a very awkward place. With a beam arrangement for the leg and a drip stand for the arm, and the boy lying on a mattress on the floor, we had both limbs slung up, and he tolerated it very well, making a satisfactory recovery. Of course it made things difficult for the nurses, and also for this doctor who was not perhaps as agile as she had been!

I had one very prolonged out-patient session each week. It started at 8 am and continued far into the afternoon. Being a weak

'Mzungu' I found I must walk firmly away at around 1 pm and have a snack, or everything, including my temper, would have given out. I feel sure that everyone else of whatever nationality had their solution to the problem, and "he had to go to the bank" is heard surprisingly often!

Calls to different wards, or a few days in charge of them, were welcome, as it kept me in touch with what was going on: the range of admissions, where they were coming from, and the general atmosphere. Getting to know all the nursing staff was difficult unless there was a chance to see them at work. Much of this applied especially to the children's ward, giving it an added attraction. When called to see women on the medical ward, it was good to see how Judith Mnkondo from the children's ward at Magila was adapting to new conditions of work.

One of the great assets of the new clinical situation was having Elizabeth on call, especially when medical cases or babies and small children with high fever needed expert advice. Often, malaria and another infection occurred together, and one or other could easily be missed but a quick diagnosis could save life. More staff, a better-equipped laboratory able to do more tests, and Elizabeth to call on made a great difference to my day's work.

Maternity Without CSP

In the maternity department after their three months with us, I missed the two CSP Sisters with whom I had enjoyed working for so long at Newala and Magila. But there was Jane Gongwe, and others whom I should soon get to know. Jane was the wife of Dr Vincent Gongwe, former District Medical Officer (DMO) of Muheza, recently retired. Dr John Kifua, another Assistant Medical Officer (AMO), had taken his place as DMO, spending part of his time out in the District and part on the hospital staff.

Jane had taken a course in tutoring when she knew that a midwifery tutor would be needed when the Magila nursing school came to Muheza. Already an experienced nurse-midwife she proved herself a valuable member of the new training team. She and the Sisters had co-operated in their work while they were in charge of the maternity ward and deliveries, and Jane would give the help and oversight needed until we could get replacements. We already had good staff-midwives who could carry on with the day-to-day work.

I was very glad that Tanzanian midwifery training followed the British tradition that childbirth is a normal occurrence. Midwives are trained to see the mother through pregnancy, childbirth, the postnatal period, and also the care of the infant during the first two years of life. This is all spoken of as MCH (Maternity and Child Health). The doctor is called if there is any sign of complications. It fits in well with African tradition that childbirth is women's business. Then if a male doctor has to be called in it makes it easier for him to be accepted. Don't worry, male doctors: I had plenty of problems with being accepted for much of my surgical work!

Teaching

Our aims at the new nursing school were unchanged in spite of the very changed circumstances. A good nursing school must produce good nurses, learning in their classroom studies about the body, its structure and way of functioning, and what can go wrong with it. This must be balanced by practical time in wards and departments, learning how to nurse, to give good nursing care to the patients and carry out their different treatments. New and better buildings and facilities will be a help, but we also needed plenty more Sylvesters, Salehes and Judiths to carry it through.

I enjoyed my teaching sessions in the pleasant new quarters. I was also aware of the importance of this period in the lives of the students as they prepared for the changes and chances of the world. They will go with more education than many around them and with a valuable service to offer to their patients and to their country. As a Christian training school it could be a time for Christians and Muslims as well as any others to think and study more about their faith.

Zanzibar

During these first few months at Muheza I felt almost smothered in hospital affairs, so a pressing invitation for a weekend away was very welcome. David and I were invited, together with the other clergy and their wives, to go over to Zanzibar for the centenary celebrations of our well-loved but seldom seen cathedral.

It was a momentous weekend which we thoroughly enjoyed, and of which more will be said in Chapter 12. We felt it a real privilege to be present at the centenary of this beautiful and unusual cathedral. It was built in the early days of UMCA, and so of the Anglican Communion in what is now Tanzania.

David's Activities

Arriving back at Muheza, David and I were soon back in harness. I was finding the new operating theatre convenient to work in, and as this was true for the nursing staff as well, we could fit far more into a morning's work. David too was feeling the advantage of having the church and parish hall, with activities building up around it and the parish becoming more of a community. The parish hall was being used more, and he himself especially valued the vestry. He now had somewhere to robe before services, and a safe to put the money in, instead of carrying it home in his pocket and locking it in a drawer in our bedroom.

He was keen to get out more into the deanery. Magila and Mkuzi were nearby and had well-built churches, 'old' by our standards. They were built of stone and in somewhat English style, dating from around 100 years ago when missionaries were setting up centres including schools, clinics and churches. Since then most such buildings, including churches, are of cheaper and more easily accessible materials, needing frequent repair and replacement. All of us hope to do better as soon as funds are available. Amani, up in the foot-hills of the Usambara mountains, had several tea estates and a long established malaria research centre, so there was a considerable population up there. There was a comfortable Government rest-house at Amani where later on David and I spent a weekend when

David was celebrating the Sunday Eucharist and meeting people of the parish. We visited one of the tea estates, and were shown the process from picking by the women in the fields to processing and packing in the factory. The gradient up the road was steep and the surface stony. On the steepest part we were met by a cortege of evidently 'important' Land Rovers, halting me on one side on my little motorcycle. Getting started again on the stony hillside was not so easy!

A Mini-Theological College

David's long commitment to theological training continued. Seeing this in action within their own diocese was making members of local congregations think more about a possible calling to ordained ministry. David hoped too that experienced local clergy might consider taking part in the training programme.

At Muheza it was not a flood but just a trickle of men who, after years as teachers or other 'life's work', felt called, and ready and willing for training to become priests. For those who were not suitable to go to St Mark's College in Dar-es-Salaam or elsewhere, the training that David could offer was turning out to be just right. Continuing their job they would come once a week by foot or bicycle, or else for some days at a time, staying in the guest house, which was extremely simple but which served its purpose. Catechists too could come for refresher courses.

Sylvester Ntendegea was one who had appreciated the guest house during his training. Now ordained priest, he was resident in a newly built curate's house, giving David more freedom to get out to outstations and other parishes on Sundays.

April 25th 1982 was a big day for the parish. Ordination of three of David's students was held in our own church, and Clement Mdoe, by now well known as hospital administrator, was one of them. The pre-ordination retreat took place at Muheza, and instead of them going off somewhere else for the big event the Bishop came to us so we, the congregation, were all involved.

Next for training came James Ngereza, a student from St. Mark's College, who was with us for over a year. He was keen and intelligent and wanted to study, but had found life at the College too stressful. He flourished in this more practical situation, where he could study quietly on his own, with teaching periods when David was available. He could go out on his own into the parish or on the back of David's motorcycle for experience of a parish priest's day on the job. There were weekends with services, Sunday Schools, confirmation classes, mothers' union meetings and more, where he could sit in and see what happened. It turned out to be an ideal way for James to prepare for ordination.

Clement Mdoe had followed Harold Mhando as one of the early students in this series; Harold, formerly head teacher at Mkuzi, had now returned to Pangani parish on the coast south of Tanga. Clement retired after a very useful year at Muheza as hospital administrator, because the government was able to find a suitable administrator to take his place. After we moved on he became priest in charge of Muheza parish, moving into 'our' house until sadly he died of malaria in 1994 when we were in England.

MADABA and Visitors from Canada

By the time the hospital had moved to Muheza, Clement and Sylvester and others had decided that the area of the church centre should be called Madaba, representing our names, MArion and DAvid BArtlett. This name apparently had some connection with the past, but I didn't ever hear that full story. There is a happy significance in leaving our names on hospital wards at Lulindi and Muheza, and now at the church centre, especially as the church and parish hall were built with my mother's money. At Lulindi it had been the men's tuberculosis ward, it had survived a lightning strike soon after it came into use. At Muheza hospital after we had left Africa I was asked for a photograph of myself to hang in a new children's ward, which was to be given my name.

Nine months into this eventful year I felt the need of some relaxation, so October 1980 was a well chosen time for Alan and Joy (my brother and his wife) to suggest a visit to us from Canada. Now living in Hamilton, Ontario, they had quite a small house but with a large garden, highly productive of fruit and vegetables as well as flowers. It gave them plenty of work all year round, but with summer crops gathered in, eaten, stored or handed round to friends, and winter ones planted in orderly rows, they felt free to spend two weeks with their family a few thousand miles away.

For us it was a very good suggestion, though we did have a few anxieties. It would still be rather hot, and our guest room was small; they had never visited the tropics before, and neither of them liked hot weather. How would they get on with our fairly simple diet? Also neither Christopher our 'cook-general' nor I had Joy's rather exceptional skills in the kitchen. We still had the car, so could meet their plane and bring them home and there were plenty of interesting places to visit. David, having had three weeks in England in May, would not feel he could take much time off, but some outings would fit in with places which he needed to visit, so he could go with us on those days.

As with their son Martin and his friend Rob who visited us in 1973, we did wonder about space in the car. Perhaps it was as well that David couldn't spend the day with us when I took them to Lushoto on that steep, winding mountain road. I was quite glad to hand the driving over to him when we joined him at Korogwe after his meeting there.

On another day we all had an outing to Kwa Mkono. Later, when we knew that our home would be there for nearly seven years, we were very glad to have arranged that day out. Our time at Minaki and Lulindi, and for David Namasakata too, had been so similar in many ways to Kwa Mkono. Muheza was quite different with its modern facilities: electricity, telephone and even water coming out of taps!

Kwa Mkono had a 'bedded dispensary' and a 'polio hostel', both needing a doctor on the spot. I had visited the dispensary on a tour of the medical work of the diocese 30 years ago (Chapter 3). At that time the polio hostel was an idea in the head of one of the CSP Sisters, soon to be made into a reality.

There was plenty to see at Muheza itself, the town with its market stalls piled with fruit (if sometimes little else), and the church, hospital and nursing school. The hospital and nurses training school had been in use for 6 months when our visitors came. It was a good time of year to come, not the hottest time and not usually raining, though I did think of 1961 when we were closing Minaki hospital and the rain poured on us from October 18th onwards (see Chapter 5). The roads were dusty, and piled with sand in some places, but that is more of a problem for motor-cycles than for cars.

Altogether the visit was a success. It was lovely to see them, and for them to see Magila, with all its history, and where Martin and Rob had done so many useful jobs. UMCA's work on mainland Tanganyika had started near Magila, and the CSP Sisters had built their convent there in their very early days.

Joy had brought me some very practical gifts: items like plastic bowls and containers which were damp proof and ant proof. We were annoyed to find later that rats enjoyed sharpening their teeth on the edge of the bowls, even if not actually adding them to their diet. Thirty years later I am still using a bowl with rat tooth marks round the rim!

Game parks and Kilimanjaro are two of the attractions which bring visitors to Tanzania, and to give Joy and Alan a brief sight of these we accepted the kind suggestion of a friend, Sallie Buchanan, a teacher living near Moshi in the foothills of Mount Kilimanjaro. She had room for David and me, and would book for Joy and Alan at a hotel nearby. We all hoped that while we were there the mountain would make its dramatic appearance through the clouds, seemingly right above one's head and usually at breakfast time; and it did, and looked to be floating in the clouds.

One day we drove round Kilimanjaro game park, seeing as many animals as we could, not forgetting the flocks of flamingoes on the lake. We also looked in on the Kilimanjaro Christian Medical Centre

(KCMC) which I had watched grow up from an idea in the minds of Dr Jensen at Bumbuli and others, to its present state as a centre of excellence.

Our visitors were keen to experience something of the mountain, so next day we set off to climb the steep path to the first hut. David and I had done this first bit of the climb once or twice before, and it is quite hard work, but worth it for the panoramic view when you reach the first hut.

On a previous occasion we had caused some surprise and mirth among some porters who were on a routine patrol of the route. It was out of season and it was raining. I had one arm in a sling, having just had a minor operation on one thumb at KCMC; David was carrying an umbrella, having forgotten that he might need a raincoat. After handing round some sweets and sitting down for a chat in Swahili, they realised that we were not crazy tourists who needed escorting back to their hotel!

There was no rain for our visitors, and the view as stunning as ever, making a memorable place for a picnic. The climb and the altitude take their toll, especially coming straight up from the coast, and we were quite glad when we were on the way down to our supper with Sallie.

We were sad when the time came for another visit to Kilimanjaro Airport and to say goodbye to Alan and Joy. We had all enjoyed the visit, and David and I hoped that we might be able to return it next year at their home in Canada during our overseas leave.

Malaria and Drug Resistance

This was a very tricky period for malaria in East Africa. During my first ten years there, if one of us developed malaria we thought they had been careless and forgotten to take their daily paludrine tablet, or their weekly chloroquine when that was introduced. But more exceptions occurred, starting for me with my attack of malaria on the boat on the way to Dar-es-Salaam in 1949 (see Chapter 2).

Gradually it became clear that in some countries the malaria organism, the plasmodium, was becoming resistant to one drug after another, and so not killed by them. With all its disadvantages we were having to use quinine again, and it was an enormous relief that it would almost always work when the others had failed. The problem was most serious in two groups, babies and small children, and long term expatriates who had become casual about malaria and had stopped taking regular prophylactic pills.

In the former group we were seeing the very serious complications of cerebral malaria and blackwater fever. These little ones were brought in with uncontrollable convulsions and/or passing no urine at all or very little and heavily blood stained so almost black in appearance. Immediate quinine injection could have a dramatic effect. The other problem for local children, especially babies, was the long-term effect of recurrent less severe attacks. These were brought in collapsed and gasping for breath from anaemia. The malarial parasites live in the red blood corpuscles, gradually destroying more and more of them. Our staff nurses and others became experts at putting needles into veins however small and in a restless child, so that if we could get a blood donor, lives could be saved by an immediate blood transfusion.

In our area the adults were mostly Roman Catholic priests and nuns who had no doctor in their mission. They came to Elizabeth or me, desperately ill, and a blood sample found to be loaded with malarial parasites. As for children, immediate quinine injection was usually life saving, followed of course by quinine tablets and expert nursing care. It was drastic treatment for a critical condition. Blackwater fever and even cerebral malaria were also being seen again in adults, as in the old days when they were frequently quoted as the cause of death of pioneer missionaries.

Quinine by injection is a horrible drug to give, whether into a vein or muscle, but marvellously effective. We followed it as soon as possible with pills, but it is so bitter that for babies and small children not at all easy by mouth!

Roman Catholic missions in Tanzania must be famous for their generosity! Invitations soon came to visit their mission settlements in lovely places in the Usambaras, both Gare near Lushoto, and Rangwi further on and up to the north. These were Irish Rosminian Fathers and Sisters from Germany and Holland. As well as definite invitations we were soon told to call in at any time.

David and I had two or three short breaks with them. Days were spent walking in the hills with a picnic lunch, or restfully at the mission, and enjoying their company in the evening. To our surprise sometimes they would put on a film in the evening, inviting all and sundry in to see it. When we left our already loaded back packs would be further loaded with a bag of home grown coffee beans, which we found on our doorstep when we were all packed up and ready to go, and on one occasion a bottle of home grown wine for me and one of whisky for David!!

We travelled on David's motorcycle to Lushoto and Gare and he managed to keep on the road in spite of its load and the surfaces and gradients which had to be manoeuvred. Passing Soni on the way home we would call in on Dr Leader Sterling and his wife Anna, then in retirement at Soni after Leader had finished his five years as Minister for Health. Down on the plain we passed Makuyuni, where Bishop Neil Russell lived in retirement. He was a former long term UMCA missionary of the diocese who became Suffragan Bishop of Zanzibar before his retirement. After a few years in Scotland, he retired 'home' to spend his last years at Makuyuni near Korogwe. It amused us that calling in on him in his simple dwelling, we would offer him coffee and biscuits out of our bulging packs, as we always made room for a flask of hot water and something to go with it.

First Year Completed

My memories of the first year's work at Muheza hospital must be deceptive, as they are almost entirely of administrative matters. I see myself in my office, either alone ordering drugs and equipment, or drafting letters, or interviewing staff; at other times I would be over at the nursing school doing much the same with Sylvester Chizazi.

During the first six months Clement Mdoe and I had the final stages of the building project to handle. We had expected to have Jim Flood doing it, and his sudden departure was a serious disappointment to us, and no doubt to him as well. There was quite a lot to finish and also to correct before the final payment could be made.

Meetings of the hospital board were a new experience, clearly necessary in this type of hospital, but not something which I was used to. It took time to learn how you could get things done, how much was my decision and how much to consult others first, or to refer to the next board meeting.

From theatre records I know that we had a full operating programme, and that I did most of it, but it is strange that I remember few individual patients or operations in the way I remember them so vividly at Magila and Lulindi. But in one of my newsletters to friends and supporters during this period I have said, "We need a young and energetic surgeon here, as the work will soon be too much for me." An obstetrician or gynaecologist would be quite at home with much of the work. I had almost forgotten that my specialist training had not included these skills!

David and I both had diocesan committees to attend at Korogwe and one of them, the Diocesan Finance Committee, gave us a day out together. David was already a member and I had recently become one with the retirement in 1979 of Dr Lesley Sitwell, who had given thirty years of devoted service to the diocese. She had been the senior doctor in the diocese, so was officially in charge of all our medical work. Her retirement left me in that position, and the finance of the medical work was one of the responsibilities.

Lesley Sitwell was a very good friend, and we always enjoyed staying with her in England when we were on leave. After we retired she returned the visits, and as gardening was her hobby she did wonders in our garden. No job was too much for her, as was true of her years at Kideleko, Magila and Korogwe. Nurses as well as patients loved her.

Farewells

Our first year at the new hospital passed quickly. Sadly we said goodbye to the two CSP Sisters who had been running the maternity department, Sisters Jacqueline and Gillian Mary, with whom I had so much enjoyed working for so many years. Jane Gongwe had plenty to do in her teaching role for the midwifery students, but would give time to the maternity ward until someone else became available. With Elizabeth ready to take the hospital on, at least for my time away, and Ernest Barabara, the retired priest who lived near and grew citrus trees, to look after the parish, David and I set off to England for leave in May 1981.

Overseas Leave

Leave would be different this time, our first without David's mother's home to go to when we arrived in England. His elder brother Edward and Susan his wife very kindly made us feel 'at home' in Ibberton, a tiny village in a lovely country spot in Dorset. We soon got hold of a car, and set out on our usual visits all over the country. Meetings, talks and sermons, visits to supporters and to family and friends gave us a fairly full programme in England. There was also my visit to Hamburg to report on progress at Muheza DDH, and to get more help and advice from SIMAVI about instruments and equipment. Now that we were up and running at the long awaited Muheza Hospital, we had a better understanding of what was lacking. Returning to England there were visits to USPG Headquarters, and orders to put in for drugs and equipment at our usual suppliers.

Maureen and Bill Jones

A long weekend at St. Alfred's College Winchester had been booked for us by USPG, to attend their annual conference. My memories of that weekend are two: my first visit to Winchester's magnificent

Cathedral is one; meeting Maureen and Bill Jones at the conference is the other. Maureen was an experienced and skilled nurse-midwife; Bill an experienced and skilled teacher. They were USPG mature candidates for work overseas, who had a family of three, the youngest within sight of leaving university. As a family they had spent time together on less well-known routes to places less often visited at the time.

Now Bill and Maureen were keen for a period of overseas mission work, and their destination was still in the balance. We from Muheza could make attractive suggestions to each of them, and could explain how urgent our needs were. It was not difficult to see Maureen running our maternity department, strict about standards I felt sure, but friendly and helpful to the students and other staff.

Hegongo secondary school, which had taken over unused buildings at Magila and also those at Hegongo, was desperate for an experienced English teacher. The couple seemed cut out for both jobs. As we told them more of the history of Magila and the present situation there and at Muheza we could see their enthusiasm increasing. With a huge sigh of relief, we soon heard that they would be with us, though it would be a year before they could come. They had told us enough about their lives and interests to make us feel sure that they could fit in well and enjoy the challenge of both jobs and of life at Muheza.

Canada

Joy and Alan had moved to Hamilton, Ontario, since our last crossing of the Atlantic. Alan's job was similar to that in Flint, Michigan, and it was a time when there were many exciting developments in the world of radiotherapy. Their new home was a small but comfortable house in a very large garden. With their gardening enthusiasm, the sizable front area was full of flowers, and at the back were rows and rows of vegetables and soft fruit like strawberries and raspberries. These were interspersed with fruit trees, and a few flowers in any space in between. All this was carefully harvested and put to daily use and as gifts to neighbours.

Joy also made pots and pots of jams, jellies and chutneys, and the rest was stored for winter use in their ample deep freezers. These were defrosted in midwinter, when deep snow outside the back door could keep all the contents deep frozen over night.

Naturally we both offered to help in the garden. David helped Alan with one of his energetic projects, while I was commissioned to make an attack on dandelions which were threatening to take over in any space they could find. Joy and I were amused that she had seen in a gardening guide, 'Plant dandelions now for winter use'. We wondered who needed to do that. They are beautiful flowers but a thorough nuisance to many gardeners.

We didn't see much of the nephews on that visit: Martin pursuing his medical career and Jim far into the exciting, but to me rather obscure, world of physics. This was soon to lead on to astrophysics, which I find even more obscure.

Back in England we had to spend time in my sister Gertrude's bungalow in Norwich which was left to me in her Will. It was twenty years since she died; Eva Hilliard, sister-in-law to Fred and Elsie Hilliard, had lived there since then. She had looked after it well for us, but had now moved to an Abbeyfield Home in The Close in Norwich. We had been advised, unwisely we found later, to let the bungalow furnished. We enjoyed having some time there, dealing with an assortment of things left by Eva, Gertrude, and even my mother and I myself in the spacious loft. We could also see friends in and around Norwich. Sadly the letting was a failure, with damage done to house and furniture, so we were thankful that the Hilliards had taken care of the grandfather clock during this period. They also dealt later with the sale of the bungalow and storage of such furniture as remained serviceable, so that we had something to come back to when we retired.

The Opening of Muheza DDH: August 1981

Arriving back at Muheza in August 1981 it was really good to see that progress was being made, and that Elizabeth was getting on well. While we were away the official opening of the hospital and nursing school had taken place. We had been honoured by the President, Mwalimu Julius Nyerere, finding time to come for the occasion. I feel sure that Elizabeth would have been more at home at the centre of an event of that sort than I would have been, but naturally I was sad that we had missed it.

For such a great event many had come in from all around the District. They didn't want to miss the rare opportunity of seeing our very own popular President, and of seeing him at their own new hospital. I expect some were wondering why David and I were not there, and I hope they were not putting it down to the wrong reasons.

I had first met Mwalimu Julius Nyerere at Minaki soon after I arrived there in 1949 (see Chapters 2 and 4). He was then teaching at the Roman Catholic secondary school at Pugu, only about 3 miles from Minaki. Our students, secondary, teacher training and medical, of St Andrews College Minaki met those from Pugu from time to time for sporting and other events, so we got to know the staff.

At our first personal meeting he was the anxious husband, bringing his wife as she needed some minor surgery after the birth of their first baby. Julius was deeply into politics then, and during the next few years became the leader of the party which took the country to Independence in 1961.

I had met him several times since, but only as part of the crowd, and with hardly an opportunity for conversation. The last occasion was in 1968 when an official sundowner was given to bid goodbye to Bishop Trevor Huddleston. Bishop Trevor was staying with us at St. Albans Rectory, Dar-es-Salaam, when he was on his way to England after 8 years as Bishop of Masasi Diocese (see Chapters 6 and 7), so we took him to the sundowner. He and President Nyerere had been really good friends during Bishop Trevor's time in the country.

I was thankful that both our previous Government and our first President were keen on the co-operation which had developed between the Government and the churches and missions in the struggle to improve the country's medical services. It was an honour and I think also a sign of his desire for joint action on the development of medical services that he found time for the opening of our hospital and for similar occasions around the country. The President was a Christian and a loyal Roman Catholic, and applied his beliefs to his life and his policies.

Co-operation

It was some years later that I realised that during over 40 years in Tanganyika/Tanzania, one of the important themes which ran through it all was co-operation between the Government and all Christian medical work in the country. Missions and Churches were undertaking an estimated fifty percent of this work including training. Progress which was very much needed would be made only if we worked together.

Dr Mary Gibbons, my predecessor at Minaki, and other doctors including Leader Stirling and Wellesley Hannah, an Australian CMS doctor, had made a big difference to this relationship (see Chapter 3). They had set up a Mission Medical Committee (MMC) which included all doctors working in Christian organisations in the country. The Christian Council of Tanganyika brought most Christian groups together, but not Roman Catholics, so the MMC could not be affiliated to it. We doctors were determined to speak with one voice in our medical planning and our relations with Government and with each other.

Of all the places where members of the MMC were working, Minaki was only 18 miles from Dar-es-Salaam where all Government Departments had their central offices at that time, while for others the distance was measured in hundreds or thousands. This and Mary's determination and ability made her the obvious choice as secretary of the MMC, and as such made her responsible for all interchange with Medical Headquarters.

Within six months of my arrival Dr Gibbons went to England on leave; unexpectedly she had to retire; as a new young missionary I found myself persuaded to take on Mary's position as Secretary. It was a job I felt in no way ready for, but one which gave me a lot of very interesting experience, including my visits while at Minaki to Tanga Diocese, Manda and Liuli down on the eastern shore of Lake Malawi, and Ndanda and Peramiho, both large Roman Catholic Benedictine centres with sizable medical units. After almost 12 years at Minaki I moved to Masasi diocese in the south of Tanzania, to Lulindi hospital (Chapters 6 and 7). There the co-operation was needed first between the dioceses supported by UMCA, as to whether we should develop one hospital such as Mkomaindo Hospital, Masasi as a joint project (see end of Chapter 5). I feel sure we were right not to go ahead with this. Instead, with approval of the new Health Ministry, we built a new nursing school at Mkomaindo, and planned developments there. Lulindi nursing school was transferred to Mkomaindo during 1966-67, Lulindi hospital becoming a rural health centre with special responsibility for leprosy work. This chapter and the last are about co-operation in building 'Muheza DDH': one new hospital in place of two old ones; one a mission hospital and the other the district hospital. This was made possible by a new Grant in Aid agreement for a Christian hospital to take the place of the district hospital, and so become a 'Designated District Hospital' (DDH).

The first year at Muheza DDH before I went on leave in May 1981 certainly needed a spirit of co-operation, and my own experience of differences which I was having to get used to was just one example. Others had similar experiences in wards, OPD, laboratory, and especially perhaps in the MCH Clinic which was central to the service to the whole District and had some pretty senior staff in charge as well as the DMO. Government and mission salaries, though basically equal, had advantages on the Government side.

Elizabeth Hills, straight from England when the DDH opened, must have found it all strange at first, but her very different past experience as a consultant in a UK Health Service hospital instead of a local person may have been just what was needed at the time. Things were certainly going well when David and I returned.

What of Our Future?

Back at Muheza I realised how mentally drained and exhausted I was after the years of working on the Muheza project with all its problems, while still having a lot to do at Magila. I was happy to be back at work in the hospital wards, enjoying the present mixed staff and the improved working conditions. What I could not face was any administrative responsibility, and also, strangely, any social activity or even just meeting people and talking to them. This latter even made me flee to the kitchen if I heard anyone approaching our front door.

It was an enormous relief that Elizabeth was happy to continue as acting Medical Superintendent to the hospital, and was soon made Superintendent in my place. David did his best to help me out of what was becoming a sort of phobia, but it was time and prayer, and perhaps a change of scene which we realised were needed.

As well as my problems there were other reasons for us to have a move. David was one of two priests working in the diocese who came from overseas; Paul Hardy, the other, was on the island of Zanzibar. David had been in charge of Muheza parish since it was created 11 years ago, so this in itself could well be a reason for the parish as well as David to have a change.

Kwa Mkono

At the same time, we badly needed a doctor for Kwa Mkono, with its 'bedded dispensary' which needed upgrading to hospital status while continuing its outreach to the villages in the area.

The situation there had been on my mind for some time, especially since Dr Lesley Sitwell's retirement in 1979 which had given me more responsibility in planning. Lesley had supervised the dispensary from Korogwe 30 miles away where she was in charge of St Raphael's Hospital.

As well as the 'bedded dispensary' at Kwa Mkono there was the Polio Hostel. This was another enterprise of the CSP Sisters which had by 1980 become a well-known haven for children disabled by an attack of poliomyelitis. I had visited Kwa Mkono with Paddy Shiel on our tour of medical work in the diocese in 1951, described in Chapter 3. Sister Magdalene was one of the Sisters working in the dispensary at that time. She noticed the number of children unable to stand up and walk, and so not able to go to school. The Sisters were at the forefront of the national effort to get all babies immunized at dispensaries, hospitals and MCH clinics, but poliomyelitis was still far too frequent a cause of death and deformity.

By 1972 Sister Magdalene had started a hostel for these children, who came from near and far. At home the children would be just sitting on the ground or managing to scramble or crawl around; at Kwa Mkono the staff would manage somehow to get them to the nearby school. If needed, they would be given some preliminary teaching to make up for lost time.

Now the hostel (as well as the dispensary) needed a doctor on the spot to advise about physiotherapy, calipers, crutches and general rehabilitation. Facilities were also needed to perform the simple operations which would enable the children to learn gradually to stand up and walk. We must start a 'Kwa Mkono Project'. To find a doctor and a salary for one would make a good start: both money and doctors were in short supply!

The Diocesan Treasurer relied a lot on Government grant, as agreed with Christian medical representatives, for salaries for doctors and other medical staff (see Chapter 3). Salary for an assistant medical officer was high by local standards, and for one with a university degree a lot higher (though still not comparable with those in 'the West'). We could apply for salary grant when a doctor had worked in a new post for a year to show the value of the appointment. At Kwa Mkono we should have to do a lot to buildings and provide a lot of new equipment, and probably employ other new staff as well as the doctor, paying for it all for a year or more, with still no certainty of approval for continuing payment.

There are advantages in being a woman and in getting older. Now at over 60 I could apply for my English pension: a man would have to wait a few years for his. So if we moved to Kwa Mkono I could solve both problems of doctor and salary; Bishop John might think it a good move too for David. A 'Kwa Mkono Project' would still be expensive and so it would need the approval of the Bishop and Treasurer and perhaps others, but a start would have been made.

Mary Archbold

The treasurer at the time was Mary Archbold, and as such was an important person for the Bishop to consult about a development of this sort. Mary had come long ago to the diocese as schools supervisor and UMCA missionary. She had spent years going round the diocese on foot, bicycle, bus or latterly sometimes by car, spending the nights in the villages, camping at the back of the church if there was no rest-house, and doing wonders in developing a network of good primary schools in the villages. She was also a keen botanist and collected rare plant specimens wherever she went. She was in close touch with Kew Gardens, and dozens of her specimens must have found their way into the Kew collections of plants from all over the world.

When the schools were taken over by the State, Mary turned her hand to accountancy, assisting the treasurer until he retired and then taking over when no-one else was available for the job. Her predecessor was, by the way, the teacher Paul Mhina who had come down to Masasi for our wedding as David's best man.

Mary died in harness soon after we retired, well over 80 by then. At the time she was helping St Mark's Theological College in Dar-es-Salaam to get their accounts in order. She died quietly one night, just calling her long time cook and general helper, and is reported to have said, "I am dying but please don't call anyone."

Dear Mary! Determined, awe-inspiring and rather over-powering in her early days, especially for new missionaries, but mellowed by the time I got to know her. Admired, and I am sure much missed by many, and an example to us all in her calm and trusting end to life on this earth.

Our diocese used very little red tape in making a decision like that of transferring us to Kwa Mkono. Bishop John would consult some of his staff, especially the diocesan treasurer; for medical ones I should now be the one to consult, and of course Elizabeth Hills because of the gap it would leave on her staff at Muheza until a new surgeon was found. The Bishop was very quick to agree that for us to move to Kwa Mkono would fit in well with diocesan planning.

Thoughts and Plans

For me it would be 'back to the bush' in the hospital, on my own and with far fewer facilities. The challenge would be to build up and improve the medical and surgical facilities. It was now well on in 1982, and the move was fixed for early January 1983. Moving house and job always causes mixed feelings, but also there is the excitement and challenge of something different as well as the sadness of leaving familiar faces and places, and the support of trusted fellow workers. Now we must make good use of the short time left to us at Muheza.

At Kwa Mkono we would be back to paraffin lamps and a paraffin fridge, no running water in or near the house, and no telephone! Cooking would be on a small round charcoal stove, just a single ring, and we must get a brick oven built in the back yard for bread making. The nearest shops for bread (if any) would be in Handeni, 30 miles away. Christopher, our 'cook-general', would not be coming with us.

The two CSP nurse-midwives working at Kwa Mkono were Sisters Thelma Mary and Jacqueline. Sr Thelma Mary was an expert on MCH work and did a great job with the mobile clinic, taking a small staff with supplies in a Land Rover to a number of villages every month, and supervising the sessions at Kwa Mkono.

Sr Jacqueline and I would have to put our heads together to plan a small, convenient and affordable operating theatre. Good light and ventilation made it difficult to keep dust and flies out as by day we would use daylight. At night it would be pressure lamps which are hot, noisy and not entirely reliable. We had an electric spotlight, but getting it recharged would be difficult. The solar panel which we tried was not strong enough. We had to try to get electricity. Meanwhile Sister Jacqueline would find a way to use another building so that we could make a start, especially for a few of the polio children.

David also would be having thoughts about 1983. In a sense it would be just the same job, but among different people in different surroundings. The Wazigua people were cattle people with a strong loyalty to their tribe and their homeland. I'm sure this is true of many tribes, but I was very aware of it among the Wazigua. At Kwa Mkono there was also a small Maasai encampment. This was turning into more of a settlement; they had started planting fields of maize and vegetables, instead of relying entirely on their cattle for food as they had in the past. My memory of Maasai cattle is of huge, gentle, slow moving animals, but supplied with long, curved and really dangerous-looking horns!

David would have the long established parish of St Francis Kwa Mkono to look after with its outstations scattered over an area 15 to 20 miles in all directions. As Rural Dean (Area Dean) he would also have nearby parishes like Handeni, Kideleko, Mandera, Kwa Chagga and others to visit, so his time would be full and his motorcycle in constant use. Church and parish hall were already there at Kwa Mkono, so our planning for new buildings would be only in the hospital this time. He was keen to continue his training work in Zigualand, and in fact opportunities soon arose. He also hoped that other experienced parish priests would take on this much needed programme, and that the work might continue at Muheza. As in England, there was a tendency for various reasons other than ill health for teachers, medical workers and others to retire early, a number were feeling a strong call to ministry in the church. For these as well as those with a few more years before retirement, local study was far more appropriate than moving to a college with its more academic type of study.

Thankful that I could still enjoy the day's work, especially when teaching the nurses or in the operating theatre, I was aware that it was likely to be the last time I would have the luxury of having someone who knew how to give a general anaesthetic. Nurses would be doing their best, with me doing my best to advise them. Some nurses seemed to have a natural instinct for it, but there's nothing like a few good lessons. Sister Jacqueline and I would both miss the luxuries of Muheza DDH theatre; for me good lighting and good supplies of the right instruments would have priority, also the air conditioning for the hottest days (not always on because of expense) because I was in cap, gown, mask and rubber gloves most of the time. Sister J and the staff nurses would miss the sterilising facilities; a primus stove with a steriliser sitting on it is not the easiest arrangement to handle. There would be many times when I found Sister J crouching over one when I expected her to be back in the convent having a meal or saying the evening office in the chapel.

A Passion Play and Some Coconuts

Sylvester was a popular name in our area, and there was an elderly man of that name living in a small collection of houses about a mile from Muheza church. Several of his elderly neighbours found that mile more than they could manage, and led by Sylvester were determined to have a tiny church, or synagogue, as they would call it, of their own. I could never remember Sylvester's second name, so called him Sylvester the Coconut. The reason was that we frequently caught sight of him walking past with a basket of coconuts on his way to take them for sale at the market. Perhaps I should say 'hobbling', as even without the heavy basket of coconuts he found the church just about as far as he could get.

Sylvester assured David that they could themselves build the walls and roof supports, but would have to use palm leaf thatch, as they couldn't find money for a more permanent roofing material. It didn't take long for us to find a parish in England who would finance such a worthy cause, although the price of corrugated iron or aluminium was rising rapidly at the time. David could soon add this new little outstation to his monthly visit for Eucharist and meeting with the old people, and they could use it for prayer and bible study at other times.

David had produced or taken part in passion plays in English parishes, but it would be rather different here. An outline script was available to build on and early in Lent he invited those interested to come for rehearsals. Plenty showed enthusiasm, at first anyway, and many showed talent. Traditional acting is extempore, often straying far from the theme. Rehearsals went well, but as usual there were plenty of anxieties when it came to Holy Week. All the key figures turned up and remembered their parts with only occasional promptings. David and I were probably the only people who were aware that there were thirteen apostles that day instead of the usual twelve. Perhaps his name was Matthias.

New Arrivals

Newcomers from overseas were always a rather special event, or had been up until now. However, as our new 'Hospitali Teule', Muheza DDH, developed, various experts gave weeks or months of help working in their own speciality and we got more used to newcomers. Also medical students came from overseas for their elective periods, and staff exchanges were arranged, especially through the Hereford Link.

Maureen and Bill Jones were planning for a longer period at Muheza. After passing the hurdles of USPG interviews and health checks, they spent a year at Selly Oak Missionary Training College and came prepared to settle in. In fact they spent three years at Muheza and then family affairs took them back to England.

One of Bill's early purchases was a Suzuki motorcycle. He would be faced with riding the Muheza to Magila road with its rocks, sand and mud every day as I had been. Bill and Maureen were fortunate in having a month in Zanzibar on first arrival for an intensive course in Kiswahili. I should have valued that. I never became confident except perhaps in the limited areas of hospital and church use.

Bill was valued at Hegongo Secondary School not only for his experience as a teacher, but also for his willingness to help wherever needed, and for his pleasant friendly way of doing it. Mwalimu John Keto, an old friend of ours from Minaki days, was now headmaster at Hegongo. John and Bill became good friends: Bill appreciative of John's wisdom and long experience, and John grateful for all that Bill could give for the development of the new school.

Bill's experience at Hegongo was very valuable to him when a few years after leaving Muheza, Wakefield diocese in Yorkshire sent him to Mara diocese in the north of Tanzania to start a boys' secondary school on the Serengeti Plain. Maureen's skills were not wasted. At first she cared for the health of the boys and helped in many other ways in the school. Then she extended her services to the local people. She started with maternity and child health (MCH), and was soon providing a much needed service to all comers. It sounded to me that she was providing a much needed GP service to the area! Bill wrote about this in his book, 'School for Serengeti'.

Maureen did a great job in the three years in Muheza Maternity Department. Her skill and experience as a midwife and her teaching abilities were much appreciated. Bill and Maureen both settled in well to the life at Muheza, getting on well with those with whom they worked and local residents. They were keen to get to know about local agriculture, and especially to make their garden flourish and become productive. Dr Hills was another keen gardener and often successful in producing fruit and vegetables as well as flowers in her garden.

We Needed a Surgeon

John Kifua was now District Medical Officer, Muheza, so a lot of his time was spent out in the villages and in his office. His interest and ability in surgery were valuable, but he had little time available.

Also he was an Assistant Medical Officer with no further training or qualification.

Judging by the hospital's progress during its first two years and the theatre operation book, a full-time surgeon would soon find plenty of work to do. Of course, he must expect a wide range of surgery, taking on gynaecology and obstetrics, fractures and a bit of orthopaedics, and as far as possible anything that turned up. Referral to a specialist was not often a practical option.

Some surgical teaching was needed for the nursing students and the medical assistants would benefit from having some regular help with minor operations and further refresher lectures. This would also give an opportunity to assess their ability to be recommended for surgical training.

An Interim Plan

As the year wore on we still had no offers of a new surgeon, just an American showing a mild interest "perhaps by the end of next year (1983)", so we had to make an alternative plan for 1983. Elizabeth and others felt that they could manage temporarily with the routine work, but obviously the hope for development of the surgical side couldn't get much further until we had a recognised surgeon in the post and on the spot. Elizabeth asked me to go over about every six weeks from Kwa Mkono for a week of intensive surgery, outpatient clinics and teaching during 1983, hoping that the post could be filled by the end of the year, perhaps by the American. Another possibility would be a surgeon seconded by Government, thus providing local surgical training for Tanzanian medical students. My work at Kwa Mkono would build up gradually, so David and I thought it reasonable to arrange a six weekly visit. We should have to plan our journey carefully. It was 70 miles from Muheza to Kwa Mkono on a 'made up' road that was always breaking down, sometimes a dirt road, sometimes awkward with sand, and then what in England would be described as just a muddy lane. It could be dry and easy in the Land Rover or on the motorcycle in good weather; in the heavy rains even David on his Suzuki trail bike and our skilled driver in his Land Rover could get hopelessly stuck. I still had my motorcycle. What we hadn't got were cell phones or in fact any other sort of phones at Kwa Mkono! Some safety net must be arranged, as a puncture or any other problem would leave me stranded!

We should have to arrange details of my travel nearer the time. The trouble with a motorcycle is that if something goes wrong, even a puncture, there is nothing I would be able to do about it, and at times there is no other vehicle on the road, so no offers of help. With the Volkswagen and a puncture I would hope to be able to change the wheel.

On one of the earlier visits from Magila to Dar-es-Salaam, I was returning with an elderly CSP Sister but neither of my normal male companions. About halfway home the engine just stopped, so quite soon we stopped too. We were not short of petrol, the battery leads were in place and that was about all I knew about a sudden stop. Of course I tried the starter several times after an interval with not even a cough, and of course there was no crank handle to struggle with as there had been on the car which Alan kindly lent me on my first home leave. I got quite good at cranking it after judging just how much to wedge the accelerator down with a tin can that lived in the car. I'm sure that both Sister and I were praying silently, when along came a large lorry with a Kenya number plate. To my relief he stopped, and (using English, or was it 'Kenya Swahili', anyway not an obscure language), asked what was wrong. The problem, of course, was that I didn't know what was wrong. Very quickly he found out, put it right (though unfortunately he didn't explain in a way I could understand) and firmly refused any thank-offering. Then making sure that we got off safely, I could see in my rear mirror that he resumed his journey. It was another occasion for "Tumshukuru Mungu" (Thank God). I wonder whether the driver was Muslim, Christian or Animist; he was certainly a kind man.

A Visit to Kwa Mkono

Before the end of the year (1982) I paid a visit to Kwa Mkono with Felix Mhina who knew the area well and hadn't yet gone for his upgrading course. We went on the Muheza to Handeni bus and I remember that it was so full that Felix had literally to push me in as hard as he could before he could get his feet on the step. Eventually someone kindly dragged me into a seat and plonked a child on my lap.

We got to the bus stop at Sindeni, where the 'road' to Kwa Mkono turns off as we had heard that there would be a bus to Kwa Mkono. However it had stopped running and it was too late to set out on foot, so we called in on the Khans, a very friendly family who lived in Sindeni. As it was the month of Ramadhan, and the sun was setting and so time for their meal, they invited us in to share the meal, and then took us in their Land Rover to the care of the Sisters at Kwa Mkono. The Khans became good friends, as did other Pakistanis in Handeni. Often we were able to help such families with their medical problems. In one particular case a son of the family had contractures from previous poliomyelitis and the Polio Unit had restored him to a fully active life. In that case I feel sure that we were repaid many times! They were extremely generous, frequently laying on for our staff a good meal when returning from a visit to one of the village clinics. The garage that serviced and repaired our Land Rover didn't send me bills for almost a year and when I asked, they said they'd charge for spare parts only, not for labour.

Arriving at Kwa Mkono, Felix went to the village to friends, while the CSP Sisters gave me a comfortable room and a cup of tea; I then joined the 3 or 4 Sisters for Compline in their wee chapel and so to bed.

Next morning after looking round the hospital and staff housing, Felix and I had a great discussion with the two Nursing Sisters, and the Senior Medical Assistant, Michael, about staff, finance, and buildings. We agreed that the first new building would be the

Maternity and Child Health (MCH) Clinic, leaving the operating theatre until after we moved in. Sister Jacqueline had ideas of how we could use an existing building temporarily. Staff housing would also have to wait, but we actually called in Simon, the carpenter, and Mohammed, the mason, and arranged the site and plans for the clinic which they would start on at once.

Sister Joan Thérèse, formerly Sister Tutor at Magila Nursing School, was in charge of the Polio Hostel. My responsibility there would be the children's health and especially their mobility. Sister introduced me to the staff and showed me round, and we discussed the urgent needs in their buildings. Paved pathways in the hostel and through the hospital to the nearby primary school, were the most urgent needs.

The headmaster at the school was Mwalimu Henry Lugembe, who was active in church and parish affairs. His wife, Monica, a trained nurse-midwife, was hospital matron. Monica soon had my respect and admiration as matron, nurse, midwife, wife and mother. The word 'friend' was soon to be added.

Our Future Home

The general layout of Kwa Mkono was convenient. Coming in from Sindeni, the primary school came first, then hospital staff houses and hospital, with a small daily market on the roadside. Next was the Sisters' convent and the parish priest's house, and then the church. The polio hostel was nearby and a little further on quite a large village and then the second primary school.

Church and hospital were dedicated to St Francis. It was a large church which at that time had two rows of benches near the front and mats for all others, some right in the front for children. An attractive small stone altar was in the sanctuary. On the right was a small Blessed Sacrament Chapel with vestry on the left. There was no east window, as a much needed parish hall had been built onto the east end of the church a few years before.

My memories of our visit were of a friendly place where David and I would both have interesting and quite challenging jobs. Many aspects were similar to Lulindi, but for me a very different hospital. A lot of work to do, funds to find, and other people's help would be needed to turn it into a real working hospital.

The remainder of 1982 passed quickly, with daily work including full and interesting operating lists. Muheza hospital was getting busier, with many more night calls, as we were so near the main road linking Dar-es-Salaam to the Tanga area. Of course there were more of us to share them, so I was on call just for surgical and obstetric problems, which others were not happy to handle. That made a welcome change, as for much of my time in Tanzania I was always on call when a medical assistant or sister on duty needed a doctor. Now we must face the upheaval of our move to Kwa Mkono.

CHAPTER 11
Zigualand – Handeni District

The Move

We had reached January 1983 and prepared ourselves for the move to Kwa Mkono. We knew we had to take everything – except of course electrical goods. Now it would be paraffin (kerosene), charcoal, firewood ('kuni' in local language). Taking 'everything' did include the kitchen sink this time.

We expected the lorry to arrive next morning with the incoming priest and his family and their possessions. After unloading, the driver would come and load our things. Instead it arrived the evening before and would come at about 8 am to load our things and set off for Kwa Mkono. We would follow on our motorcycles. We set our alarms suitably early and got to our beds.

Then the phone rang – "Please come quickly. We have a desperately ill patient". Then came some explanation. It was clear when I saw him that he needed an urgent operation if we could resuscitate him from his shock and collapse sufficiently to have any hope of success, and even at Muheza we didn't have anything like the facilities expected in a modern hospital. By the time I had decided it was now or never I did operate, but sadly had the only 'death on the table' which I remember in Tanzania. The night had gone by the time I could get away.

Back home by about 8 am I found all our things already on the lorry. David was nearly desperate, but had managed to keep a piece of bread and a cup of milk for me in the fridge (electric, so not being taken). The cat that we were to take with us had (understandably) got terrified and ran away. After a quick look round we went back to the hospital, where Maureen Jones took time off from the maternity department to give us an ample breakfast and we set off for the 75-mile ride to Kwa Mkono. Calling in at the diocesan office at Korogwe to tell the Bishop that we were on our way, we took the good but sandy road roughly south, towards Handeni.

January is hot. The sun blazed down on us. Our packs got gradually heavier. Then the tsetse flies came, just like large horse flies, with vicious bites. Thirty miles to Sindeni seemed like three hundred.

At Sindeni we turned eastward into the country lane to Kwa Mkono with its ruts and bumps, but trees gave us some shade, we were not looking into the sun, and the tsetse flies left us. Not far now to our destination.

Welcome to Kwa Mkono

Our welcome soon revived us! We were to use a house in the polio hostel complex until the parish priest's house was ready after some necessary repairs. The polio children in their excitement rushed to be the first to greet us. Some could run, but others could only scramble along the ground. With them came some of the helpers to see the newcomers, but also in their role as carers. With them was Sister Joan Thérèse CSP. She had been Sister Tutor at Magila, but now that Sylvester Chizazi had taken over that job when we moved to Muheza, Sister JT as I called her was using her skills to run the polio hostel.

There were usually five or six CSP Sisters at Kwa Mkono. Sister Etheldreda was the one in charge most of our time there and was soon to give us some welcome food and drink. At the same time she assured us that she would look after our needs until we could get our own domestic arrangements made. Two of the others, Sisters Jacqueline and Thelma Mary, would be with me in the hospital, and the others I should soon get to know.

Another who gave us a special welcome was Father Edward Kihala. Recently retired, and with his home in Kwa Chagga, which was a village quite near Kwa Mkono, he still spent a lot of his time at Kwa Mkono. He was a much valued assistant priest for David, very often to be seen in the hostel and hospital, and for us it was a real luxury to have not one but two enthusiastic chaplains! He freed David to get out more into Kwa Mkono parish and also to get to know Handeni Deanery, for which he had responsibility.

Starting Again

We slept well after our exciting arrival with the special welcome by the youngsters of the polio hostel and Sister Joan Thérèse CSP and her staff. All the staff took part in caring for the children. They had their special work – cooks, office staff, and teachers. Those with special skills had the title 'Fundi', and were the men who made callipers and the shoes to go with them, and crutches. They also kept the wheelchairs in order for the hard work on the rough roads, and they knew something of the physiotherapy which would help with posture and mobility as the children tried to get upright and start walking. They were skilled craftsmen who had learnt their craft on the job, rather than by a recognised course of teaching. Their work would be increasing when we could start on some surgery for the children.

As you may imagine, surrounded as we were by the children of the polio hostel, my mind was quickly on the subject of what surgical help I could give them to get upright and to walk. David, who had always loved teaching children and bringing them into church and parish activities, was thinking how best to do this in view of the fact that many were from Muslim families. However, the children didn't want to miss anything, and all turned up together and were soon taking part in the plays when David started to put them on in church after the Sunday Eucharist.

Handeni District

Handeni, a small town about 65 miles south of Korogwe, is the headquarters of Handeni District with the district offices and hospital, as well as shops, post office, bank, schools and other facilities. It is the country of the Zigua tribe, who are essentially cattle people. Their cattle and goats roam the land with its areas of scrub or bush, open country and forest. Clearings are made for crops, mostly basic food like maize and beans as well as vegetables and fruit, but not in the quantities that were all around us in the Muheza area.

Because of the frequent periods of drought, the people in such areas were, in my early days in Tanganyika (as it was then), being encouraged by the administration to plant cassava. This is a valuable 'famine crop', and has made a great difference in periods when the maize (corn) crop has failed. A 'root crop', the part used for food is like a large and rather tough looking sweet potato. It can be dug when needed over a period of two to three years and the thick stalks are then set into the ground to produce the next generation of the crop. After boiling well it is used as a potato-like vegetable, or dried in the sun; boiling first is vital because of its cyanide content. When completely dry it can be ground into flour as a substitute for corn-meal in ugali, the almost solid porridge (which is the staple diet) or for 'uji', in English, gruel or porridge.

Now of course there is much moving and mixing of tribes. Near us was a small settlement of Maasai, who had started to plant crops like maize and beans instead of living entirely from their cattle. Here they did not have the vast area for grazing which they enjoyed when they roamed between Kenya and Tanzania along the Rift Valley.

In Handeni a small Roman Catholic Benedictine mission was concerned with Maasai in the town and the area around. There were also Lutherans in the area, and David's catechist Raphael was a Lutheran Maasai and that was very useful. Many Maasai women spoke only their own language, which is a difficult one, and not obviously related to Kiswahili.

Home: The Parish Priest's House

The layout of Kwa Mkono has been described in Chapter 10. Soon we could move into our new home. Being so near to the church it was obviously right for David and right for me too, as it was only five minutes' walk to the hospital and less to the hostel or to the Sisters' little convent. Space would be limited and rooms multi-purpose.

As I remember it the house must have been about 28 feet long by 16 feet deep and facing onto the church. A narrow covered strip along the front was used for parking bicycles and motorcycles. The six tiny rooms would not have been easy for us, but the builder who built it assured us that it was safe to knock down two middle walls. This gave us a long thin multi-purpose living room in the middle which we used for meals, for motorcycle repairs and garage at night, as well as for my evening office work. The long room at one end made an office for David with a sitting room area at one end; our bedroom and a tiny narrow guest room were at the other end, the latter soon to become more of a 'place to put things'. A yard at the back had an underground rain water tank at one end and space for a brick oven to be built at the other. I planted pumpkins in this closed-in area one year, but the monkeys found that they could get onto the roof and jump into the yard, so we had no pumpkin pie from them.

A tiny kitchen, a store, a wash room and a pit latrine formed the back wall of the yard. The water tank was our only source of water, and hardly ever failed. We dipped the water out with a tin on a piece of cord. No-one thought of a more sophisticated method! We were very thankful for it. The brick oven got built, the mud bricks soon becoming baked bricks when we had used it once or twice to bake bread. We had to teach our builder about building a brick arch. His first one, straight up and then straight across fell as he picked up the last brick. Thrilled when he found the solution to the arch he built an oven for the Sisters and also made them popular in the village.

The back yard was a useful extension except when it rained, but that filled the underground water tank and made the crops grow, so it was usually very welcome.

We had no telephone, so night calls were "Hodi, hodi" outside our bedroom window. Even a quiet call by a nervous junior nurse would wake me. (I must have mentioned the 'hodi' bird at Minaki whose night call would sometimes get me out of bed.)

When at last we had a generator, to give us good lighting for night emergencies (fortunately not common), David was the one to start it for us. It sometimes failed, and if an operation was in progress a junior nurse was told: "Run to the parish priest's house; shout through our bedroom window; if no response bang on the burglar bars". (David was quite deaf by then, and had no hearing aids in use at night.) I felt sorry for the girl or boy, as they would find it hard to shout at the parish priest through his bedroom window!

Priorities

Our priorities in the hospital were the new MCH clinic now ready for use and the temporary operating theatre. By April the operating theatre too was up and running. Cases were few so far, mainly because local people took time to get used to us. I think most wanted someone else to go first, except for injuries and urgent small problems. However, by October I reported in a newsletter a number of hernias, two prostatectomies, contractures corrected for two polio children (sometimes difficult to get permission) and one cæsarean section, as well as a lot of smaller operations! A transparent panel had been put into the roof, giving much better lighting in time for the caesar.

Before long we found that Wazigua working in Dar-es-Salaam and elsewhere were sending relatives or coming themselves to make use of our 'bedded dispensary' for their surgery. This was complimentary but could easily overload our staff. A cæsarean section needed a large proportion of them to provide safely for mother and baby, including complications like severe maternal bleeding or resuscitation of baby.

Hospital Routine

My day started soon after 5 am when I lit the charcoal stove (not always easy), and got a kettle boiling to make the increasingly necessary cup of early morning tea. David liked to get over to the church by 6 to be ready to celebrate the Eucharist at 6.30. I tried to get breakfast prepared and a few household jobs done, in time to join him and others for the service. I could usually get to the hospital by 7.30. A local girl came in soon after 7 for two or three hours to clean, do washing and ironing and odd jobs during the morning. One who did this for a year or so was Teresa, who then left to marry Daudi Michael and start a lovely family. Daudi had been a 'polio boy' in his time. Now he taught tailoring in the hostel and took part in many church activities.

For the hospital day-staff work began at 7.30 am with reports from night staff and preparations for the day's duties. At 8 am we met in the outpatient reception area for a hymn and short morning prayers. The half hour before we met was useful to me to see any especially ill patients and hear about any urgent problems.

After hospital prayers we all went off to our places of work. The two or three medical assistants (MAs) settled in their small rooms to see the daily stream of outpatients; a 'dispenser' got ready to give out medicines; the lab worker set his microscope up to get the best light from the window to examine blood especially for malarial parasites. A few other blood tests could be done as well as examining specimens of stool for worms (hookworm being much less common than when I arrived in 1949). Examining urine for signs of infection was useful, but there wasn't a lot more our laboratory could offer at that time. For blood transfusions we could do only direct cross-matching. HIV/AIDS tests were added in the 1980s when it became a problem.

Another useful person in the outpatients department (OPD) with a little room to work in was the outpatient nurse. Dressings were the special duty, but he or she was there to be called on to do, or help with, any other job that needed doing. Other nurses and the prenursing students who were 'learning the job' went to their places of work. Meanwhile, the midwife on duty was either so busy that she had to call in help, or make use of a much needed quiet period to get the routine jobs done and to get ready for the next admissions. Problems would be referred to one of the Sisters who would call the doctor on duty if needed, and that of course was me.

The Operating Theatre

Now that the operating theatre was in regular use there were always jobs to do under the watchful eye of Sister Jacqueline or her deputy. On the two days in the week when we had a planned operating list, one or two of the staff came on early so that we could start by 8.30. On the other days routine jobs were done and days off were fitted in. Caps, gowns and masks as well as drapes had to be washed, ironed and packed ready for sterilisation in the small autoclaves. Dressing packs for the wards had similar treatment, and our operating gloves were still being re-used after patching any small holes and autoclaving. Needles and instruments had various methods of sterilisation. Looking back on it I am amazed at how little post-op infection we saw. I scarcely remember prescribing an antibiotic, except in conditions already infected like peritonitis.

Our routine operating lists on two mornings a week were short at first, but became too much for the temporary theatre while we waited to get the new one built. The response to almost every building supply order was "Bado" ("not yet") or "Next week"; and that often meant next month or even next year.

Finally on New Year's Day 1986 we celebrated the opening, blessed by David accompanied by a troop of robed servers and smart looking nurses. What a joy to start using it for the increasing number of routine operations, from hernias to eyelid operations, the huge fibroids that we had got used to in other hospitals, as well as cæsareans and other emergencies and injuries as before. The polio hostel children were an addition which I enjoyed, and Sister Joan Thérèse made sure they were well cared for afterwards, bringing them along for change of plaster and getting them onto their feet as soon as possible.

As before in surgery as well as other activities I was 'Jack-of-all-trades'. It made me long to be an expert in something – especially what I was just doing! Prostatectomies (by the abdominal approach) were very serious operations for us and often exacerbated by delays before the patient would commit himself to the operation.

Two mornings a week I saw outpatients in my room in the new MCH clinic. Some were people referred by the MAs from outpatients, others were asking for an operation such as for a hernia. The MCH nurses made their referrals from the home clinic or the mobile one, and there were 'follow-up' patients from wards and outpatient departments including fracture patients. Theoretically, the session was 8.30 to 1 pm (with a very necessary break for a cup of tea or one or more bananas, often both); often I could be found struggling on after 2.30 pm.

That left me one morning a week for serious ward rounds when a little teaching could be done for staff as well as students. I tried to get a rest before getting back to the hospital by about 3.30 and to use that time till 6 pm for some administrative jobs. The Matron, the senior MA and the MCH Sister (Thelma Mary) occupied that time. Sister Jacqueline and I usually saw plenty of each other in the theatre!

MCH: A Continuing Priority

The design of our new home-base MCH clinic worked well. My outpatient days were usually quiet and orderly, but not the clinic days. Then it was silent when the Land Rover took the mobile clinic out, but with plenty of turmoil when filled with mothers and their little ones from a few weeks to two years old. As at all clinics these must be weighed, some measurements taken to help assess their state of health, given immunisations according to schedule and often food supplements given too. Pregnant mothers had a full examination, and were advised about their delivery. Health education was fitted in about hygiene and diet, especially protein for the 2-year olds when breast feeding stopped. Even agricultural advice was given because milk, eggs and meat were in short supply and vegetables like beans and pulses could be used instead. Malaria control was difficult especially before impregnated mosquito nets were available.

National policy aimed to have MCH and other medical help available within five miles of every village. To do this the DMO Handeni allocated six or eight villages to the Kwa Mkono 'mobile clinic'. Our Land Rover took out a team consisting of a fully trained nurse-midwife and three or four others, mostly prenursing students, with all their supplies and equipment once a month to each of these villages.

Preparations were made overnight one or two days of the week for the MCH team to go out for the next day's visit. Sister Thelma Mary was the expert here and her days were totally devoted to mothers, babies and toddlers, unless she was almost dragged off to do some other service. Vaccines, dried skimmed milk with bags of flour or maize meal when available, medicines and first-aid items were packed and put ready.

Also very important, flasks ready to be filled with sweet tea, and large bags of 'maandazi' (small rather solid little doughnuts) which were very popular, were assembled for use during the day when the team could take a few minutes off. These would keep the team going until their evening meal.

I was quite surprised at how keen people were to be chosen for the team; it was often a very long day as they tried to carry out the full MCH routine for both mothers and children. Journeys were often long and delayed by bad roads or Land Rover breakdowns. Conditions for work were often cramped, with poor lighting, heat, flies and often too many people to see, or of course too few if bad weather made it impossible for the mothers to come.

If the route taken passed through Handeni, help was at hand on the journey home. The mother of one of the friendly and kind Pakistani Muslim families always put on a really good meal for the team, including the driver, at whatever time they arrived. Our connection with this family had started some years ago when the eldest son had an attack of poliomyelitis leaving him unable to stand or walk. The Kwa Mkono polio unit had taken him in hand and with callipers he could now lead a normal life and so take part in the family business.

My main contact with the family was when they gave me my least favourite surgical job! Their business involved welding, and they were not careful enough about using eye-protection glasses. Removing tiny flakes of metal from the cornea, which is so vital to good eyesight, needs skill, practice and good magnification, as well as excellent sight and a steady hand. It is all too easy to cause permanent damage to sight, and I fell far short of a number of these assets. The nearest specialist eye department was at KCMC in Moshi, well over 200 miles away.

Our mobile clinic drew in others besides mothers and babies. The staff gave advice and simple remedies like paracetamol, and chloroquine if malaria was the likely problem; dressings for minor wounds or ulcers were often asked for. One morning a poor lady arrived who had given a big yawn the evening before and dislocated her jaw. She must have had a terrible night, and now, as no-one on the team knew the fairly simple trick of putting it back, she had to wait all day to be brought to the hospital as the clinic was going on to another village that afternoon. When they reached Kwa Mkono I had the great advantage of being able to sedate her quite heavily, and with my thumbs well padded and small but strong fingers and hands as I had then, was able to slip it back as if by magic. Sister Jacqueline's big yawns were subject for occasional teasing, so I was called on to explain the exact technique to the other Sisters just in case!

A Visit to Masasi

Not long after our move to Kwa Mkono David was asked to lead the annual Retreat for the Clergy of Masasi diocese. For me it would be a few days really off duty, and for us both a chance to see old friends. We would stay with Bishop Richard Norgate, now the diocesan bishop but priest-in-charge of Mkomaindo parish when we were in the diocese. We could use the Land Rover as far as Dar-es-Salaam airport as it would go on to government medical stores to collect drugs and other supplies. We could then take a flight from Dar-es-Salaam to Mtwara on the coast near the Mozambique border. The Bishop's Land Rover would meet us there for the last 100 miles to Mtandi, the diocesan centre near Masasi town. As we drove in to Mtandi we should see the Cathedral where we were married and beyond it the Bishop's house.

As we were being welcomed by Bishop Richard a young chap with an anxious face rushed in and handed a note to the Bishop: "Please could we borrow the Land Rover to take Brother James Anthony SSF to Ndanda hospital?" Ndanda was a large Roman Catholic Benedictine centre 15 to 20 miles from Mtandi. The Brother they said had a dreadfully painful back. He was an old friend of ours from Muheza days. He with two or three young Tanzanians were then living at Kiwanda in the hills above Magila and used to call in when they came down to Muheza for any reason. The Franciscans had for a time had a Friary in Dar-es-Salaam which we had visited once or twice. They were there for a few years, but it was evidently not just what was needed by Tanzanian youth at the time. However, James Anthony was now at Masasi helping a few young men to explore the idea of setting up a similar community.

Ndanda had an excellent medical centre, but the thought of 20 miles in a bumpy Land Rover on a bumpy road (as both were then) for poor James Anthony broke through my weariness and I found myself saying, "Shall I come", hoping that a quarter of a mile of path could save 20 miles of misery. Pain relief and some advice about rest, graduated exercise, what not to do, and a few other things relieved Brother Anthony, and also his small community as well as myself of our anxiety.

After the retreat we visited Lulindi, Ndwika and Nagaga one day (see Chapters 6 & 7). Lulindi 'hospital' now had only dispensary facilities, but some of the buildings were in use as a school for handicapped children. A health centre was planned but not financed yet. Ndwika girls' secondary school and teacher-training centre was flourishing including their rather special chapel. Nagaga, at the turning to Lulindi off the main Masasi to Newala road, was the climax to our day. We arrived late at a crowded church, the one David had been so determined to help the village to get built before we left. David celebrated a sung Eucharist, which was followed by dancing and singing outside as it had been at the Midnight Mass in 1966. There was a thunder storm just ready to start then and we were going back to Lulindi on a motorcycle.

We hadn't time to go on up the steep escarpment to Newala, the climb I knew so well, but it was our one chance to spend a night with the CMM Sisters at Kilimani. These are the Community of Mariamu Mtakatifu (St Mary) and their mother house is at Kilimani, near Masasi. There they had fishponds, a productive garden and some farm land, to be increased later on. They did a lot for the people in the villages around, and the Reverend Mother and her helpers had responsibility for the other Sisters in smaller houses all over the country and even one in Zambia, as well as those working or in training. My meetings with them before had been mainly while I was at Lulindi when they needed operations!

Rondo and St Cyprian's College we did visit on our way home. David had been there for seven years as Warden of the theological college (see Chapters 6 &7). Now there is also a secondary school or 'Junior seminary'. The whole visit to Masasi was memorable for our visits to old haunts and for seeing old friends and making new ones.

Christian Witness in a Muslim Area

Within our diocese discussions were in progress about our relationships with the largely Muslim population. David was involved in discussions with other clergy, catechists and teachers in the schools about our Christian witness: the dangers of 'hiding your lamp under a bushel' on the one hand, and on the other a lack of respect for other people's search for God. We with our patients, students, medical staff and the polio hostel staff needed to think about that too.

Getting to know the people of the village was a good start for David. We, in giving medical care to people in the area, hoped it would show something of God's love if we could give an efficient service with sympathy and kindness.

David was working hard on ideas. It was increasingly becoming acceptable to invite local Muslim clerics to events and celebrations. Plays such as those being shown at Christmas, during Holy Week and at Easter, telling a definite Christian event, were included and gave no offence. One year they performed two short bible scenes in the marketplace during the Sunday market (with permission from the village chairman). These were the healing of blind Bartimaeus, and Zaccheus climbing the sycamore tree to see Jesus pass by. Zaccheus was played by Daudi (David) Michael, with his paralysed leg. Calliper off he scrambled up using his three other limbs. The market crowds were fascinated and delayed their shopping with plenty of clapping and cheering.

Daudi did some other surprising things. He used to go out with David on the back of the motorcycle, taking his calliper off and carrying it. At bad bits of the track, due to rocks, heaps of sand or quagmires of mud, he got off, put on the calliper and found a way of getting past the obstacle. Also when an acrobatics club was formed among the local youth he joined it and joined in!

One year, because the parish and hospital are dedicated to St Francis, the life of St Francis of Assisi was celebrated early in October with a play performed in the church after the Sunday Eucharist. All was going well, and David out of sight on one side of the stage had little to do as the prompter. Suddenly a member of the congregation rushed in and up the aisle shouting "chumvi hakuna" (we have no salt). Someone had forgotten to order it for the delicious meat and vegetable stew which was being cooked nearby in a huge cauldron, and which we should all enjoy after the play. It was hardly likely that David would be carrying several ounces of salt in his cassock pocket!

When our Land Rover driver was on holiday or off sick David did the driving. This gave him a free ride to one of the villages without taking up much-needed space on a mobile clinic visit, and getting to places was always a problem. On several occasions he spent hours in a village, talking to people and holding informal meetings. Occasionally a local church choir could join him. After one such day, in an almost totally Muslim village, a village leader got up and made a speech at the end. "Well", he said – followed by a pause – "we have had people come here to talk about health, about improving our roads, giving us new ideas on agriculture, digging pit-latrines, as well as the maternity and child health clinic, but no-one has ever come before to discuss religion. Please come again."

There were six villages in what was called an 'outstation' in the parish where a group of Christians were living, and meeting for prayer and bible study. David or Fr Kihala would try to visit each on one morning in the month to celebrate the Eucharist. Some built a small 'tabernacle' (tiny church) as a place of meeting, but in others any table or even a box would serve as an altar and the back seat of the motorcycle often came in useful too. This had always been on a weekday, but they planned now to go on a Sunday, even if it meant David leaving rather late after the 10 o'clock celebration. This was possible if he could keep his motorcycle on the road.

The hospital outpatient hall was multipurpose – we could even hold staff parties there. We met there for daily prayers, and then the outpatients started to arrive, admissions waited there or the urgent ones were quickly taken to a ward; it was a centre of activity by day and useful too for the staff on duty at night.

It had one special day in the year – Palm Sunday – the mid-morning Sunday service started there. Congregation, choir, servers and priest, palms and hymnbooks, all collected there, but no donkey as they were not available and a goat or calf would be less appropriate. After the first part of the service and with plenty of enthusiasm and waving of palms we set off singing on the short walk up to the church for the Palm Sunday Eucharist. Polio children joined the procession if they could or else were wheeled to it or to the church.

David and Fr Kihala always made the major festivals of the Church 'special' partly because of the children, but I'm sure that we of the congregation enjoyed the special services and were helped by them just as much. Many from the villages came in for these special days, finding it refreshing to worship with those at the parish church.

All in a Day's Work

David's days got increasingly filled up and I could see how pleased he was when the first few men turned up on foot or on bicycle asking for theological training, hopeful of ordination if the Bishop agreed.

He was soon to find himself responsible for keeping not only the hospital Land Rover and his own and the polio hostel motorcycles on the road, but also the diocesan 'fleet' of motorcycles. For those parish priests who were able to ride, or keen to learn, there were various sources from which we could get financial help. David was very keen on this project and it appealed to donors. The most difficult part was getting spare parts. In Tanga (100 miles away) he could seldom get what was needed, and even Dar-es-Salaam was 'touch and go'. Orders from England via ECHO or any other agency took a long time to arrive in port and sometimes a long time for us to hear of their arrival and arrange to fetch them. So it was important that all used the same make, and Suzuki was the one they decided on.

I didn't need a motorcycle then but got an occasional ride. I continued to need occasional visits to Muheza which was on the way to Tanga, and we could fit that in with taking or fetching a motorcycle with which David needed help. The problem for me was the height off the ground of a Suzuki Trail. Increasingly they seemed to be building them for men of the taller build! When mine was no longer needed David could satisfy a life-long wish to take a motorcycle apart. He then packed it in a box and sent it down to Tanga to be sold!

When much-needed spares arrived our living room was frequently in use as a repair station, which I suppose was fair enough as I used it as an office in the evenings.

A New Land Rover

When at last a new Land Rover arrived for the hospital we set off on one motorcycle for the docks in Tanga. Other small jobs done we arrived at the docks and went through the rigmarole of clearing the vehicle and actually getting possession of it. But – no windscreen wipers – they had been stolen! More forms to fill in, time wasted, tempers frayed, and it had started to rain. After a quick lunch with the CSP Sisters in Tanga we had to set off with about 100 miles to go to Kwa Mkono and with a call to make on the way at the diocesan centre at Korogwe.

The rain was increasing. One of us must ride in the rain, the other drive without wipers on bad roads, tarmac with potholes to Korogwe, unmade-up road to Sindeni, then country lane to Kwa Mkono. I started on the motorcycle but David decided we should exchange places before long as the rain got worse and worse. It was slow progress. At Korogwe David set off up the long track to see the Bishop, while I settled down in the new vehicle. Having pen and paper with me I could ignore the weather and draft one of our newsletters to friends and supporters in England, America and elsewhere. Only 35 miles to go when David reached me again, but it seemed twice the distance as it had when we moved to Kwa Mkono in blazing sun and with clouds of tsetse flies meeting us. It was an enormous relief to have a new Land Rover, registered in my name; but I never drove it again. If I was out of Kwa Mkono they would have the vehicle for emergency use.

Prenursing Students

There were always plenty of teenagers, boys and girls who wanted a place at Muheza nursing school. However, in rural areas like ours, few would have enough English to cope with the entry exam and nursing course in English, or have the confidence required to take on the training. A year or more working at St Francis Hospital, getting a little teaching and practice in the use of English and hearing hospital terms like 'syringes', 'dressings', 'stretcher', 'operation', etc gave some just what they needed to pass the entrance exam and do well in the nursing course. They didn't get a salary, just various 'hand-outs', and the boost to their hope of a career.

Paul was one of them, a bright young man with ambition and not afraid of some hard work. He had a bout of fever which didn't respond to anti-malaria pills. Instead of staying for more help he was taken home, only ten miles away fortunately, and though a Christian family, the 'mganga', the local 'medicine man', was called in. David knew the family and soon told us what was going on and it went from bad to worse: herbal medicines, yes, but also drumming, dancing, exhausting ceremonies and 'treatments' that seemed like real cruelty to us; and no hope it seemed of getting him back to our care. Then on a visit David found poor Paul quite out of his mind and out of control with high fever, shouts of pain and misery, and tied up to a pole in the dark old-style house. David spent time there, prayed, pleaded with the family and finally they agreed and brought Paul back to hospital. By then I could quickly see what was causing all this, so it was safe to give him strong sedation as he was still raving mad, and to go ahead to relieve the situation.

He had a huge liver abscess. When he was quiet I used a large needle to drain the abscess, emptying it by aspirating well over a pint of thick reddish brown pus which confirmed the diagnosis: 'amœbic liver abscess'. I had never seen anything to compare with it.

To my great relief the fever responded quickly after this to injections of emetine and tablets by mouth which were the standard treatment at that time, and as far as I remember no further aspirations were needed as the amœbic infection of the liver responded so well to the medication. But Paul remained 'out of his mind', and several weeks later when physically fit and ready for home his mental state was far from normal. He remained on largactil, the only antipsychotic drug we had then, for three or four months, gradually reducing the dose. After two or three more months without sedation Paul turned up for work. Next year he passed the entrance exam and took up his coveted place at Muheza NTS. One of the leading students, he sailed through the nursing course and exams and was soon at work as a reliable staff nurse. I hope and pray that all continued well in his life and work after his amazing recovery.

Paul was a rather special example of our prenursing students, but many others were helped by it, and even those who couldn't pass the entrance exam were seen to leave us with more confidence. More at ease in using the English language, they had the chance to get a simpler training such as nursing assistant or village midwife or in lab work or some other job in hospital or dispensary.

Our Health

I went to Tanganyika in 1949 as a healthy young thing, so on the journey out on the 'Llangibby Castle', after five days in dock at Mombasa it was a shock to be admitted to the sick bay on the ship. I had high fever, a terrible headache, and was seriously unwell on this my first journey to Tanganyika. It was diagnosed as malaria, and it was followed by various problems over my first year at Minaki (see Chapter 2). But health returned and I developed the much-needed attitude: "A doctor doesn't get ill".

During David's periods at Minaki I was often giving him bottles of medicine which we used then for digestive troubles, and I also knew of his back troubles which started during his cricket career at Cambridge. Before going to Masasi Diocese in 1961 he had a serious attack of sand fly fever which gave him some heart problems. These went on for several years, not improving until thankfully he got himself off the out-of-date treatment that had been prescribed! Of course we both had the annoying mild attacks of malaria which were all too common because of the problems of drug resistance. Motorcycles were not ideal for back sufferers and the old-style Land Rovers on rough roads not much better.

However at Kwa Mkono we did both have problems. One very hot day in Dar-es-Salaam David was trudging round the town looking for Land Rover and motorcycle spares. He was getting more and more thirsty and given a sweet cold drink at each Asian store he visited, the sugar just increased his problem. Meanwhile I had finished my necessary jobs and was feeling totally exhausted. A few well-earned minutes on my bed (we were staying as usual at St Mark's Theological College) turned into a deep sleep, and I missed an important appointment!

Next day we reached home all right but I realised that it was time I faced the fact that David was probably developing type two diabetes – I had noticed recently how often he went to the fridge for some cold water.

When tests for sugar were strongly positive, I knew we must go to Muheza for further tests and advice, as I had no experience of diabetes control using the oral medication now available. We got safely to Muheza on David's motorcycle and Elizabeth Hills soon got David's tests done and was ready with her advice. Just as I turned some thoughts onto my own increasing ill feelings the cause became obvious – jaundice.

Infective hepatitis was quite common in white people who spent time in East Africa. Local people must have had some immunity. We got home safely but by then for me it was straight to bed, really ill, and it was only a few days before Christmas. The CSP Sisters looked after David and his new diet and urine tests for sugar. They looked after me, and Sister Jacqueline found time to do some real nursing, as for a few days I needed it. Thankfully mine was a short very sharp attack but the service of Christmas Communion had to come to me through the bedroom window: we were not many yards from the church.

For David it was a hard struggle to keep going with all the extra services and parish activities at Christmas time. Sister Etheldreda the housekeeper ensured he kept to a diet to bring his blood sugar nearer to normal, but I soon realised that thin as he was he needed plenty of carbohydrate and medication to cover it, rather than the low carbohydrate diet normally prescribed at that time.

Safari Ants

Then came another excitement. On the first day that I could get out of bed and safely walk about we went to bed as usual soon to be very wide awake again. The safari ants had come and were all over our mosquito nets, some already inside. These are black biting ants, some large some small but all with a really sharp bite and they cling on until they are pulled off. They march through the forest in a column of many thousands with large sentinels guarding the smaller ants. When they come to a building they break up and swarm all over it, clearing out every living thing. Insects and spiders are eaten, while large animals like ourselves flee tearing off the ants and any clothes we are wearing, and it is a real hazard for babies and small animals.

Now that I could stand and walk David and I fled to the nearby church, grabbing a fairly ant-free covering as we left the house. Church benches are very hard and we felt surprisingly cold, but it was much better than hundreds of ant bites! The one useful result is that after an invasion the house is totally clear of unwanted insects and other invaders until a new supply settles in.

Punctures

David's jaundice came later when he was on insulin and having difficulties controlling his blood sugar. My diet had for a few days been just sweet lemonade, with ample lemons from our tree outside the front door, and sugar, which incidentally at that time was in extremely short supply. Illness in diabetes sufferers warrants a larger dose of insulin than usual with of course enough carbohydrate to cover it, sugar of any sort not being at all the best supply of it in the normal way. Specialist advice was needed, and when I did get a chance to phone from Korogwe to Muheza I could hardly hear what the doctor was saying. When he very kindly came over to see David a few days later, the worst was over and we were thankful that a little knowledge and a good supply of common sense had dealt with the crisis.

My visit to Korogwe had been a very necessary one in spite of David's illness and our Land Rover troubles. It was for the twice-yearly meeting of the diocesan medical committee. The meeting went well, but transport was the problem. Land Rover tyres and inner tubes and even repair kits had been unobtainable and orders were delayed for months if not for years. Our driver was clever, but there were limits. Returning home at dusk, the first puncture came after ten of the thirty-plus miles. The driver had warned me that he had only the one spare wheel to use so he put it on. He had used his last patch during the day and could get no more in Korogwe. With darkness, but with a rising piece of moon, came the second puncture with still 15 miles to go. Headlights, the moon, patches made out of old tubes, and glue from a tree near the roadside got us through that problem. Three miles from home came the third puncture. We were stuck in the middle of the track with no verge to get onto and no way for another vehicle to pass. What should we do? We had passengers on board, so several strong men were asked to stay on the spot, while the rest of us set off on foot, the driver planning to hunt up some patching materials and return on a motorcycle owned by the polio hostel. As we started on our walk I said to the driver: "Please leave the car keys with the men who are staying". Naturally he replied that none of them could drive, but I persisted. Why, I don't know!

It was quite a pleasant moonlight walk, but my anxiety about David's state returned. I had been out all day; how would he be at this critical stage in the illness? A while after 10 pm, on reaching home, I was just about to assure the Sisters that we were safely home when we looked back down the track and to our amazement not one, but two pairs of headlights were coming towards us.

Impossible – but there they were! A man from the village who worked elsewhere occasionally brought his Land Rover to Kwa Mkono for the night. Knowing us well he had put his spare wheel onto our Land Rover, a brother took our keys and cleared the road by driving it home followed by their own.

I could leave further Land Rover plans to our driver, and after what I hoped was an adequate expression of thanks to all three drivers and the others, I hurried off home. I found David sleepy after a long day, but well looked after of course by the Sisters. He was doing quite well, and in fact it was the turning point of his illness.

St Columba's Church Mkata

Another complication to David's jaundice was Mkata Church and its very active catechist Paul Msezigo. Paul was an albino, and had to go to Dar-es-Salaam quite frequently to have skin cancers dealt with. Albinos are persecuted in many countries, but down near the coast in Tanzania this problem didn't present for them real danger as it did in some places inland. Paul was absolutely determined to get a church built for the Christians in and around his largely Muslim village. David was his rural dean, so to David he appealed for help: money for building materials and advice about plans.

From Mkata to Kwa Mkono, some 30 miles, Paul could get help with transport, but it brought him to us at about 9 pm. He had to leave at 6 next morning, and the most serious stage in the enterprise came during David's jaundice! How David managed discussions well into the night, and how Paul with his health problems led such a hyperactive life I don't know, but they succeeded. Mkata church was built and in use before we left in 1990 and dedicated to St Columba. Sad news of Paul's death came to us in England not long after our retirement.

Mzundu

Eight or nine miles from Kwa Mkono was Mzundu village which had the best-built outstation church in the parish. It was dedicated to St John the Evangelist, but on one of his yearly festivals the preacher gave us a sermon on St John the Baptist. One day I was struggling through the remaining outpatients at about 1.30 pm when a chap on a bicycle rushed into the clinic without any preliminaries. He was quite unintelligible at first but we soon realised that David was very ill and I had to come quickly to Mzundu.

A first-aid kit, a flask of well-sugared coffee and some rapidly made sandwiches were quick and easy to assemble, and assuming it was a hypoglycaemic attack I included the most urgently needed injection of intravenous glucose which was what we used at that time. But how could I get there? Our Land Rover was out on a visit. There were no other vehicles in the village at the time, and I did not relish the idea of riding there myself or even being taken on the polio hostel motorcycle to handle an unconscious David on my own. Suddenly a vehicle turned up from Handeni with some of our Pakistani garage friends. Ernest, an excellent staff nurse, was bundled into it with me and Sister Jacqueline; a full team and off we went.

Arriving at Mzundu Church we found the whole congregation in their places praying. It was now about 2.30 pm and David had collapsed at about 10.30 am. David was lying on a 'low bed' in the sanctuary letting out the occasional moan; a small heap of sugar lay on a ledge bedside him on a piece of newspaper, but no-one had been brave enough to try to get him to swallow it! To my relief Ernest, the staff nurse, soon took up the glucose syringe and confidently injected it into a vein. A hearty shout from David relieved the medical team enormously, though not I think the congregation until they saw David gradually return to full consciousness. With thanks to the congregation for their care in staying so long with David I said, "Please go home now". But no, they had to see him safely off home first.

With sweet coffee and sandwiches inside him David said he felt as good as new and insisted that he would ride the motorcycle home. Of course I said he must go in the Land Rover and I would ride it, but no, there was a deep dry gulley to ride across and I would find that difficult on his larger-sized motorcycle. Does patient obey doctor or wife obey husband? Anyway, we in the vehicle went anxiously behind David on his bike. When we reached the village people were at their doorways waving and singing as though we had come home out of a fiery furnace or a den of lions. It was good to be home. Glucose tablets and often bananas were in David's pockets, but not easy to use at the right moment sometimes.

Surgery for the Polio Children

As soon as we had an operating theatre in use, among the first patients to come to it were polio children for simple surgery and plaster of Paris. Sister Joan Thérèse gave what I had to call 'Intensive Care' to the polio children. To my joy, I have a list from her of all the children on whom I operated. The temporary operating theatre was in regular use by September 1983 and by the end of the year, while I was still spending time at Muheza, we had released the contractures (joints fixed in bent position) of our first five children. The whole procedure is a long one. First comes the operation and the plaster of Paris cast to hold the limb as straight as it will go without strain. Then changes of plaster at intervals until finally it is straight enough to start walking with a calliper. And then the great day comes: "Now I can walk". A little later perhaps: "When can I go home?" The calliper might be a 'life sentence', but sometimes different muscles grow strong and the child can say good-bye to the calliper.

In 1984 there were seven operations recorded on polio children, 17 in 1985, and in 1986 the record shows a total of 25. The new operating theatre gave us better light, more space and much more convenient facilities for the nurses (who could even see that I got a cold drink between cases). All this made for more time and less weariness for us all in a busy morning. The children were brave little things, and encouraged by the staff and seeing others in the hostel with plasters off and able to get onto their own feet made them quite excited about it all.

I loved seeing their games of football, limited of course to those who were safe on their feet in their callipers and crutches if they had them. The ball, a real light football if they had one, could be 'kicked' with anything available, certainly a crutch or a calliper and I think also a clenched fist or flat hand. I once saw a lad swing himself up on one crutch and kick the ball while still high in the air with the opposite foot.

Maasai Worship

One Sunday morning David took me with him to the Maasai settlement for the Sunday morning Eucharist. Their church was a ring of fast-growing trees with bushes between. David used a makeshift altar. The congregation of about 30 needed no seats but kindly gave me a stool.

The service was in the Maasai language and David reckoned that he could read a short lesson from the Bible in that language and be understood while understanding hardly any of what he read. Raphael Lengima the enthusiastic catechist interpreted his sermon given in Kiswahili. My experience of the Maasai was of their sincere spirituality whether or not they had become Christians. It was very noticeable in the women as patients themselves or when bringing their children. Raphael and the group near us were Lutherans.

Raphael had three wives. At the time Roman Catholics, Lutherans and Anglicans were discussing what to do when a man and his two, three or four wives wanted to become Christians. As I understood it the Roman Catholic Church said, "No", and looked for solutions for all but the first wife; the Lutherans said "Yes, come in all together but then no more wives"; but we Anglicans had no decision made from above so we accepted what the priest thought right. David found himself encouraging one man to keep three wives; but it was the senior wife that the husband wanted to send away.

Good Rains: Bad Malaria

"Good rains" were of course those that came at the right time and over the right period, in the right quantity and with sun and warmth (not too scorching hot) to give the best possible harvest. No-one doubted that: food was the first necessity of life. But there was a flip side. Mosquitoes love pools of water, in fact any collection of water, even that caught in plants in places like the bases of banana clumps. Good rains brought bad malaria because the female anopheles mosquitoes could lay thousands of eggs which matured quickly and were soon sucking blood and infecting their victim with malarial parasites. Babies and small children suffered worst. Good rains meant bad roads interfering with our mobile clinics, David's parish visits, transport of food and almost all our activities.

Our elderly MA Michael was on duty one evening and came to me almost in tears: "Doctor, I have got the benches in the outpatient hall covered with children with malaria and high fever, just come in from miles away and the children's ward already overcrowded." Fortunately we did have an empty room, more like a shed, and we found from somewhere some usable beds. The staff worked overtime and the supply of anti-malarial injections didn't run out as more and more children and adults arrived. Some, especially tiny ones had lost too much blood to the mosquitoes, and getting blood donors from their family was the next job: testing the blood and taking it from the donor and then the skilled and tricky job of putting it into tiny veins.

Measles

A similar problem occurred in a measles epidemic. Measles for us and other tropical countries is a much more vicious disease than in the UK. Chest problems are often severe, but also cerebral symptoms with convulsions can lead to early death.

One afternoon I was asked if as a special favour our Land Rover could go to Luiye, a village about ten miles away which was one of David's outstations with a small 'synagogue' (tiny church) and some Christian families. Many children there had measles; could they bring some to hospital? We didn't usually do this, because the so called roads were really just bush tracks and the Land Rover was already nearly worn out. With strict instructions to send only the really ill children and very few adults I had to agree. Returning to the outpatients department at dusk it seemed that every bench and even the floor was covered with children and a number of adults as well. I asked no questions and did no counting. Examining and arranging for treatment and accommodation for all who were too ill to go to a relation or friend in the village took all my time and energy as well as that of the other staff.

These worrying measles epidemics were one thing that made the MCH vaccination programme so important. The measles vaccine needs meticulous care with refrigeration or it is useless, and this was very difficult to achieve for a mobile clinic.

Our Last Overseas Leave: 1987

We were now coming towards the end of our time in Tanzania, and it was rather a strange leave. We did not have the usual amount of time for visits and meetings and sermons. We both needed medical advice and David needed some surgery. We needed a lot of medical and other supplies and David needed two motorcycles and lots of spares; also we wanted to see my family, some in Canada and others in the USA.

Margery Moncrieff, a former USPG doctor, and her husband, Gavin, had retired to Eye Manor near Hereford. She put David into the hands of a surgeon whom she knew well at Hereford Hospital, and referred me to Doctor John Wood, physician. Someone had mistakenly reported that I had a large liver, and Doctor Wood was able to declare me free from the after-effects from the hepatitis. We agreed that after all the midwifery and other things we did with bare hands or unsafe gloves an HIV test would not be wasted. It was negative we were glad to know.

It was interesting to meet John Wood again a few years later, the leading figure in the link which had developed between Hereford Diocese, NHS Hospital, and Muheza DDH. Doctor Elizabeth Hills had been responsible for this valuable link as she had for 'Medicines for Muheza' (see Chapter 10).

Our shopping in England had included the usual order of drugs and medical equipment from ECHO, the wonderful medical supplies company where I always shopped when in England. They had gradually widened their range of supplies to include motorcycles and spares, so David had put in his order: two Suzuki motorcycles and plenty of spares. He was assured that to send them by air was hardly any more expensive and much quicker, safer and more convenient than by sea freight. A lot of the medical supplies could be packed around them as well as the spare parts, tyres, tubes and patches.

By August David was fit enough and we paid a brief visit to Canada where all the Phillips family met up in Hamilton. It was a hot summer and fruit and vegetables in plenty from Alan and Joy's garden were enjoyed by us all. Soon after returning to England we were off again on a plane to Dar-es-Salaam.

Two New Motorcycles

The Land Rover met us in Dar-es-Salaam and the motorcycles had already arrived. David's first job was to get them unpacked, onto the road and ready to ride. Our own luggage and all purchases in England had to be put onto the Land Rover. The driver would then pick up other hospital orders and then set out for home.

David and I left early next morning on the motorcycles. It would be rather a long ride for me on an unfamiliar motorcycle. Did we have to 'run them in' or were the days for that over? Opinions differed. It was a good ride and surprises awaited us when we turned off from the main road near Mumbwi. The track through field, bush and forest had been smoothed out and tidied up, people came out and waved to us, and then we noticed the flags: they couldn't be for us – they were neither St George's nor the Union Jack! We discovered that our much-loved and admired 'Father of the Nation', Julius Nyerere, would be passing this way next morning on his last official trip round the country on a farewell tour to see as many of us as possible. Sadly I missed his cortège passing through Kwa Mkono, as a young woman with severe internal bleeding from an ectopic pregnancy turned up. We had to get her onto the operating table at the first possible moment. Little did she know that she was more important that day than the President!

One of the motorcycles was for Kwa Mkono parish, which David would enjoy using for the next three years. The next I heard of it was ten years after we left. A letter with a photograph of the writer, Fr John Karozi, arrived asking for help. John was then priest-in-charge at Kwa Mkono. The motorcycle, said to be David's still, was worn out in use on those rough tracks for 13 years – so, "Please could I send them a new one?" Now in our retirement bungalow in North Walsham (Norfolk) I put out an appeal through our church and between us we soon collected the money, and by then Japanese models were on sale in Tanga. One generous and touching donation was £100 from 'a fellow motorcyclist' – I never found out who he was. Photos were sent to us of Fr John and his new motorcycle, and I made sure the donor got a copy.

Some Large Gentle Animals

Our trips to Dar-es-Salaam continued though far less frequently than while our building programmes, church, hospital and nursing school at Muheza, were in progress. With no car they were on David's trusty motorcycle.

One day we set off early for some business there. But by early I don't mean at 'first cock' (about 2 am) but before 'second cock' so it was still dark. With headlights on we set out along the forest track which after about 15 miles would bring us to the main road.

Before we had gone far on this narrow track which David knew well, we saw in front of us what looked at first like a troop of people carrying lanterns. Soon, as we slowed gradually to a halt the lights had turned into torches pointed straight at us. Then we realised that we were looking at animals' eyes and as David turned off the headlights we could dimly outline a herd of huge Maasai cattle with enormously long curved horns. We knew their reputation for gentleness, so hoping and certainly praying that this was true we just sat very still on the motorcycle. Soon we were feeling their huge rough bodies brushing gently past our legs. With an exchange of greetings with the herdsmen and thanksgiving to our Heavenly Father we renewed our ride.

With my country upbringing and a deep love for animals this was a very special experience. The Maasai really care for their animals, handle them with respect, and while traditionally living on their milk, and blood cleverly drawn from their veins, the large powerful animals remain gentle and peaceful, showing no fear, but obedient to their herdsmen. My childhood farm experience had shown me a similar relationship on English farms, even when the animals were being bred for food.

I don't know how much the Maasai kill their cattle for food. However a meal with our local Maasai consisting of almost raw liver was thought to be the cause of my very troublesome attack of jaundice!

More Punctures

On another trip to Dar-es-Salaam, on the return journey I remembered that our mobile clinic would be at the turn-off from the main road near Mumbwi, one of our outstation churches. (I have two memories of Mumbwi: one of the kindness of Bishop John making time to come and confirm an old lady in her home, and the other the live hen I was given when I went there with David, and of packing her into my pack for the ride home.)

We stopped and looked into the clinic and found they had a lady needing an operation 'urgently' – a leaking ectopic pregnancy I felt sure. We left before the Land Rover but were brought to a halt by a puncture with all the difficulties that motorcycle punctures produce. At the side of the track I looked after all the bits and pieces as David skilfully took the wheel off and did all that was necessary. As he was finishing along came the Land Rover. They had also been delayed by a puncture.

We were all quite weary. Nearly 200 miles on rough roads with heavy packs on our backs and the puncture too made it a long day! With relief I found that rest, relief of pain and some fluid replacement was what our patient needed; my hands had steadied by morning, the weariness had worn off and the operation went well. Some emergencies must be dealt with whatever I or the other staff were feeling like, but I was thankful that delay this time was better for this patient as well as for us.

Our motorcycles fortunately had relatively few punctures, but a troublesome one came when David and I were on our way home from Korogwe after dark. We came to a halt half way home. A kind lorry driver from Handeni stopped and lent us a huge torch and we walked to the nearest village. The people welcomed us and gave us a flat place to work on between their small thatched dwellings. We spread something on the ground, and as it was a front wheel that had to come off David started to undo a lot of connections by the light of a hurricane lamp with a very smokey glass which the villagers had brought. My job was to look after a whole series of bits and pieces, all very important. But out of the darkness came a troop of little boys, all wanting to pick up and study or play with them!

I was relieved when David's job was successfully completed. At this point a little figure crept out of a house totally covered in black cloths. Not a word was said when from the front of the cloths came two lighter blobs. The useful torch showed me that they were tiny club feet; there must be a very tiny baby hidden under the cloths. Then I was allowed to see the baby. I explained to the mother and some of the men that they could be made into almost normal feet, but it would mean repeated visits to Kwa Mkono over quite a long period. I knew quite well that it was virtually impossible for them to do that. About a 15-mile walk each way, no transport available, other children and shamba (field) to look after, as well as doubt in their minds as to whether it would work. Sadly I never saw them again.

We had a success story though in a family who had many troubles with their legs. Danieli taught tailoring to some of the polio children in our efforts to send them home when ready with a skill to help them to earn their living. Living on the spot they could come to me very soon after birth when their second baby had two club feet. They brought the little girl regularly, and by the end of the year the toddler was learning to toddle quite normally.

The family had an extraordinary story. Mother had club feet, untreated but she could get round on them. An older brother had had a serious deformity of one foot and ankle treated fairly successfully before my time; Danieli himself had had very serious deformity of both legs following polio. Sadly the attempted treatment had gone completely wrong and the end was amputation of both legs. His tailoring skill enabled him to earn a living, and he walked well on artificial limbs which KCMC, the large medical centre at Moshi could supply. Travel and the cost of the prostheses were the problems.

Serious Injuries

Our meat supply at Kwa Mkono was mainly wild pig. Simon who supplied us was stone deaf. The thought of hunting in the forest without good hearing, let alone absolutely none, gave me the shudders. We saw plenty of animal and gun injuries, and Simon was a bad asthma sufferer too. His delivery service was efficient and generous. He came just after dark (so as not to offend his Muslim neighbours) and banged on the door continuously and loudly until I came from the kitchen and opened it. Coming in with a bucket of pieces of wild pig he tipped them out onto the concrete floor and told me to take what I wanted. I chose a piece, paid for it, and he went off with his bucket. Next day there was banging on the door, and another offering appeared – a huge bunch of tiny ripe bananas.

Very sadly when we returned from an overseas leave we found that Simon had died on one of his hunting trips. It was from asthma they said, not a wild animal. Occasionally at a festival, the polio hostel would celebrate by killing a goat for the children and we were given a joint. Both pig and goat were delicious, while cow really wasn't worth buying: he or she must have walked hundreds of miles and I had once seen one recently slaughtered at the roadside. Later, in Zanzibar, I hardly went into the meat market, as the goats were bleating outside. I really couldn't put meat on our table under those circumstances.

But gun wounds from gun explosions or accidental shooting as well as wild animal wounds were not uncommon as described before. A memorable case at Kwa Mkono shortly before we retired in 1990 came from the village of Luiye. The man was attacked by a lion, very fortunately not far from where other men were working in their shamba (fields). Determined to save him they rushed to his help, now covered with claw and tooth wounds, and they managed to drive the lion off. The victim was wrapped in various cotton garments which stopped the flow of blood as no large vessels had been pierced, and the next job was to get him to the hospital, 11 miles away.

Nothing daunted they made some sort of stretcher and set out on their long rough walk. The patient arrived safely, but shocked from the lion attack, pain, blood loss and tissue damage. I expect his rescuers settled down on the well-used outpatient benches and went to sleep after their valiant effort.

We gave him pain relief and took him to theatre and settled down to hours of careful work with syringes full of local anaesthetic. I examined the many wounds, cleaned them and stitched where possible, drained where it seemed necessary. I just hoped I was making the right decisions, as the book of rules in my day said, "Don't stitch animal wounds". But he was one who certainly got plenty of antibiotics.

It was a long haul for him and the nurses. Inevitably some wounds took many days and many dressings and the whole incident had been really traumatic for him. His discharge from the hospital was a 'siku kuu', a day of rejoicing. ('Siku kuu' means literally 'high day' and is used for any festival, religious, secular, national or personal.)

People from his home village, from Kwa Mkono village and of course hospital staff lined the road and sang and danced and made speeches to welcome him back into circulation. I thought that the very realistic woodcarving of a lion which was one of our farewell presents must have been in memory of the incident.

Most Things Come to an End

By 1990 both of us knew that it was time to retire. USPG had found for us two doctors, Heather and Richard Scott, recently married, who they hoped could come out in April 1990. I should get gradual relief from what had become a very heavy schedule of work as they got settled in and we could leave later in the year. The Bishop would have plenty of time to arrange which priest should take over Kwa Mkono parish and also the deanery. Soon we heard that the Scotts were expecting their first baby in June, but she didn't arrive till July. Meanwhile by April I noticed that I was getting breathless as I walked up the slight slope to our house. Then one evening I had a bad attack of 'indigestion', feeling really ill that evening and the next day. It took several days to convince me that there was something wrong and then I noticed my grossly irregular pulse.

At the time we had a vet Chris Tomlinson from England at Korogwe. He was running one of the 'Send a Cow' projects, trying to improve the local stock, while helping poor widows and others to make a living. His wife was staying at Kwa Mkono, hoping that our staff would help her deliver her fifth baby who was well overdue. With no success so far they decided to take her home and Chris offered to take me on to Muheza for investigations. We dropped the very expectant lady off at her home. As soon as we reached Muheza we heard by phone that the bumpy ride had been just what was needed and number five had arrived safely! My ECG showed signs of a recent coronary thrombosis so I had to admit that I must have had a heart attack. It is surprising now that I was not only put on medication but also told, "Bed rest and no worries for a month". I was reasonably good about the rest, but nursing staff and medical assistants were in and out of my room with their patients' files and their questions, some of them quite tricky. Word must have got around the villages that I was out of action, and the staff told me that there was only one case that they sent straight on to the district hospital 30 miles away for an urgent operation.

However as time passed I really felt well and the test case came. At intervals during the day midwifery staff came to the house to discuss a tricky problem. An otherwise healthy lady at full term with four or five children already had high fever not responding to antimalarials. She had a convulsion and was restless and the staff feared that she was developing eclampsia. What more should they do? But their story was confusing and not so clear as I have put it.

In the end I decided two lives were at stake, mother and baby, and worrying would do me as much harm as a gentle visit to the hospital. So when no-one would be around to tell me not to, I went down to the maternity ward. Several of the staff were gathered round the bed and they made no secret of their relief at seeing me. Very soon I could see that the first thing needed was a quinine injection. As the staff-midwife was preparing that I put my hands on her very large abdomen, felt a very strong contraction and said, "And straight to the labour ward next or you will have the baby in the bed". Next morning it was a joy to hear that mother and baby were doing well, and as I felt no harm I was soon back at work. I even started operating again before long, but I did look forward to the Scotts' arrival.

Still Building

Wherever I went I was building! At Minaki it was our three well-built wards, 24 beds in each for men, women and children respectively. Solid foundations, concrete block pillars with cement floors, sundried bricks between, and 'bati' (corrugated iron or aluminium) roofs. At Lulindi the TB ward which was struck by lightning within the first few months, but ward, patients and we staff inside all survived. Muheza DDH should surely have been the finale, but no. At Kwa Mkono it was the MCH clinic, operating theatre and staff houses, and now it was the Scott's house and one for the RMA Wallace. At Muheza we had built the church and several houses around it and here David was hard at it helping to get several outstation 'synagogues' built as well as St Columba's church at Mkata.

We had a standard plan for medical staff houses, so signing orders for cement, wood and bati – and paying the bills of course – was all I had to do, but a house for a new doctor needed much thought and planning as well as bigger bills. Also we had to do our best for this couple just entering a different stage in their lives in a new country and climate, new surroundings, new jobs, as well as the new baby. When my generation of missionaries came, mission stories had led us to expect 'grass huts' to live in, and so as long as the house kept rain and wild animals out it was fine. (Later on it needed to be burglar-proof too.)

The Scotts Arrive

At the beginning of July we were delighted to hear from the Scotts that Jessica, their firstborn, had arrived safely and that mother and baby were doing well. Very well it seemed, as by early August they were all three in Zanzibar for Richard and Heather to do a short course in Kiswahili. This meant a further delay in reaching Kwa Mkono, but one that was well worthwhile. In the brief time I had with them I realised that Richard knew his surgery and could put it into practice and that Heather excelled on the medicine and children side, so they made a strong combination. I wondered who would handle what I thought of as the 'Jack of all trades' side – building, admin, staffing etc. Richard would do the surgery and Heather the MCH, and Heather would be loved by the women, especially the staff and their families.

By early September the Scotts had taken over the hospital and we could start packing up and must face the fact that we really were leaving.

Several Surprises

It certainly was time for us to move on. We had both had a long innings and we were weary. My fingers were losing their agility. My sight was not quite perfect and I was forgetting even common drug doses. David had a heavy schedule, with parish, deanery and other jobs. Both deafness and diabetes made it all the more difficult. Another trip to Dar-es-Salaam was needed for travel arrangements especially heavy luggage and its despatch, tax clearance, permits including re-entry just in case, the airways office and so on. We used our usual two-wheeled transport, and were staying as usual with Mary Peake at St Mark's theological college.

On arrival, quite ready to sit down with a large glass of cold water, we found Mary, who was approaching her ninetieth birthday with one or two others clearly worried: "What shall we do?" – - – "shall I try – - – ?" " – - – or perhaps – - – ". Then we discovered that a Bishop had got locked in his room and that neither Mary nor anyone else had a screwdriver which they needed to take off the lock. David's hand went to his pocket, out came his scout knife with its various useful components, and off came the lock. George Briggs, our friend from Masasi days, emerged quite unruffled though understandably glad to be let out. He had moved on now from Masasi to become the first Bishop of the Seychelles when they became a new diocese. It was very good to see him again. (I still have that very useful penknife!)

Knowing that Mary's ninetieth birthday would be just after we went to England, we were in the town next day and we bought an enormous screwdriver at an Asian shop which we knew well; they gave us an even more enormous cardboard box and several newspapers; we put the screwdriver among all the newspapers, and labelled the box to Mary with our good wishes for her birthday. I don't know whether she or anyone at St Mark's ever found any use for the screwdriver, but a letter showed that they had enjoyed the joke.

Before leaving Dar-es-Salaam we called in at St Albans Rectory where the office of the Tanzania Christian Medical Association (TCMA) was now well established. The Secretary (not now Ursula Hay) greeted us: "Shall we send a message to Kwa Mkono for you?" We replied: "We are going back there early tomorrow, is someone going today?" "Oh no, we'll phone through. Do you want to speak to them?" Discussions about a radio-phone to link up centres within our diocese, and the diocese with the provincial headquarters at Dodoma, had taken place between two and three years ago. We had found out all we could and then there had been complete silence. Now we heard that technicians had arrived unannounced, put in our radio-phone and gone away!

Next morning, a Thursday, hoping we had got all we needed for the journey to England done, we set off early. We were armed with sandwiches for the ride to Kwa Mkono and sheaves of papers (armfuls really) to cover health, tax clearance, exit permits, tickets, insurance, re-entry permit, and so on.

Half way home we met Bishop John in his Land Rover and said our farewells to him. He couldn't come to our farewell parties as he had to be in Dar-es-Salaam to meet the Pope on his August 1990 visit to Tanzania. Arriving home there was much for us to do as our heavy luggage was to be dispatched almost at once, and there was a string of farewell parties to attend.

On the Saturday morning, Fr Dunstan Mainde, parish priest of Handeni and soon to be Area Dean, came to the door looking very upset. I greeted him as he crept into David's study. But the next thing was laughter from both. His first words to David were, "Nataka kuungama", "I want to confess". David replied, "Then I think we had better go over to the church", assuming that he wanted to make sacramental confession of some serious sin. Dunstan replied, "We've had your party". David asked, "Did you have a good time?" – "Oh yes we did." – "Did you eat all the food?" – "Yes, all of it." – "Did you enjoy it?" – "Oh yes very much". Then Dunstan came back to me to tell the story, much more at ease now. The date for the party had been changed without letting us know and had been held the day we were riding back to Kwa Mkono from Dar-es-Salaam!

Dunstan had brought the presents which the different parishes had brought for us: walking sticks, grass mats, baskets and carvings. One of the carvings, beautifully done and realistic, was a lion, but rather to my horror there was a very unhappy looking man underneath the lion.

While I had the carving (over 20 years) it stood discreetly partly hidden behind a curtain, but when I was 'down-sizing' into one room, my American niece-in-law Barbara was really keen to have it, so with other valued possessions I was happy to see it go off across the ocean to its new home with the Phillips family.

Some five or six years later when we were in Zanzibar we were able to visit the mainland part of the diocese where we had spent nearly 20 years, and we had a Sunday at Kwa Mkono. From there we went in search of Dunstan, now in retirement. He was not in his house but we were given some vague instructions how to find him and at last we saw him walking towards us. Now elderly and clearly nearing his time to leave this world, he did his best to rush towards us, seized us one in each hand and somehow found a way of embracing both of us at the same time. I think too that a few tears were shed from our side as well as his, our search had been well worth the trouble!

Saying Goodbye

As we finished our necessary jobs at Kwa Mkono an unexpected trip gave us our first opportunity for a round of farewells. I had one of my all too common dental events which needed urgent action. Our dentist, Sister Eileen, worked at Lushoto, 100 miles away up in the Usambara Mountains. With the Scotts now in charge of the hospital and nothing booked for two days we set off on the motorcycle. However, taking a short cut through unknown country we thought we were lost. At last someone appeared and told us that we weren't! Arriving up the long winding road to Lushoto we found lodging at a guest house and were advised to bring the motorcycle into our bedroom for safety. Some hard boiled eggs were found for our supper.

Next morning the Roman Catholic Sisters welcomed us and Eileen quickly dealt with my problem. That done we thought: "Gare, where our friends the Roman Catholic Rosminian Fathers live, is less than ten miles up the hill, let's go and see them". But we hadn't been that way before and didn't know that hill. Very soon we realised that I, with my recent 'heart problems' must get off and walk or rather climb, or else we must go back and go 30 miles round to get there or else we must go home. I climbed, and was quite glad when I could be picked up again!

We were welcomed by Fathers and Sisters, given a pleasant room and excellent supper with the community, and seen on our way next morning. Next stop was at Soni, part way down the hill to say goodbye to Dr Leader Stirling, a friend from Masasi days, and his wife, Anna.

Setting off again down the hill towards Korogwe we remembered that it was the day of the diocesan finance board, and we had both been excused because we were 'busy packing'. Our only hope of lunch was to join them at Korogwe, and enjoy the chance to talk to so many people we knew, so we decided we should call in. An ample lunch, much talk and a chance to see some of the Wazigua priests whom we had missed at the Handeni party made it well worthwhile.

The staff at Kwa Mkono gave us a good party in the multipurpose outpatients waiting area. Then it was Muheza where they decided we should hold the main event, as the Church of Christ the King and its parish and the hospital were our main work in the diocese. It seemed as though everyone we knew was there except Bishop John, who being also Archbishop of the Province of Tanzania couldn't miss the Pope's arrival. Presents, some large, piled up, and our heavy luggage had already been taken from us, a problem surprisingly solved when we actually reached the airport. All the kindness and generosity were overwhelming.

Included in this trip, undertaken as usual on the motorcycle, was a lovely service at Lusanga, the nearby church which David had taken a lot of trouble to protect from the weather. Shocked at my longish journey on our usual transport not long after the heart incident, they treated me as a delicate invalid. With Modi, their valiant catechist, I was given a seat in the sanctuary, looking down on the small crowded church. Modi, in spite of serious heart problems, spent her days walking in the hills, telling the gospel story and encouraging the Christians. Sadly we heard of her death not very long after. To both Modi and me that Eucharist, celebrated by David at Lusanga, was very special. They all made us feel so 'at home' that we didn't know whether we were leaving home or going home.

By mid-September, packed up, cleared up, and ready to go David's last celebration of the Eucharist in Uzigua would be on the way to Dar-es-Salaam. The small church at Mkata was now finished, a triumph for catechist Paul Msezigo's determination. Our Land Rover stopped there on the first part of our journey for the Eucharist and dedication of the church and parish to the missionary saint, St Columba. It was an occasion for much rejoicing: "Tumshukuru Mungu", Thanks be to God. The fact that I had left our sandwiches behind didn't seem to matter; within a few hours we should be in Dar-es-Salaam, and we had some coffee and biscuits we could have before that.

Our luggage now needed thought and action. We had with us two suitcases, together weighing about 40 kilo which was our allowance. Then came one huge basket, packed with all our heavy gifts, and enveloped in an old rug stitched and roped so as to secure the lid and preserve the basket. Next, a rather smaller one which would be my hand luggage. The small one was heavy and the large one too heavy for me to lift. David had his pack and several other things, and the walking sticks etc. were in our hands. Clearly someone was needed who could make allowances.

At the airways office we told our tale: 80 years between us serving the country and now really ready for a rest: our grossly overweight loads were due to the generosity of those with whom we had lived and worked, friends to remember. The girl at the desk disappeared briefly. She returned with a smile: "That's OK. Just ask for Judy when you get to the check-in desk at 5.30 in the morning and she will see you through", and she did. We staggered to the plane with our hand luggage and on arrival at Heathrow Airport found all the rest on the luggage belt. Our good friends Harold and Pat Wheate, leprosy workers in Tanzania when we first met them, were there to meet us and take us home with them. Before long we moved to a flat provided for us by USPG in Bournemouth to start getting used to England and retirement. Should we find it boring? I don't think so.

Blessing new operating theatre, including on left tall figure of Sr Jacqueline, CSP

Archbishop John Ramadhani at a Confirmation

Marion and David at Kwa Mkono, with the church in the background

After the Eucharist, with Abp John Ramadhani

CSP and CMM Sisters

Arriving back from school at the polio hospital. The children's crutches and callipers were made by local craftsmen ('fundi').

Daudi Michael, standing on left, Fundhi Danieli in middle, Teresa, Daudi's wife on right

Zanzibar Cathedral painted by John Paul, a local artist

Marion and David in retirement

Edith Fox with Marion on an outing in Derbyshire

CHAPTER 12
Zanzibar and Retirement

Retirement

England in Autumn is one of my favourite times of year. Changing colours, fruit in the orchards, berries in the hedgerows, the harvest gathered in except of course the root crops, especially sugar beet if you come from Norfolk. I love the changing seasons and the changing times for sun and moon rising and setting.

A flat on the outskirts of Bournemouth was provided for us by USPG for the first three months. We could rest on our own, start to make plans, arrange to get English driving licences – I had driven a little with an 'L' during and after the war when there were no tests and David had an army driving licence, now long out of date of course. Our international licences lasted a year in the UK. Then there were family and friends to see and some very necessary shopping.

Our bungalow in Norwich inherited from my sister Gertrude had been sold and the furniture put in store and David soon felt ready to look for just the right 'house for duty' offer. He would enjoy renewing his experience of an English parish and I should at last have a taste of being a 'vicar's wife'. Before long we received a phone call from David Hope, then Bishop of Wakefield, asking us to go up and see him. Would David like a 'house for duty' job at Heptonstall, about a mile and a thousand feet above Hebden Bridge in the Calder Valley in West Yorkshire? Anyone of our age who has walked up that hill knows that it really is above! David had done his three years' curacy at Brighouse, not far away, so was familiar with the area. Very soon we would be driving up to Yorkshire to see Bishop Hope.

'House for Duty'

The Bishop was offering us a five-bedroomed Victorian vicarage in a village with a large cold Victorian church next door with the moors on one side and the Calder Valley on the other. David would be in charge of the parish. During the interview they realised that Bishop Hope would have been a choir boy who sang at David's ordination to the priesthood in Wakefield Cathedral in 1952! The vicarage would be free with various other assets, unfurnished, and it would be theoretically a part-time job for David. What an offer! By early January 1991 we had moved into the vicarage. We were welcomed and made to feel at home very quickly, and we had over three really good years at Heptonstall. But the first thing that happened was snow, the heaviest they had had for years. Buses couldn't run, supplies couldn't get up the hill, animal food had to be dropped by helicopter on the isolated farms. David and I had to hang onto each other to get the few steps from vicarage to church wading through deep snow. How kind people were making sure that we were all right and offering bread or anything else we needed!

David gave himself to the job and soon got to know people. I was trying to learn to be a vicar's wife and secretary. Cooking was in a large cold kitchen with no heating except the gas cooker. All modern office equipment was new to me. Copying the parish magazine or sheets for occasional services such as for the death of Martin Luther-King (see Chapter 8) had previously meant turning a handle and getting purple ink all over the hands, and that was only during our three years in Dar-es-Salaam. I could use an old fashioned typewriter. Everything in England was strange at first, even cooking.

We both did some walking and enjoyed it but my heart made me avoid steep hills which was not easy in that lovely hilly countryside.

We had plenty of visitors which encouraged us to take some trips to interesting places like Haworth which was a short drive on a moorland track. We also visited York and Whitby, including the Abbey, and had plenty of visits to Wakefield and its attractive little cathedral and also to Blackburn for David to speak about Tanzania. We spent a night with friends up in Cumbria on a farm among the hills, Bevis and Ann Cubey. He was one of the doctors who had spent time at Mkomaindo Hospital, Masasi, during its development. It was all a part of England that was new to me.

Norfolk: Rest at Last?

In February 1994 David was 70 so he must again 'retire'. Our homes had been Norfolk and Salisbury respectively in the early days and we decided to look for a bungalow in Norfolk. If we could enjoy the Yorkshire moors in all weathers we could surely stand up to Norfolk's east and north winds straight from the Russian Steppe or the North Pole as people like to say. The kind vicar of St Nicholas', North Walsham, Martin Smith helped us find just the right little bungalow and in August 1994 we sadly said goodbye to Heptonstall and moved down to North Walsham. Joy and Alan had spent our first Christmas with us in our large cold vicarage there; we all enjoyed it, but they said 'never again'; we hoped the bungalow would be more to their liking, and later they did spend Easter with me there in 2002.

Meanwhile we planned to visit them in Hamilton, Alberta, in mid-April the following year. From there Alan and I would pay a long-planned three-week visit to China; David would have the chance to visit his brother in Minnesota. We would return to England at the end of May.

Bishop John Ramadhani

Bishop John had been part of my life and David's since the 1950's at Minaki. Outstanding during his time at St Andrew's College he had been head student and then a top class teacher. He was soon snatched by the Ministry of Education where he became head of the English department.

John had always felt that he had a call to the sacred ministry but not yet. He did not marry. The time came in 1973 when he went to England to Queens College Birmingham to study and train for ordination, which took place when he returned to Tanzania in 1976 (see end of Chapter 9). After brief ministry in parishes and at St Mark's Theological College in Dar-es-Salaam, he was chosen on Bishop Yohana Jumaa's retirement to take his place as Bishop of the diocese of Zanzibar and Tanga at the beginning of 1980, and so became our Bishop. Magila hospital moved to the new Muheza hospital on April 1st 1980, so Bishop John was the one to bless the new hospital and its chapel. He also became chairman of its board of governors. We had ten years with him before our retirement from Kwa Mkono in 1990, so knew him well as our diocesan bishop. Bishop John was also appreciated by others of the Province, and so was chosen to be Archbishop in 1984, continuing until 1997 although ten years is normally the maximum in Tanzania.

Before we left England for our planned visit to Canada, USA and China came two bombshells. First a letter from Tanzania, Bishop John Ramadhani would be in England in mid-March; could he spend a night with us? The obvious reply was, "Yes of course, you are most welcome". He arrived a bit late in the day and was going off in good time the next day. He made several telephone calls, had supper and helped with the washing up and then the vet, Chris Tomlinson, formerly at Korogwe now in practice round North Walsham came to see him but was soon called away to see a sick cow. Then Bishop John asked David if he could come to Zanzibar to the cathedral to look after it and the parish for at least a year and preferably more! He as Bishop was still living at Korogwe on the mainland until the division of the diocese took him back to Zanzibar to live near the cathedral.

Luckily we had guessed the purpose of his visit to England, and knew that a somewhat younger priest, Michael Westall, whom he was visiting first, was not free at the time. Michael had served in India for some years and then at St Mark's College in Dar-es-Salaam. He was later made bishop of South West Tanganyika diocese. So we had some warning and were able to say, "Yes of course" again, but we did feel torn between a quiet life and another interesting and exciting project. Father Paul Hardy who had been priest-in-charge in Zanzibar for seven years was retiring at the end of June, so could we be ready by then? To that the reply could only be, "We'll try".

We saw Bishop John off next morning and the following day I had an appointment with Dr. Liam Hughes, a consultant at the Norfolk and Norwich hospital about my heart, expecting advice about medication. It was five years since this had been reviewed. Instead he said I probably needed heart surgery; should he set in motion the necessary investigations? I must have shown surprise and concern. Feeling that he would understand I told him what we had just agreed to. His reply, "Oh that's all right, just come back on the first plane if you get worse, otherwise we'll do it all when you come back". He adjusted my prescriptions and we said, "Au revoir". Later I heard that Dr Hughes was one of those who raised large sums of money by energetic activities like cycling and rowing for various good causes. I was glad I had not been sent to someone who kept saying, "Do be careful"!

An Amazing Holiday

The Canada, USA, China holiday was a never to be forgotten success for Alan and myself. As well as seeing the country where our Dad had worked for 30 years, mother for 9, and baby Alan with them for the last one, we really enjoyed doing it together. Alan saw everything, wanted to know everything and to discuss everything as we went. Then there was the time we had together after supper in the evenings, when we wrote up diaries, drank different China teas, and talked – just as we did I suppose during the many hours we had together as children in our country home.

Realising that there was something in what the consultant had said about my heart I was pretty careful walking on hills and especially on the 'wonderful wall' as I called the Great Wall of China. Alan, at 75, happily took the 'hard route' while I enjoyed the easier one which also had amazing views of the countryside, pointed hills, deep valleys, and the wall winding away in the distance.

Back in Canada we were all soon off to Lexington near Boston to stay with my elder nephew Jim and his wife Barbara before getting the plane to England to prepare for Zanzibar. There was plenty to fit into that last three or four weeks in England.

Arrival

Zanzibar airport was just a mass of people and luggage and noise. Somehow Paul and two men from the cathedral congregation shepherded us and our luggage out to a Land Rover and off to Mkunazini, the area around the cathedral. We should be taking Paul's place in a small but convenient bungalow with little but the tall diocesan office building between us and the cathedral. From our front door we looked straight out onto the north side of the cathedral. Opposite us was a building which two or three CSP Sisters had run in the past as a clinic with a few hospital beds and their own flat above. Now it was a hostel for tourists as well as local people, and a restaurant which supplied simple meals to all-comers.

'Mkunazini' means literally 'the place of the Chinese date, or jujube tree', the tall palm tree standing even until our day in the centre of what in England we should call the Cathedral Close. Stone Town, the old part of Zanzibar Town, could be compared in shape to Norfolk (on a very small scale) as it had sea on three sides. We could take an evening walk out in one direction, round the sea shore, and back to complete the circle, but not if there was a very high tide! As we walked round the beach and saw all the hotels going up I did wonder if the island was going to be swamped by tourists or alternatively if some hotel firms would find they had been over-optimistic and lose a lot of money!

From the beach we didn't get the most impressive picture of the old buildings which came into view after we had passed the modern development area. Coming in by dhow or other open boat there would be no aroma of cloves now but still the impressive row of buildings: the Sultan's palace with its high spire, the Bet-el-Ajeib or 'the house of wonder' (now put to more prosaic use like offices), and the eighteenth century Portuguese fort. These heavy stone buildings in their distinctive style made a good introduction to Zanzibar for passengers on the enormous tour liners. They would not be using the hotels, but were encouraged to spend money when on shore. In the town the walls, the narrow streets, everything was made of stone except the marvellous carved, heavy brass-studded wooden Arab doors on the stately buildings. The Roman Catholic cathedral was in the centre of Stone Town while ours was on the edge, with the main food market – fruit, vegetables, fish, meat, rice, sugar, all we needed to live on – very near. Not much further away is a street market with all sorts of household goods and fabrics of all colours displayed on racks outside the shops. The new town spreads landwards, but I found that I didn't need to go further for our daily needs.

We had only a few days with Paul, and then it was our turn to take him to the airport. He would occupy our bungalow in England briefly and then drive 'our' car off to Bromley College where he was soon given a flat.

Settling In

David had a nice little study in our bungalow which I'm sure was in perfect order as left by Paul. The phone was a problem. It was good for the few long distance calls we had – USA and England – but often very bad for mainland Tanzania. I had to take most calls because of David's deafness, and I had some difficult occasions when I couldn't get hold of the one key word in Bishop John's message to David. Bishop Donald Mtetemela, soon to be Archbishop in Bishop John's place, fortunately came through better. He was calling about a planned visit to a youth gathering in Zanzibar. The gathering sadly had to be cancelled because of a small cholera out-break. It was not serious but deprived us of the meeting with Bishop Donald. I did meet him briefly in England but that was after David died. He was a much loved and admired Archbishop in the province.

My first days and weeks were spent sewing! Of course I had to go marketing to keep food on the table and then cooking it but we would be short of bed linen and curtains, and – for myself – of thin dresses. It was hot. At sea level or a bit below, the sea breeze helped a little but not much. Jocelyn Tayari from the Mothers' Union turned up like magic soon after we arrived and took me to the marvellous road-market where we bought yards of material at what I'm sure were not tourist prices. Then she said that the MU had a sewing machine sitting in a cupboard, not in use at present, would I like to borrow it, so I was all set up. Thank you Jocelyn, I am still using some of the things I made then.

Minaki Remembered

St Andrew's College Minaki when I was there from 1949 was one of the three boys' secondary schools in Tanganyika: at Tabora was the government one, at Pugu, only three miles from us, was the Roman Catholic one, and the Anglican one at Minaki where increasingly more non-Anglicans were accepted. So in 1995, 45 years later, there were a number from the college now retired in Zanzibar including some 'important people' and some who had been my rural medical aid (RMA) students or staff members (see Chapter 2).

Adam Mwakanjuki I specially remember because I had nervously removed a tumour (benign I hasten to say) from the roof of his mouth, doing it under local anaesthetic as I had no anaesthetist. He was determined to get it done and was extraordinarily tolerant. He rose to the very top of the army before retirement.

Lawrence Kamnonyele from Masasi, not at all an outstanding RMA student, worked for a local authority for a time. He then studied successfully for a law degree and became a judge before retirement. Joseph Angwazi had trained as a medical assistant (MA) at Bumbuli and spent a few years with us as a very useful member of staff before Minaki hospital closed. After much interesting work and experience, I found he had become manager of our hostel at Mkunazini.

One of Joseph's big interests was in women's position and rights, a very worthy cause I felt. Giving women the chance of education was important to our mission and others from long ago, and made the training of nurses and midwives of particular importance to me. These trained women, some of whom had risen high in their profession and in local and national government, now needed to be treated with due respect in public as well as in the home. It was Joseph who made me fully aware that whatever the position in the West, 'women's lib' still had importance here and in many other countries.

Slaves

Zanzibar and the east side of Africa had to wait until 1873 for the Sultan to sign the decree making slavery illegal in the islands. He controlled Zanzibar, Pemba and the surrounding small islands but not the mainland which was then under German control, and not the sea. Zanzibar had been a staging post for slaves from the mainland sold on to the Indian sub-continent and the Gulf. This could still be done secretly on the rugged coast and small islands which were difficult to control.

The story is told of an Arab slave ship after abolition, which was boarded by a British naval vessel. In haste a group of slaves were battened down under a tarpaulin on deck. The naval officer shouted, (in Swahili) "Anyone here?" The reply from the crew, "No, no one except the crew." Then the cover of the tarpaulin moved and a little voice, "Mimi hapa" (I'm here) is heard; the result is freedom for one more load of captives. The little girl was called Monica. She came from Masasi, and two men of her family went with David Livingstone on his final journey across the mainland.

The slave market had been near the edge of the old town, Stone Town, near what became the main market area where I did my daily shopping and where Jocelyn had taken me to buy material.

The Cathedral

The land made available for the cathedral had been part of the slave market. It was built by Bishop Edward Steere in the early days of UMCA, when the work of those courageous early missionaries was well established on the island. Completion was in 1880. The main building material was coral, to us an unusual building material but apparently a good choice. At the time the Sultan (Muslim of course) had, it was said, predicted that when the Christians gathered in it for the first time the wide coral arch over the sanctuary would crash down pulling the whole roof with it and killing all the Christians. Happily in 1980, 100 years later, that tragedy had not occurred. At the centenary the Muslim leaders of our day were well represented under that same roof for the celebrations. Another story told is that the Sultan gave the clock for the cathedral tower on the understanding that the spire would not be as tall as that on his palace on the harbour front!

The time shown on this and any public clocks on the island is Swahili time which is like biblical time. Midday is 'saa sita' (six o'clock), and midnight 'saa sita usiku' (six at night). In the bible 'the third hour' is nine o'clock, so 'saa tatu' (three o'clock) in Swahili. Confusing for new arrivals and for tourists if they see a public clock. To us who lived there it seemed quite normal to call midday 'saa sita', six o'clock.

Under one of the hostel buildings near the cathedral, down some well hidden stone steps, is a maze of stone apartments with hardly any light or ventilation and just a stone slab to sit or lie on. In this underground prison the captives, men, women and children, were kept until they were brought up for sale in the place where the good news of God's love is now told. Going down into such a place gives one an appalling insight into the whole horrible story of slavery. Ironically the prison has benefited the island now as a tourist attraction.

When at last the great news of 'Uhuru', freedom, came it was not easy to put into action. [The slave trade in most of East Africa was abolished in 1890]. But as the slaves were freed, those waiting to be sold and those 'slaving' on the estates, working in shops and houses and even the Sultan's palace were gradually handed over to the UMCA missionaries. The mission owned a large area of well cultivated land at Mbweni on the coast about three miles out of town. There the adults could build their own houses of simple materials and the lone children were provided for. Medical care was needed and schools for the children, and soon a lovely church was built. This building programme provided employment for some of the freed slaves.

As paid work became available in town and in the estates these unfortunate people could struggle back to a more normal life. A fortunate few even found ways of getting back to their own tribal area. Gradually the settlement fell empty and the church was out of use.

By our day Mbweni was flourishing! The land was being used for retirement housing for those with some money, and the church was well cared for. I always enjoyed our visits there for the Sunday Eucharist.

A Joyful Celebration

A hundred years later it was our privilege to be there. We were at Muheza in 1980 (see Chapter 10) and that mainland area was still in the diocese of 'Zanzibar and Tanga', so with many of the clergy and their wives we went over for the centenary celebrations of the Cathedral. As our party of clergy and wives landed in Zanzibar we were met on the tarmac by Augustine Ramadhani, Chief Justice of Zanzibar and nephew of our Bishop, John Ramadhani. We had known him in Dar-es-Salaam as a university student from Makerere College Uganda. With some introductory teaching there in playing the organ but otherwise self-taught, Augustine had made good use of our church organ at St Alban's for some serious practising, and evidently used it to good effect. He would be playing for the celebration service, and had become a very competent church organist since graduation. Taken off to our accommodation, David and I were relieved to find that we should be with our fellow clergy, and not at a posh beach hotel with the other 'Wazungu' and VIPs. Ours was what I call 'second class tourist accommodation', an attractive old building in Stone Town, the old part of Zanzibar town.

It did however have its problems, as the main water supply got cut off after we arrived. A tap in the basement was working, but there were no jugs or buckets to be found. In our room there was a clean, new-looking plastic waste paper basket, so we got a little water for ourselves and took some round to the others, telling them where we got it.

We were well fed and had bottled water with our meals. One evening we went to the beach hotel for the VIP dinner, and enjoyed it. We met the guests from Dar-es-Salaam and further afield, as well as having an excellent meal.

The service was a wonderful celebration of a hundred years of Mission starting in the Islands of Zanzibar and Pemba. It was from Zanzibar that they took the Gospel to mainland Tanganyika, and to the Magila- Korogwe area. From there they continued south to what is now the Southern Region and, settling in Masasi, they built churches and schools later forming the Masasi diocese. After a period of growth there, these ardent missionaries, local Christians as well as from overseas, continued westwards to the shore of Lake Nyasa (Malawi), and then on across the lake into Nyasaland (Malawi) and Northern Rhodesia (Zambia). We were celebrating much more than a building.

With the choirs of both St Alban's Dar-es-Salaam and Zanzibar Cathedral, we all sang local worship songs heartily, and also hymns with good translations and the tunes from our usual hymn book which is based on the English Hymnal. The cathedral was packed with a rejoicing crowd from Zanzibar and Pemba Islands, as well as from the mainland especially our diocese. It was a joy as well as a privilege for us to be part of it.

Hot and weary we came out from the long service, and were relieved to find not only food but fluids laid out to revive us. It had been hot and airless inside, and very crowded. Predictably I was soon asked to go and see an elderly priest who had been taken ill during the service, and I was quite surprised that there weren't more. What he was most in need of was a good drink of water, some anti-malaria tablets and paracetamol, and then some rest and light refreshment.

We were always short of money for hospitals, schools, churches and for people themselves, so why did we spend money on festivities like this? Travel, hotels, food, is it worth it? In spite of my reputation for economy (I remember Brenda Stone once saying to me "Oh doctor, we're not that poor.") I would say "Yes", and yes again. Our fellowship as Christians is vital to our Christian life, and occasionally we need to celebrate it with people from all over the place, remembering those of the past and looking towards those who will follow our generation.

Tanzania is a country where Muslims and Christians live closely together, and on the islands the Muslims are in well over 90% majority. Our respect for each other had grown, and was vital to our relationship, allowing Muslim leaders to join us in worship and celebration that day, just as at Christmas in our hospitals the patients enjoyed our Christmas tableau and carols.

The Market

I really enjoyed visits to the market for our almost daily needs, and it was encouraging that in spite of heat, uncertainty about my heart, and sometimes a really heavy basket, I felt no ill effects. Our fridge was tiny, necessary for our whole year's supply of David's insulin: we were warned not to rely on the local shops either to get the type which he used or that it would be still valid. If the power failed for long David had to pack it up and rush to Mbweni where the 'Mbweni Ruins Hotel' had switched their generator on and kept it cold until the power came on again. We were friendly with Flo Liebst, the proprietress of the hotel, who spent time at our house studying the cathedral archives. Flo was an artist who gave us a copy of a beautiful little book which she had written on Zanzibar past and present. It included some of her own illustrations and some old photographs of people, places, buildings and doors as well as information about the island and especially about Mbweni. The Mbweni ruins had been used as a base for the Mbweni Ruins Hotel which she had built.

Our diet, almost all from the market, was mostly fish, eggs and beans for the protein. Cheese was an expensive import. Meat from the meat market was a problem for me as goats were tethered outside bleating – waiting to be slain. I hated going there! The fish was delicious: however some were enormous and brought in on the top of lorries or buses, looking as though they could fall off and kill someone passing by. Rice, sugar, potatoes (English as well as sweet ones) were in plentiful supply and stacks of wheat flour were on the stalls, so bread making wasn't a problem and I had a little oven I could use when the power was on. Pineapples, mangoes, pawpaws, oranges and many other fruits were piled on the stalls, and various types of bananas, yellow, green and red with different delicious flavours, as well as the big green cooking bananas.

Co-operation in Zanzibar

Another interest for me on my marketing trips was the people, mainly Africans and Arabs and some Indians and Pakistanis. The stall-keepers were mostly Muslims and would greet me with, "We saw your husband on TV last night." David with a Roman Catholic and a Lutheran priest had the privilege of having a slot each week which they took in turns on both radio and TV to give a short reading or talk, and clearly many Muslims didn't turn it off. Zanzibar had its own president, inevitably a Muslim as they were in such a large majority; he was vice-president of the United Republic of Tanzania.

In Zanzibar I was doing no medical work and so I had no reason to be in contact with the government as I had before where many on both sides wanted to work together to improve the country's medical service. David's contact was minimal. However he and the leaders of the other religious groups were summoned by the President one day when there had been a tragic ferry disaster on Lake Victoria with many lives lost. As a result the President wanted to call a gathering at which leaders of religious groups would lead for a short period in whatever way they wished – prayer, reading, and singing – to show their concern and sympathy. We met out in the stadium and there was a real atmosphere of prayer. We were praying together despite our different beliefs about the one to whom we were praying and about life after death about which our beliefs were certainly very different.

The Parish

David had responsibility for the cathedral and for its parish, which was the whole of the island at that time. He had a curate, Immanueli Masoudi who with his wife Agnes and children Harietti, Edmond, and Alban (often shortened to Bani) lived next to us. A second curate for a time was Douglas Toto. He was an NSM who worked in the post office. He then gave up the job and went to England to St Stephen's House, Oxford, for some further study before returning to full-time ministry in Zanzibar.

A few years after we left Zanzibar the Diocese of Zanzibar and Tanga was divided. The mainland part with Korogwe as its headquarters became Tanga Diocese, with Philip Baji its first Bishop, while Zanzibar, Pemba and the small islands continued as Zanzibar Diocese. John Ramadhani continued as its bishop for a few years until he retired. Although not many years ordained, Douglas Toto was chosen in his place. Popular, though with many different gifts from his predecessor, to everyone's sorrow Douglas died after a very few years in office, to be followed by a long interregnum ably overseen by Matthew Mhagama as Vicar General. By this time we had really retired to UK.

The parish also had a very active catechist who I soon learnt was a student in the town named Stanley Lichinga. To me he was 'the chap on the bicycle': a streak past the front door, then a knock, and then Stanley.

We had a daily Eucharist at 6.30 am usually celebrated in the Lady Chapel at the cathedral; and other services during the day. There were four outstations, soon to become individual parishes. An elderly Land Rover was in use (with driver) but David soon and not unexpectedly bought a motorcycle, a joint Chinese-Japanese make, small, not expensive and it turned out to be a good bargain. We were quite lightweight between us, and we used it a lot; it would have been light enough for me to ride but I was quite glad not to have to at 75 and five years or more out of practice.

When David went to the outstations I nearly always went with him. Stanley Lichinga, the catechist, was usually there, either with us in the Land Rover or on his bicycle if we used the motorcycle. He was a real help to David. On one particular occasion Stanley and I were each thankful that the other was there. David got as far as the end of the sermon and then collapsed. Glucose tablets and coffee revived him, but he couldn't go on. He had shingles as well as his usual diabetic problems. We were very lucky that a vehicle was available to take him home and a volunteer to ride the motorcycle so I could go with him.

I wish I had taken the opportunity to ask David what Stanley and I should have done if the priest collapsed part way through the consecration prayer. Could we give the bread and the wine to the congregation at whatever stage in the prayer he had reached? In circumstances like ours perhaps catechists and even wives of clergy should be given some teaching on that. David's collapse was at Machui, the least-developed of the outstations with only a small mud and stick church like most of the Kwa Mkono outstations. Dole and Mahonda had larger congregations and better buildings.

At Mbweni was the beautiful old church built by the early UMCA missionaries, and many well known early missionaries' names are on the stones in its grave yard. Much needed repairs were in progress.

While the slave settlement and the missionaries were there it was in regular daily use. Now it was coming to life again with the recent developments. Near Mbweni is Kiungani. This was the home of St Andrew's College, the boys' secondary school which was in 1925 moved by Canon Robin Gibbons to Minaki on the mainland, 18 miles inland from Dar-es-Salaam. It was soon well known as St Andrew's College, Minaki, boys' secondary and teacher training college. Medical assistant training (MA) was added by Canon Gibbons' wife Dr. Mary Gibbons in 1931 (see Chapter 2). This was where I spent the first 12 years of my life in Africa.

Of necessity David's work in cathedral and parish involved meetings which his deafness made increasingly difficult. Annoyingly some got the idea that not 'hearing' was because of language, and David's Swahili was really good (unlike mine to my shame!). I could help him with phone calls in either language but not of course meetings. There was an occasion too when we had to post his hearing aids to England for urgent repair and return. A delay of some weeks made us phone and get someone in England to make enquiries. The reply came back that they had been sent to David's executors! There was no point trying to find out what gave them that idea. "Please just return them NOW."

The Island

David and I were not in the prime of youth when we moved to Zanzibar, but we did want to see something of the island. The town and its surroundings we soon got to know with our visits out to the small churches, but that didn't take us far. Zanzibar Island was being developed for tourists. Around the bit of coast where we often took an evening walk there were the tourist hotels springing up, some already in use. Otherwise on the west side, facing the mainland there was the modern harbour with cargo ships and huge tourist liners coming in and out. Their size seemed quite out of scale with their surroundings, and they must have been a boon to the economy, though most of the passengers would be sleeping on the ships not in the hotels.

The other developments we heard of were Chwaka on the east coast, and Nungwi up at the northern tip of the island. The former had been going on for some years, but the latter was quite a new enterprise. We visited both, but didn't go down to the south part of the island. The east coast faced right out across the Indian Ocean – sea, sky, sun and lovely beaches. As we gazed out we could imagine it in a storm, but the tourists didn't come at that time of year. We tried getting home by a different route across the island, shown on the map, but the track soon disappeared into impenetrable bush and forest.

The land had been cultivated in estates which included many clove estates, but these had been broken up for shambas (fields) and Pemba was now the main place for clove trees. A few estates were turned into tourist attractions, showing the many herbs and spices which could flourish there. Some restaurants in the town specialised in exciting dishes making full use of them.

Another day we went up the west coast to the northern end. The main roads east-west across the island and north along the west coast from Zanzibar town were good, except the last ten kilometres to the north when we were there which were terrible! There was one hotel near the northern tip, and with our experience on the motorcycle we felt like advising them to get the roads seen to next! The beach was a dream! Miles of sand, broken in places with gullies or rocks, and one or two fishing villages with their assorted craft on the beach. How different it would be when the hotels were built and tourists everywhere! It was very hot, with sun blazing down on sea and shore. I hoped visitors would avoid severe sunburn and would take salt as well as fluids. They might need a serious first aid post to minimise problems.

On our return we passed a sign towards the coast, 'Mkokotoni'. How could anyone pass such a name especially as we were very near the coast? After only a mile or so we came to a delightful fishing village. The seashore was crowded with fishing boats, from simple canoes to dhows. The commonest were outrigger canoes with large sails and we had seen these skilfully sailed in and up onto the beach during our evening walks round Stone Town beach. Everyone looked cheerful and busy, preparing to go out that night, so I suppose they were 'mending their nets'. A gentle whiff of fish filled the air which completed the picture but would not be appreciated by all.

Pemba

Another trip we made was to Pemba. No, we didn't go in a dhow. It was just the ordinary ferry service for passengers and goods. From Zanzibar harbour it sailed up the west coast in complete calm, but with wind and huge waves, coming I suppose from the East Indies, when we reached the northern tip of Zanzibar Island. Nearing the southern end of Pemba we smelt cloves and soon saw them spread out on sacking on the beach to dry. In the old days Zanzibar was the 'Clove Island', but with fewer clove estates, modernisation of the harbour and sea front, and air travel for people like ourselves, we had to go to Pemba for that lovely smell to greet us.

An over full little bus gave us a bumpy and swinging ride as it took us north to Chake Chake and on to Weti where our Anglican church is. The priest-in-charge, Matthew Mhagama, had a small but loyal and enthusiastic congregation. We already knew Matthew as he came over to Mkunazini quite often.

Scholastica his wife known as Schola had recently had their first baby. They welcomed us, showed us the church and their house and surroundings, and gave us refreshments.

Accommodation was booked for us at the opposite end of the town with apologies that it was an entirely Muslim area. However, we were extremely well looked after and were not aware of any ill feeling although we knew that politically there were problems at the time. A friendly incident sticks in my memory. It was hot and we had done a lot of walking. Some men were sitting by the roadside drinking and selling 'dhafu', the delicious drink from the unripe coconuts with the top chopped off. Ours were neatly opened for us and we were invited to share their doorsteps and tell them our news as we enjoyed our cool drinks.

In Chake Chake there was a Quaker mission centre run by local people now. We didn't have the chance to visit them but I realised there was an interesting connection with my childhood days (see Chapter 1). Our dear farmer friend Emelene fairly late in life married George Burt, also a farmer. His family were Quakers and well-known in their Lincolnshire home for their connection with the Quaker mission in Pemba.

Out to Dinner

Not surprisingly Flo Liebst invited us out to dinner one evening at the Mbweni Ruins Hotel. Her father, in his eighties, lived there and was their handyman. 'Baba' is 'father'; 'Babu' is 'grandfather' or 'granddad'; and to everyone – staff, visitors, everyone – he was Babu. Clothing and transport had to be considered. It would be the motorcycle this time not the rickety old Land Rover. Our last invitation out to dinner in Africa had been to the Hale power station when we were at Muheza and had the car. But my 'best dress' survived this occasion as I had no best trousers.

A rather amusing complication was that this was during Lent, and we normally gave up our small intake of alcohol during Lent. This Lent we had decided that there was no point as Zanzibar was alcohol-free except for tourist hotels! Babu would have thought what odd friends Flo had if we had asked for lemonade and there was no point in upsetting him unnecessarily. We enjoyed our dinner including the drinks in this lovely hotel and were glad to get to know Babu and Flo better. Sadly Babu died not long after.

The other extra special evening meal I remember was an invitation from a couple from England who were visiting Zanzibar. They had done their homework and found a small rather hidden upstairs restaurant that served a real Zanzibar meal. Several different and delicious herb and spiced dishes were served in a very select and quiet atmosphere. Their coffee was good, but the extra special coffee I remember was with Francis Mdoe, son of my old friend

Father Clement Mdoe. Mrs Mdoe brought small cups of strong black coffee flavoured with iliki (cardamom). It would not be to everyone's taste but I remember it after 15 years.

Food and Finance

There was one rather awkward fiasco over food. An expert in accountancy and finance was coming from the mainland to give some advice and instructions to the keepers of our cathedral, parish and hostel accounts. Since I had been helping with the hostel accounts I felt I must give those who were responsible a warning to be sure to make full use of the visit. I told them that the visitor was a very clever person and that we should pick his brains and get all the help from him that we needed. To do this we must ignore his quick temper and actual rudeness, alike to me or David or to them, not wasting this valuable opportunity. To their credit they took his visit and words well and made good use of them: we all knew that help was needed.

He was to have a room in the hostel and have his meals with us. He arrived at our door at supper time. Almost his first words were, "You know I am a vegetarian". I didn't, and I had braved the meat market for this special occasion; with only one oil stove to cook on at the time I had made a hot-pot with meat, potatoes and several vegetables in one delicious stew! "Oh, don't worry" he said, "I'll just have the vegetables", but not vegetables plucked out of a savoury meat gravy! I could hardly offer bread and cheese even if I had any of the luxury of cheese, so he had to go out and find a meal in the town. Not a good start!

Visits to the Mainland

While in Zanzibar we made two visits to our old haunts. Each was in the weeks before Christmas for the diocesan clergy retreat for David either to attend it or to conduct it. It gave us the chance to meet a number of the clergy in Korogwe for the retreat. For me it was sad that Clement Mdoe had died. He had been a medical assistant at Minaki and much later in life, hospital administrator at

Muheza while receiving training from David for ordination. Then he was priest-in-charge of Muheza parish after we had gone to Kwa Mkono. Bishop John Ramadhani was still diocesan bishop.

On the Sunday after the retreat we went to Kwa Mkono for David to celebrate the Eucharist and to preach. We saw many old friends and had lunch with the CMM Sisters, now settled happily in the CSP convent buildings. It was after that enjoyable visit that we set off to look for Canon Dunstan Mainde as described in Chapter 11.

Meeting old friends, and for me especially patients, was an enjoyable feature of our mainland visits. Fr Dunstan Mainde was one, as was John Barabara the hypertensive driver at Magila whom nephew Martin got to know so well, who had been cured of his blood pressure problem, though not by me. In Muheza there were Muslim leaders, friends of David's and for whom I had done some surgery who were still extremely friendly and drew us into their house to meet family and neighbours.

Clergy retreats have to be midweek, so we could have a Sunday at Muheza as well as the one at Kwa Mkono, staying with Dr Hills. In the hospital good developments were taking place and I felt that Elizabeth was just the right person to have followed me as medical superintendent. HIV/AIDS was starting to be important by the time I left and much more so now. By 1995 when we were visiting Muheza the hospital had started a comprehensive centre for the problem – prevention, treatment and care, especially for children, and an early emphasis was on the prevention of infection from mother to newborn baby. Soon the centre had an excellent reputation for this. Research projects too were being taken on, and the nursing school had started plans to take students for the higher grade of general nursing training.

The visits to Kwa Mkono and Muheza had gone well and been thoroughly interesting. Now we had to get the bus to Dar-es-Salaam and then the ferry over the water to Zanzibar.

Next year, 1997, we should be back in England at this time of year, and at Cambridge, celebrating the lecture of David Livingstone in the Senate House 140 years before, in which he called for young university graduates to come to Central Africa to bring the good news of the Gospel, thus inspiring those valiant pioneers who gave their lives to the early years of the 'Universities Mission to Central Africa' (UMCA). David Hope, now Archbishop of York, gave the lecture in 1997.

The Living Dead

While living in Tanzania I had very much appreciated the consciousness and respect people had for the 'living dead' which was part of their strong sense of 'family'. This was beautifully demonstrated in Zanzibar when it came round to the All Saints' and All Souls' season. After celebrating All Saints' Day, November 1st, with an early Eucharist in the cathedral, the day was spent by those who had time to tidy up and decorate the group of family graves in the cemetery just outside the town. In the evening we went out from the cathedral to sing evening prayer in the cemetery for the Eve of All Souls' day. While we, the congregation, sang psalms and hymns, the priests and servers progressed round blessing the graves, and then came back to us to complete the service. It was a moving way of combining local culture and custom with our faith in the Living Church, and the future life when we leave this world.

The difference in our attitude to death and in our way of expressing our emotions had first come to me suddenly in my very early days at Minaki during a typhoid epidemic. In spite of all our efforts, including anti-typhoid injections, one of the quite young college students died. He was far from home. Suddenly I felt a deep sense of sadness: "There's no one here to mourn for him" – meaning that there was no relative here to start the normal loud wailing of the women. As well as expressing their feelings in a way we 'Wazungu' couldn't, it was done in honour to the dead and to support them as they passed on to the next life. Yes, it had come down from pre-Christian beliefs, animist, pagan or whatever label their beliefs had been given, but it was equally fitting within our Christian beliefs about our life after we leave life here on earth.

Thinking and speaking of 'the living dead' reminds us that our sadness is for ourselves in losing those near and dear to us. I was gently reminded of that by a kind and caring priest after David died.

Finale

For us the two years in Zanzibar was a wonderful finale to our lives in Tanganyika/Tanzania. It is the place where the work of the valiant early missionaries really took root, and from which the Gospel was taken to the mainland.

By August 1997 David and I were both tired and ready for rest. For me the heat was now difficult; for David deafness and his diabetes were the main problems. We had to face another round of packing up and then farewell parties, speeches, individual goodbyes which would with Bishop John be 'au revoir' as he would be in England next year for the Lambeth Conference. The leaving present was a large painting on canvas of Zanzibar Cathedral, just exactly the view we had from our front door and painted by the local artist John Paul, who did his work in the hostel building.

Welcome to England

Partings are always difficult but we had our bungalow to go back to, and a kind god-daughter, Sue Hansell, to meet us with her car at Heathrow. There was just a small crisis at the airport when we had to go to the freight area to clear some freight. While Sue was valiantly arguing for us about the freight that hadn't arrived, David's diabetes started giving trouble. The biscuits and sweet coffee were in the car, all we needed were the car keys, which Sue among her other cares and responsibilities for the two 'old returning missionaries' had locked inside the car! Huge relief when someone told us there was a rather basic cafe upstairs in a very unlikely looking building next door. They had both sweet coffee and large sugary buns which were just what was needed. Meanwhile, Sue had finished arguing, the RAC had opened the car (just 20 seconds after their speedy arrival) and Sue was getting us into her car for the drive to North Walsham.

Our special welcome continued next day when our old friends Edith and Timothy Fox turned up. Our damson tree was laden with fruit; Edith had brought a basket of damaged Victoria plums from their garden. After we had stripped the damson tree she prepared the plums for freezing as we sat together in the conservatory and I dealt with the damsons. Timothy and David pruned the garden shrubs so that we could gradually tackle the neglected garden. It was a very English welcome after the years in Tanzania.

Past, Present and Future

Since I first set foot in Tanganyika in August 1949 until we finally returned to England in August 1997 the changes in that country have been phenomenal. The name, now 'United Republic of Tanzania', tells the political side of the story, following independence on December 8th 1961 and union with Zanzibar in 1963.

Still 'missionaries' at least until we retired from Kwa Mkono in 1990, our much loved missionary society, UMCA ,united in 1964 with SPG to become USPG, now more recently named 'Us'. Our diocese had just one Tanzanian bishop and few expatriate clergy. Going to Zanzibar in 1995 we were simply recruited by our bishop, John Ramadhani, who was then also Archbishop of the Province of Tanzania; we were not 'sent' by any missionary society.

David and I were both sent to Tanganyika by UMCA to the Diocese of Zanzibar (which then included the Tanga, Korogwe, Handeni areas and Dar-es-Salaam as far south as the Rufiji River). Our diocesan bishop was English, Bishop William Scott-Baker; the administration was British, a United Nations Mandate under the Governor, Sir Edward Twining. David was sent to take part in Theological Education: this he did at St Cyprian's College Namasakata and as Warden for six years when this moved to Rondo. Also he was Warden during part of the short life of the small college at Kalole, Minaki. During the 24 years after our marriage he continued what I called his 'mini-theological college' at Muheza (Chapters 9 and 10) and other places.

I was sent to Africa in response to a cable from William Scott-Baker, Bishop of Zanzibar diocese to UMCA headquarters (see Chapter 1). "Send Phillips Surgeon Zanzibar". You will have seen that I did no medical work at any time on the island of Zanzibar. Was I a 'surgeon' or a 'Jack-of-all-trades'? I sometimes use the term 'bush surgeon'. I was always thankful for the surgical training I had, and enjoyed the surgery and obstetrics when I felt we had done a good job especially when it hadn't been easy but resulted in a happy patient! Zanzibar was different. We were asked by Bishop John, a Zanzibari, to go there and we informed our Mission that we would be going. It gave me the chance to take more part in the life of the church and do more with David; I was called 'mama canon' now instead of 'mama daktari' by many.

Instead of Sir Edward Twining, Governor of the UN Mandate of Tanganyika, our leader following Independence was first Julius Nyerere, and then Benjamin Mkapa President of the United Republic of Tanzania. The Bishop who asked us to go to Magila in 1971 was Yohana Jumaa, not William Scott-Baker from England. John Ramadhani followed him as bishop.

In 1970 Tanzania became a Province of the Anglican Communion and gradually priests and people were becoming aware of this. Our Mission Medical Committee had made mission doctors aware of other Christian groups in the country; now we Anglicans of the coastal area were in touch with the inland and northern dioceses supported by the Church Missionary ('Mission') Society (CMS). We had a common liturgy and more were getting used to using it and getting to know each other's customs.

Within the country medical services, including training of all grades, from auxiliaries to medical officers and specialists as well as nurses of many grades and specialities, had made progress. Government services were extensively supported by missions and churches working together, an example being the Kilimanjaro Christian Medical Centre (KCMC) as well as Designated District Hospitals, ours at Muheza and others.

Unable now to visit the places where David and I worked, those are the areas from which I most look for news. But first I must express my thanks.

Looking back to the country where I lived and worked for so long it is gratitude that comes out above other memories; gratitude for the many kind, welcoming, interesting and generous people I met and especially those I worked with.

Also for the many, varied and extremely interesting experiences it gave of medicine and surgery, and of many other things like teaching, building and medical planning. All this was spread over 40 years and work in six different mission and church hospitals.

Gratitude also is for the people who keep me in touch with changes and developments at the places where David and I worked and of their hopes and plans for the future. I receive reports from the Hereford Muheza Link and copies of 'Masasi (now Masasi and Newala) News' several times a year and from friends and parish groups who have visited Tanzania recently; the occasional visitor from Tanzania is specially welcome.

Two such visiting bishops have been here recently: Bishop Patrick Mwachiko of Masasi just before his retirement and Bishop Maimbo Mndolwa of Tanga diocese within a year of his enthronement in 2011. What follows below is some of what they and a few valiant correspondents have told me. Co-operation, and teaching at different levels were central to our work while I was in Tanzania, so their further development are of particular interest in the different places.

Minaki 1949-61 and Medical Training

The closure of Minaki hospital before I left there at the end of 1961 means that the only medical interests I now have related to my work at Minaki are the developments in medical, paramedical and nursing training in the country. These have been significant. In my day most senior nursing posts needed expatriates, whereas enough are now trained within the country, except for a few specialist and advisory posts. Different paramedical trainings are provided now from both government and Christian medical centres. The number of medical officers trained in the country has increased enormously, including specialists in different medical and surgical subjects.

I have been able to follow the careers of most of my former Minaki students who were later ordained priests in their diocese, but I think all have died now, Denis Mhina being one of the last.

Lulindi and Newala in Masasi Diocese 1962-67

Memories of my years at Lulindi hospital are of extremely hard work and a lot of smiling faces! Staff, both local and 'wazungu' as well as nursing students enjoyed their work. On a visit to England a few years ago two Tanzanians clearly agreed with me. Bishop Patrick Mwachiko was a nursing student at Lulindi 1966-67 and then moved with the nursing school to Mkomaindo; Basil Mkata was a very reliable staff nurse now retired after a period of work in the diocesan office.

For part of my time at Lulindi I was also responsible for the maternity and children's hospital at Newala run by Sisters of the Community of the Sacred Passion (CSP), where I found the same pleasant atmosphere. It was the first of my many periods of work with CSP Sisters and we are still good friends 50 years later! Their hospital at Newala closed when Newala District Hospital expanded and was able to take over the work.

At Lulindi when the nursing school moved to Mkomaindo, the hospital was replaced by a rural health centre with responsibility for leprosy work in the area, and also for a time by a residential school for disabled children which shared the buildings. Now at last plans are in place to rebuild the health centre with improved facilities.

The big event in Masasi diocese has been that in 2009 the southern part, including the places where I worked, has been made a new diocese, centred on Newala. Both Newala and Masasi are sizable towns now with much improved communications. All-year-round bridges have been built connecting the area over the Ruvuma River in the south with Mozambique and in the north over the Rufiji with Dar-es-Salaam. Roads have improved as has the air service to Mtwara.

During the 17 years of Bishop Patrick's leadership in Masasi diocese two of the priorities have been to improve agricultural methods to help healthier living and relieve poverty, and to provide medical help to scattered and often isolated villages. Land and equipment are now in diocesan hands, with instruction given to show how local food production can be improved.

Many villages in both dioceses now receive a mobile clinic service thanks to 'Riders for Health', an enterprising charitable organisation based in England. Three existing clinics, Lulindi and Luatala now in Newala diocese and one under construction at Mtandi near Masasi cathedral, are the bases which supply the services. The nurses who run the mobile clinics are supplied with motorcycles and are taught to ride them safely. A comprehensive servicing schedule gives the assurance that 'breakdowns do not occur'! It sounds expensive, but not when compared with a Land Rover service like ours at Kwa Mkono.

Now in retirement Bishop Patrick and his wife Emmie have become enthusiastic farmers themselves on some land not far from Masasi town where they have, with some outside help, built a retirement house. It is a good demonstration to some of the younger generation who have come to regard farming as a rather degrading occupation!

Other important developments in Masasi diocese have been at St Cyprian's College Rondo and in the African religious community the CMM. In 1990 or soon after, the last of the CSP Sisters left Tanzania. The African Community of St Mary or Chama Cha Mariamu Mtakatifu (CMM) has grown and spread including a group now over the border in Zambia. Their mother house is at Kilimani a few miles from Mtandi, and at Newala they make good use of the CSP buildings.

St Cyprian's College Rondo continues to supply ordination training for Masasi and the surrounding dioceses. They also now have a junior seminary there (secondary school) which in spite of difficulties in keeping the right staff is getting good results. Two CMM Sisters have been able to study there each year thanks to funds made available in memory of Bishop Trevor Huddleston, the diocesan bishop while David and I were in the diocese.

Other CMM sisters are getting opportunities to train as nurses, teachers etc, some already qualified and in jobs. This, as well as a garden and farm, is helping the community to become more self-supporting.

For David and myself our marriage in Masasi cathedral was the start of 32 years of working together, a personal experience of co-operation in life and work, very sadly ending with David's death in 1998 a year after we left Zanzibar.

Dar-es-Salaam 1968-71

St Alban's church and parish were the centre of our lives during our three years in Dar-es-Salaam. Visitors, official diocesan as well as our own, were also a feature as we lived in the spacious and very inconvenient rectory. The ground floor rooms have become office space with a much more convenient flat upstairs still adequate for the priest-in-charge and his family.

The big change at St Alban's church is that in 2008 it became the cathedral of Dar-es-Salaam diocese in place of St Nicholas' church. St Alban's is central in the town whereas St Nicholas' is in Buguruni in the outskirts.

I get no personal news of Muhimbili government hospital where I worked, but know that its medical and surgical facilities and teaching programmes have continued to develop considerably since we left Tanzania.

St Mark's theological college, which opened in Buguruni while we were in Dar-es-Salaam with students from dioceses which found St Cyprian's College Rondo too remote, has grown enormously and is now a university college. Theology and ordination training continue alongside a variety of other subjects.

Magila and Muheza 1971-83

David and I really enjoyed working together during our 12 years in Muheza district. Together we pored over plans for a new church for the new Muheza parish, and over the plans, finances, staffing and many major problems of a 'Designated District Hospital' for Muheza. This in itself was the outcome of years of co-operation with the government health department.

Muheza parish church has had to be enlarged over the past ten years and Sylvester Chizazi has given me news and photographs of what has been done. Money for the work has come in well from local supporters he tells me, with some overseas help welcomed.

The hospital was feeling its age a few years ago after 30 years' hard use and probably insufficient maintenance. The new bishop of Tanga diocese, Maimbo Mndolwa took this in hand immediately after his enthronement in Korogwe Cathedral in September 2011. Dr Elizabeth Hills, my successor as medical superintendent, was able to be with him. I soon heard that the maternity unit had been refurbished, the first major refurbishment of those planned for the hospital. The hospital is now known as 'St Augustine Muheza Designated Hospital'.

Bishop Maimbo is planning to expand Muheza nursing school to take on not only higher nursing grade training but also paramedical trainings, with considerable expansion of buildings and facilities. New courses at the training school are planned to start by the end of 2013.

A Diana Centre for the prevention, treatment, teaching and care of those affected by HIV/AIDS has developed well. With a wide reputation for excellence it has taken part in training staff for other centres. Early work was done on preventing the spread of infection from mother to new born baby. Clare Chizazi, the daughter of

Sylvester Chizazi, trained now in administration, is taking part in the administration of the hospital, particularly in the Diana Centre.

Another development since we left has been in research, which is closely linked to clinical work in the hospital. How different it all is from April 1st 1980 when we struggled to get our doors open for our first patients!

Kwa Mkono 1983-90

I get little news of St Francis' hospital Kwa Mkono. It has had many problems since 1990 with lack of routine income and difficulty in getting medical officers. Heather and Richard Scott moved quite soon to St Raphael's hospital Korogwe and Tanzanian doctors did not stay for long because of the isolation. Even so Bishop Maimbo has it on his list for developments. A new operating theatre has been built recently by supporters in Germany but it is little used so far.

News from the polio hostel reaches me from Lesley and Keith Wright, friends of CSP and strong supporters of the hostel. They have worked on roofs, gutters and tanks for rainwater collection as plans to supply adequate piped water to hospital and hostel have been long delayed.

Bishop Maimbo has installed a new manager, John Sembuyage, who he says has "the right qualifications and the right approach to the job". The Wrights who have visited Kwa Mkono recently tell us that John is already working on ways to become more self-supporting. These include the shamba, already producing maize for daily meals, chickens for eggs to eat and sell, fruit and vegetables. They also make use of their computer to raise money as well as training children.

John is looking into the children's education, planning their out-of-school time so that they use it for exercise and other activities, as well as a definite period for homework during which those too young for homework are given something interesting and educational to do instead. The teachers say this more ordered life is already showing good effects in their school life.

There are few new cases of polio now thanks to all the efforts of MCH teams to get polio vaccine to all babies. The hostel is now taking other 'disabilities' such as those resulting from accidents, genetic problems like club feet, and cerebral palsy. Because of this Bishop Maimbo has renamed the hostel 'Kwa Mkono Disabled Children's Centre' and a Trust has been set up in that name.

Sadly Danieli, the bilateral amputee who taught tailoring to some older children, has died. However, the tailoring will continue for the children and to help raise funds for the centre.

News from David's area, parish and deanery, is scanty since 2005 when John Karozi was priest-in-charge and asked me for a new motorcycle to replace David's. We collected the money for him but he was moved soon after and I don't know his successor.

Zanzibar 1995-97

In Zanzibar I was not involved in medical services which were independent of those on the mainland. The situation in the diocese has changed a lot since Tanga became a separate diocese. The diocesan bishop now lives at Kiungani just outside Zanzibar town. The former outstations of the cathedral parish are now parishes with resident priests with a corresponding increase in priests working in the diocese. I am told that the church I was so fond of at Mbweni has now been beautifully refurbished.

Bishop John Ramadhani is now retired, but still active in the diocese. It is from him that I get most of my news not only of Zanzibar but often of other dioceses in the country and also of old friends and colleagues. He attends celebrations and church events on the mainland as well as funerals of old friends, sometimes independently, but often as speaker or guest of honour.

Life After Tanzania

David and I had a year together in our bungalow in North Walsham which we really enjoyed. He was able to take part in ministry in St Nicholas' parish church and in villages around. The garden took up a lot of my time and some of his. We tried to make it productive, the main crops being runner beans and the welcome crop from our small damson tree. Visitors came and we paid visits. We enjoyed the Norfolk broads, coast, extensive farmland and the wonderful display of azaleas, rhododendrons, magnolia and more in Sheringham Park and beautiful Norfolk churches amongst other things.

Sadly David's health deteriorated during the year. We were able to attend Bishop Trevor Huddleston's memorial service in Westminster Abbey in July 1998, but in August he died after a brief admission to the Norfolk and Norwich hospital. Before I had time to give much thought to the future my heart needed urgent surgery. The experts at Papworth hospital carried out the necessary coronary bypass and gradually I could start to work out life without David.

There was plenty to do at North Walsham, but as the years passed I began to realise that with my own close family in the United States and David's nieces all over on the west side of the country I was a bit isolated. So in January 2006 I took the offer of a flat at The College of St Barnabas, Lingfield in Surrey, with its provision of community life for retired Anglican priests and their wives and other church workers.

I had visited people at the College long ago with David, notably Herbert Sydenham, archdeacon of Korogwe in the days of Bishop Scott-Baker. Recently Bishop George Briggs has spent his last years there and others I knew were the nurse Gladys Lewis (Née Rhodes) who was at Minaki in the 1950s, with Arthur her husband.

Derek Goodrich, a cricketing friend of David's in their days at Selwyn College Cambridge is also here, having spent over 40 years in Guyana while David and I were in Tanzania. I had not met him before, but found that my flat was next door to his, with the Lewises just below Derek.

The College has very pleasant grounds, and is surrounded by woods, a golf-course, Lingfield race course and some fields in between. Walks through the attractive countryside are available while one is active; now that I have moved to the 'care' section I am thankful for our grounds for exercise and fresh air. Life here is centred round our chapel, only a few steps along a passage from my room. All the priests who are fit enough take their share in leading worship.

In 2011 the Community of the Sacred Passion celebrated their centenary. The founder of the community was Bishop Frank Weston, one of the early Bishops of Zanzibar, so it was very appropriate that Bishop John Ramadhani, with a long period of responsibility for the diocese, came to England to celebrate with them. It was a very happy occasion at which Bishop John celebrated the Eucharist and preached. The gathering for lunch and speeches was enlivened by three CMM Sisters who sang beautifully and garlanded all the CSP Sisters while dancing round from one to another.

When the excitement had died down and Bishop John felt free to leave, my kind driver Fr Robin Osborne, also a resident at St Barnabas', took both of us back to the College where the bishop was to stay for three days of his holiday in England. He met a number of the residents including Bishop Kenneth Cragg who was spending the last few years of his long life here. With his understanding of Islam and long experience in Jerusalem and the Middle East it was a highlight of the visit for Bishop John. He had visited retired missionaries living at St Barnabas' in the past but had not stayed overnight; he told me how much he had enjoyed worshipping with us in our chapel morning and evening at the Eucharist and evening prayer. I thoroughly enjoyed being a more or less silent observer as John met bishops and other priests here with their experience of leadership in different parts of our church.

Bishop John's three days at the College gave me a real sense of release and renewal: release from regrets for the past, and renewal to cope with the more restricted life which for me followed his visit. Talking to such a wise and understanding person who had known me for so long, about personal matters instead of the medical work of the diocese which we had so often discussed, was a new and refreshing experience.

For yet another blessing, "Tumshukuru Mungu". Thanks be to God!

Some Useful Contacts Mentioned in the Book

College of St Barnabas:
Blackberry Lane, Lingfield, Surrey, RH7 6NJ
Collegeadmin@collegeofstbarnabas.com

Community of the Sacred Passion (CSP):
22 Buckingham Road, Shoreham by Sea,
West Sussex, BN43 5UR

Friends of Masasi and Newala:
Mrs Gill Hucker (secretary), 6 Erme Park, Ermington,
Ivybridge, PL21 9LY; *gillhucker@btinternet.com*

Hereford-Muheza Link Society:
ellyecroyd@gmail.com
Dept of Paediatrics, Hereford County Hospital, Union Walk,
Hereford, HR1 2ER; *helenunderhill@doctors.org*

Medicines for Muheza
Drs Jeanette and John Meadway, 4 Glebe Avenue,
Woodfood Green, Essex, IG8 9HB

Rufiji Leprosy Trust:
www.rufijileprosytrust.org
RLT Newsletter Editor: 17 Harbutts, Bathampton,
Bath, BA2 6TA

USPG (now known as Us):
Harling House, 47-51 Great Suffolk Street,

London, SE1 0BS
info@weareUs.org.uk